FINLAND

Helsinki
holm
Tallinn ESTONIA
Riga LATVIA
Vilnius LITHUANIA
Minsk
BELARUS
AND
REP.
SLOVAKIA UKRAINE
Kiev
Budapest MOLDOVA
HUNGARY Chisinau
SERBIA ROMANIA
Belgrade Bucharest
KOS. Sofia
MAC. BULGARIA
ALBANIA
Skopje
Pristina
Athens
GREECE
lta

RUSSIAN FEDERATION

Moscow

Astana

KAZAKHSTAN

MONGOLIA
Ulan Bator

GEORGIA Tbilisi
AZERBAIJAN
ARMENIA
Ankara Yerevan Baku
TURKEY
Bishkek
Tashkent
UZBEKISTAN
KYRGYZSTAN
TURKMENISTAN
TAJIKISTAN
Asgabat Dushanbe

NORTH
KOREA
Pyongyang
Beijing Seoul
SOUTH Sejong City
KOREA

JAPAN

Tokyo

CYPRUS Nicosia
LEBANON Beirut
ISRAEL Damascus
Jerusalem Amman
SYRIA
Tehran
Baghdad
IRAQ IRAN
AFGHANISTAN
Kabul
Islamabad

CHINA

Midway
Islands
(US)

EGYPT
Cairo
JORDAN
Kuwait
KUWAIT
BAHRAIN
Manama QATAR
Riyadh Doha Abu Dhabi
U.A.E. Muscat

PAKISTAN
New Delhi
NEPAL
Thimphu
BHUTAN
Kathmandu
BANGLADESH
Dhaka BURMA
(MYANMAR)
Nay Pyi Taw

Taipei
TAIWAN

Wake Iland (US)

SUDAN
Khartoum
ERITREA
Asmara
Sana
YEMEN
OMAN

SAUDI
ARABIA

INDIA

Hanoi
LAOS VIETNAM
Vientiane
THAILAND
Bangkok
CAMBODIA
Phnom Penh

Manila

PHILIPPINES

Northern
Mariana
Islands
(US)

Guam
(US)

MARSHALL ISLANDS

CENTRAL
AN REPUBLIC
Bangui
SOUTH
SUDAN
ETHIOPIA
Addis Ababa
Juba

DJIBOUTI
Djibouti

Laccadive Islands
(India)

Andaman Islands
(India)

SRI LANKA

BRUNEI
Bandar Seri Begawan

PALAU
Melekeok Palikir

MICRONESIA

Majuro

Baker &
Howland Islands
(US)

UGANDA
Kampala
RWANDA
Kigali
DEM. REP.
CONGO
BURUNDI
Bujumbura

KENYA
Nairobi
SOMALIA
Mogadishu

Colombo
MALDIVES
Male'
Sri Jayewardenapura
Kotte

Kuala Lumpur
Putrajaya
MALAYSIA
SINGAPORE
Singapore

INDONESIA

Bairiki

NAURU KIRIBATI

TANZANIA
Dodoma

SEYCHELLES

Victoria

British Indian
Ocean Territory
(UK)

Jakarta

PAPUA NEW GUINEA

Port Moresby

Honiara

SOLOMON
ISLANDS

TUVALU
Fongafale

Tokelau
(NZ)

Wallis
& Futuna
(France)

SAMOA
Apia

OLA
ZAMBIA MALAWI
Lusaka
Lilongwe
ZIMBABWE
BOTSWANA
Gaborone Pretoria
Mbabane
SWAZILAND
Bloemfontein Maseru
SOUTH LESOTHO
AFRICA

COMOROS
Moroni
Mayotte
(France)

Antananarivo

MADAGASCAR

MAURITIUS
Port Louis
Réunion
(France)

Christmas Island
(Australia)

Dili
EAST
TIMOR

Cocos (Keeling) Island
(Australia)

Ashmore & Cartier Islands
(Australia)

Coral Sea
Islands
(Australia)

New
Caledonia
(France)

VANUATU

Port-Vila

Suva

FIJI

TONGA
Nuku'alofa

WESTERN
AUSTRALIA

NORTHERN
TERRITORY

QUEENSLAND

Norfolk Island
(Australia)

Kermadec Islands
(New Zealand)

Amsterdam Island
(France)

St-Paul Island
(France)

AUSTRALIA

SOUTH
AUSTRALIA

NEW SOUTH
WALES

Canberra
AUSTRALIAN
CAPITAL
TERRITORY

VICTORIA

NEW ZEALAND

Wellington

Chatham Islands
(New Zealand)

Prince Edward
Islands
(South Africa)

Crozet Islands
(France)

Kerguelen
(France)

TASMANIA

Bounty Islands
(New Zealand)

Auckland Islands
(New Zealand)

Macquarie Island
(Australia)

Country abbreviations

BEL.	Belgium
BOS. & HERZ.	Bosnia and Herzegovina
CZECH REP.	Czech Republic
KOS.	Kosovo
LIECH.	Liechtenstein
LUX.	Luxembourg
MAC.	Macedonia
MON.	Montenegro
NETH.	Netherlands
NZ	New Zealand
Russ. Fed.	Russian Federation
S.M.	San Marino
SLVN.	Slovenia
SWITZ.	Switzerland
U.A.E.	United Arab Emirates
UK	United Kingdom
USA	United States of America
VAT. CITY	Vatican City

C A

Miss Fowler

WHAT'S WHERE in the WORLD

LONDON, NEW YORK, MUNICH,
MELBOURNE, and DELHI

Senior editor Rob Houston
Senior art editor Philip Letsu
Senior cartographic editor Simon Mumford

Editors Helen Abramson, Steve Setford, Rona Skene
Designers David Ball, Carol Davis, Mik Gates
Researchers Helen Saunders, Suneha Dutta, Kaiya Shang
Cartography Encompass Graphics, Ed Merritt
Illustrators Adam Benton, Stuart Jackson-Carter
Creative retouching Steve Willis

Picture research Taiyaba Khatoon,
Ashwin Adimari, Martin Copeland

Jacket design Laura Brim, Natasha Rees
Jacket design development manager
Sophia M Tampakopoulos Turner

Pre-production producer Rebekah Parsons-King
Production controller Mandy Innes

Publisher Andrew Macintyre
Art director Phil Ormerod
Associate publishing director Liz Wheeler
Publishing director Jonathan Metcalf

First published in Great Britain in 2013
by Dorling Kindersley Limited
80 Strand, London WC2R 0RL

ISBN: 978-1-4093-7924-9

Colour reproduction by Alterimage Ltd, UK
Printed and bound in Hong Kong

Discover more at
www.dk.com

CONTENTS

Land, sea, and air

Living world

People and planet

Engineering and technology

History

Culture

Land, sea, and air

Skeleton Coast, Namibia
The Atlantic Ocean meets the edge of Africa's Namib Desert at the Skeleton Coast. Rainfall here rarely exceeds 10 mm (0.39 in) per year.

Introduction

Earth is a planet in motion, spinning on its axis as it hurtles through space around the Sun. Warmed by the Sun's rays, Earth's atmosphere and oceans are always on the move, while heat from the planet's core keeps the hot rock of the interior constantly churning. All this enables Earth's surface to teem with life.

Churning interior

The rocks in the mantle flow in currents that rise, flow sideways, cool, and then sink. These currents can force the plates of Earth's crust apart or pull sections of the crust back down into the mantle.

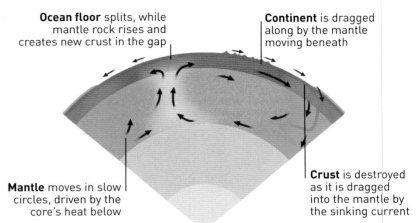

Ocean floor splits, while mantle rock rises and creates new crust in the gap

Continent is dragged along by the mantle moving beneath

Mantle moves in slow circles, driven by the core's heat below

Crust is destroyed as it is dragged into the mantle by the sinking current

Water cycle

The Sun's heat evaporates sea water, causing it to become water vapour in the air. As it rises and cools, the water vapour condenses into clouds of droplets or ice crystals. As the droplets or crystals grow, they fall as snow or rain. If it falls on land, some runs off the surface to form rivers and lakes, which return water to the oceans. A lot of rain seeps through gaps in the soil and rock. It is called groundwater, and it may stay underground or trickle to the sea. This continuous circulation of water is known as the water cycle.

Earth's structure

If we could take a slice out of Earth, we would see that the planet is made up of layers. At its heart lies a solid inner core, surrounded by a liquid outer core. Both are made mainly of heavy iron. The outer core is enclosed by a deep layer of heavy, very hot, yet solid rock called the mantle. Heat from the core drives currents rising through the mantle that keep the rock moving extremely slowly. The crust – the mantle's cool, hard shell – is made up of a number of rocky plates.

Plants
lose water through evaporation from their leaves

Rain and snow
fall, especially when air rises over high ground and cools, forming more water droplets

Clouds
form when water vapour condenses into water droplets

Evaporation
occurs when the Sun heats sea water, turning it into water vapour

Rivers and streams
return water to oceans

Groundwater may travel through rock and end up back in the ocean

Atmosphere
is a blanket of gas surrounding Earth

Mountains
form as the crust is squeezed and folded

Clouds of water droplets
form great swirling weather systems in the lower atmosphere

The Sun's energy

In the Tropics, near the equator, the Sun's rays strike Earth at a steep angle, so the energy is very concentrated. But near the poles, sunlight hits the surface at a narrow angle. This spreads the Sun's energy, giving a weak heating effect. The result is that polar regions are much colder than tropical zones, allowing ice to form in the Arctic and Antarctic. The difference in the solar heating at different latitudes sets bodies of air and sea water in motion, driving winds and ocean currents.

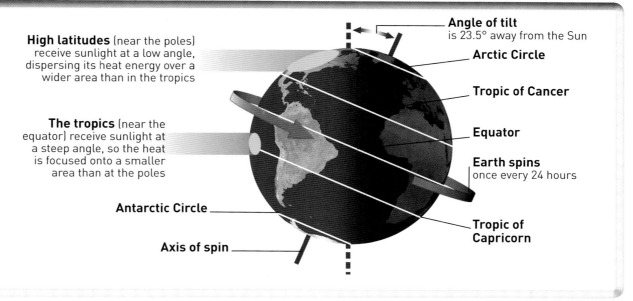

High latitudes (near the poles) receive sunlight at a low angle, dispersing its heat energy over a wider area than in the tropics

The tropics (near the equator) receive sunlight at a steep angle, so the heat is focused onto a smaller area than at the poles

Antarctic Circle

Axis of spin

Angle of tilt is 23.5° away from the Sun

Arctic Circle

Tropic of Cancer

Equator

Earth spins once every 24 hours

Tropic of Capricorn

Mantle temperature ranges from 1,000°C (1,800°F) to 3,500°C (6,300°F)

Crust consists of plates of thick, light continental rock and thinner, heavier ocean-floor rock

Convection currents circulate through the mantle. Their movement carries the rocky plates of the crust over Earth's surface

Oceans cover 71 per cent of the planet, with an average depth of 3.8 km (2.4 miles)

Solid inner core is about 7,000°C (12,600°F)

Plants, animals, and other life make up the biosphere

Molten outer core has a temperature of roughly 4,000°C (7,200°F)

PLATE BOUNDARIES
When plates meet, the collisions can form new ocean trenches and mountain ranges – or cause huge volcanic eruptions and earthquakes.

— **Divergent or transform plate boundary**

— **Convergent plate boundary**

— **Convergent plate boundary creating a deep-sea trench**

Eurasian Plate

Caribbean/North American boundary
This transform border is a region of frequent earthquakes, tsunamis, and volcanic eruptions.

African Plate

Indian Plate

East African Rift
This series of great valleys fringed in places by volcanoes are where the African Plate is in the process of splitting into two new tectonic plates.

Arabian Plate

Himalayas
The Himalayan mountain range was formed when two plates of continental crust collided. The land masses crumpled and formed enormous, jagged mountain peaks.

Mid-Atlantic Ridge
The African Plate is moving northeast at around 2.15 cm (0.85 in) per year, creating the Mid-Atlantic Ridge – a chain of volcanic mountains.

South American Plate

Scotia Plate

Types of boundary

The huge slabs of rock that cover Earth are called tectonic plates. Where the plates meet, they form different kinds of boundary, depending on the type of crust they are made of and the directions in which they move.

Convergent boundary
Where two plates collide. In some cases, one plate is pushed under the other: this is called subduction.

Divergent boundary
Where plates move apart, molten magma rises from the mantle to fill the gap, building a mid-ocean ridge.

Transform boundary
Transform boundaries are formed where the two plates scrape past each other in a sideways motion.

RELATIVE TO ITS SIZE, THE EARTH'S CRUST IS THINNER THAN THE

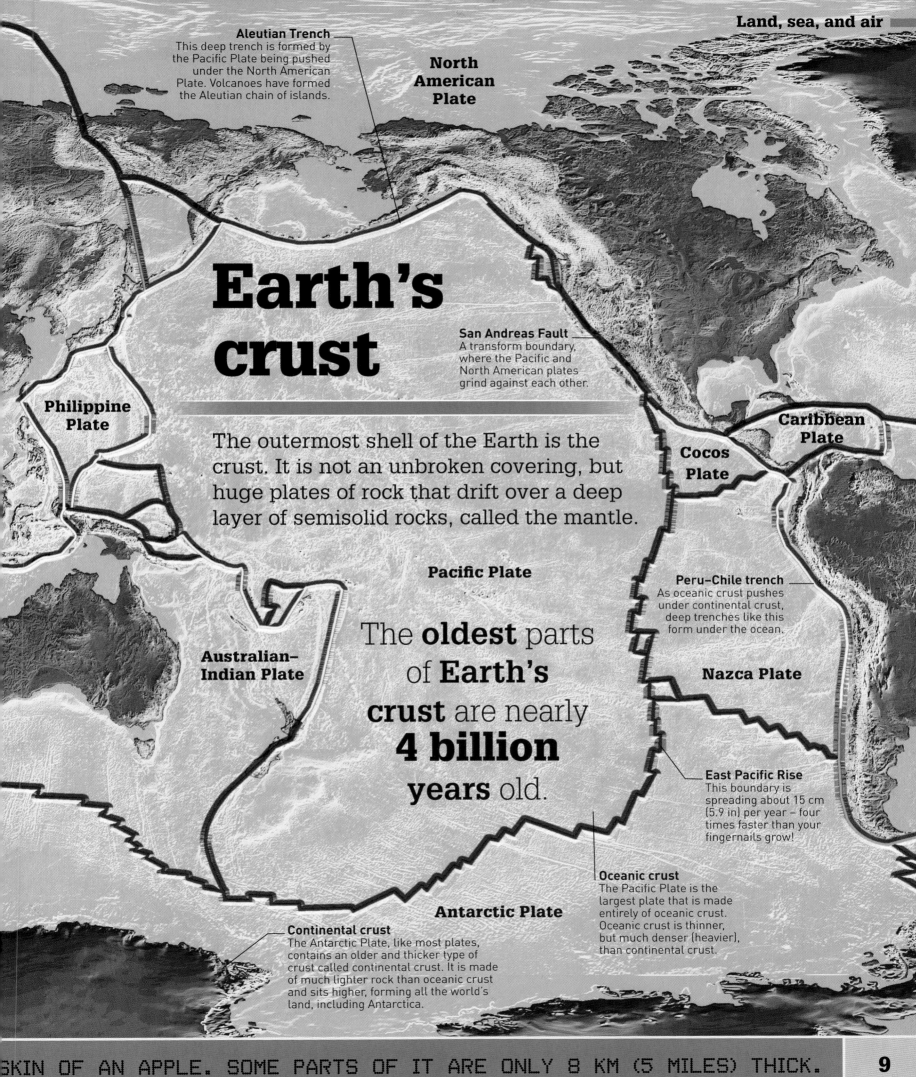

Aleutian Trench
This deep trench is formed by the Pacific Plate being pushed under the North American Plate. Volcanoes have formed the Aleutian chain of islands.

North American Plate

Earth's crust

San Andreas Fault
A transform boundary, where the Pacific and North American plates grind against each other.

Philippine Plate

Caribbean Plate

Cocos Plate

The outermost shell of the Earth is the crust. It is not an unbroken covering, but huge plates of rock that drift over a deep layer of semisolid rocks, called the mantle.

Pacific Plate

Peru–Chile trench
As oceanic crust pushes under continental crust, deep trenches like this form under the ocean.

The **oldest** parts of **Earth's crust** are nearly **4 billion years** old.

Australian–Indian Plate

Nazca Plate

East Pacific Rise
This boundary is spreading about 15 cm (5.9 in) per year – four times faster than your fingernails grow!

Oceanic crust
The Pacific Plate is the largest plate that is made entirely of oceanic crust. Oceanic crust is thinner, but much denser (heavier), than continental crust.

Antarctic Plate

Continental crust
The Antarctic Plate, like most plates, contains an older and thicker type of crust called continental crust. It is made of much lighter rock than oceanic crust and sits higher, forming all the world's land, including Antarctica.

SKIN OF AN APPLE. SOME PARTS OF IT ARE ONLY 8 KM (5 MILES) THICK.

Strongest earthquakes

(1) Valdivia, Chile – 22 May 1960
This earthquake measured 9.5 in magnitude. It killed 1,655 people and caused a tsunami that hit Japan, the Philippines, and the USA.

(2) Prince William Sound, Alaska – 1964
This 9.2-magnitude earthquake hit Alaska on 27 March. While it killed 15 people, it caused a tsunami that killed another 113.

(3) Indian Ocean – 26 December 2004
Occurring at sea, this 9.1-magnitude earthquake caused a tsunami that killed 227,898 people and affected 1.7 million more.

(4) Kamchatka, Russia – 4 November 1952
This 9.0-magnitude earthquake sent a tsunami across the Pacific. In Hawaii, no human lives were lost, but six cows died.

(5) Tohoku, Japan – 11 March 2011
This 9.0-magnitude earthquake and tsunami killed more than 15,000 people and destroyed a nuclear power plant.

KEY
Earthquakes are marked on this map according to their strength, or magnitude. An earthquake with a magnitude of 9.0 makes ten times larger seismic waves than an 8.0-magnitude earthquake.

THE LAST 100 YEARS
- Magnitude < 7.0
- 7.0–7.5
- 7.5–8.0
- Greater than 8.0

THROUGHOUT HISTORY
- Strongest on record
- Deadliest on record

Earthquakes

Most earthquake zones are at the edges of the tectonic plates that make up Earth's crust. When the plates press against each other, the pressure builds until the plates move with a jerk, sending out a shock called a seismic wave.

THE ASTEROID IMPACT THAT WIPED OUT THE DINOSAURS 65 MILLION

1.3 million earthquakes happen each year – but most are **too small** to be felt

Deadliest earthquakes

① **Shaanxi, China – 23 January 1556**
Up to 830,000 people may have died in this earthquake. Its magnitude is unknown, since seismometers did not exist at the time.

② **Tangshan, China – 28 July 1976**
The official death toll of this earthquake is 24,000–25,000, but some observers think that up to 65,000 people may have died.

③ **Haiti – 12 January 2010**
This 7.0-magnitude earthquake killed 316,000 people, but another 3.5 million suffered shortages of food and clean water.

④ **Antioch – 21 May 526 CE**
Historical sources report that a huge earthquake hit this Byzantine-Empire city in what is modern-day Turkey.

⑤ **Gansu, China – 16 December 1920**
As well as killing 235,500 people, this earthquake created major fractures in the land and devastating landslides.

YEARS AGO MAY HAVE CAUSED AN EARTHQUAKE OF 12.55 MAGNITUDE.

Mount McKinley
6,194 m (20,320 ft)
Alaska, USA

Brooks Range

Mackenzie Mountains

Alaska Range

Coast Mountains

Rocky Mountains

Sierra Nevada

Lower California

Sierra Madre Occidental

Sierra Madre Oriental

Rocky Mountains
The impact of the North American Plate and the Pacific Plate created these mountains, which stretch from Canada to New Mexico, USA.

Laurentian Mountains

Appalachian Mountains

Scandi

Pyrenees

Al

Atlas Mountains

Ahagg

Furthest from centre

Earth is a slightly squashed ball, with a bulge around the equator. Mount Chimborazo in Ecuador sits on this bulge. It is not as high above sea level as Everest, but its summit is further from Earth's centre – by 2 km (about a mile).

Mount Everest
6,382 km (3,966 miles) from Earth's centre

Earth

Earth's centre

Mount Chimborazo
6,384 km (3,967 miles) from Earth's centre

Equatorial bulge

Andes
Running from Venezuela to Chile, these fold mountains, topped by a string of volcanoes, formed when the South American Plate collided with the oceanic Nazca Plate.

Cordillera Occidental

Cordillera Oriental

Guiana Highlands

Adam Pic

Andes

Planalto de Mato Grosso

Brazilian Highlands

Aconcagua
6,961 m (22,837 ft)
Argentina

Highest fold mountains

These mountains form when two plates of Earth's crust collide. The edges of the plates are slowly crumpled and pushed upwards.

1 Mount Everest
8,848 m (29,029 ft); Nepal/China; highest mountain on Earth; first climbed in 1953

2 K2
8,611 m (28,251 ft); Pakistan/China; world's second-highest mountain; first climbed in 1954

3 Kangchenjunga
8 586 M (28,169 ft);Nepal/India; world's third-highest mountain; first climbed in 1955

4 Lhotse
8,516 m (27,940 ft); Nepal/China; world's fourth-highest mountain; first climbed in 1956

5 Makalu
8,485 m (27,838 ft); Nepal/China; world's fifth-highest mountain; first climbed in 1955

Mount Everest

Mountains

Mountains form over millions of years, thrust up as the tectonic plates of Earth's crust grind together or crack while moving slowly over its surface. Many of the peaks we describe as "mountains" are actually volcanoes – active or dormant.

Vinson Massif
4,892 m
(16,050 ft)

THE HIGHEST KNOWN MOUNTAIN ANYWHERE IS OLYMPUS MONS,

Ural Mountains

Central Siberian Plateau

Chersky Range

Kamchatka

Himalayas
When the Indian Plate and the Asian Plate met, the impact pushed up the Himalayas – home to the world's 30 highest mountains.

Mount Elbrus
5,642 m (18,510 ft)
Russia

Caucasus

Anatolia

Balkan Mts.

arpathian ountains

Elburz Mountains

Zagros Mountains

Iranian Plateau

Hindu Kush

Pamirs

Tien Shan

Altai Mountains

Mongolian Plateau

Qilian Mountains

Kunlun Mountains

Plateau of Tibet

2

Himalayas

1 4
5 3

Shan Plateau

Sarawat Mountains

sti

Aïr Mountains

Ethiopian Highlands

Ahmar Mountains

Western Ghats

Eastern Ghats

Mitumba Mountains

Great Rift Valley

Barisan Mountains

Maoke Mountains

Puncak Jaya
4,884 m (16,024 ft)
Indonesia. This, the highest mountain in New Guinea, is technically in Asia. The highest mountain on the Australasian side of the island (Papua New Guinea) is Mount Wilhelm, at 4,509 m (14,793 ft).

Great Dividing Range

Kilimanjaro
5,895 m
(19,340 ft)
Tanzania

Drakensberg

Ruwenzori Mountains
These mountains are block mountains – forced, as a block of rock, up through the floor of Africa's Western Rift Valley.

Highest volcanoes

The highest volcanoes are in the Andes, where molten rock rises through Earth's crust near the edge of the South American Plate.

▲ **Nevados Ojos de Salado**
6,893 m (22,615 ft);
Chile/Argentina;
erupted c. 700 CE

▲ **Llullaillaco**
6,739 m (22,110 ft);
Chile/Argentina;
erupted in 1854, 1868, and 1877

▲ **Tipas**
6,660 m (21,850 ft);
Argentina; isolated, little studied; no recent eruptions

▲ **Nevado de Incahusai**
6,621 m (21,722 ft);
Chile/Argentina; no recent eruptions

▲ **Cerro el Cóndor**
6,532 m (21,430 ft);
Argentina; no recent eruptions

KEY
The colours on the land areas indicate the height of the terrain above sea level

m	ft
8,000	25,000
7,000	
6,000	20,000
5,000	
4,000	15,000
3,000	10,000
2,000	
1,000	5,000
0	0

▲ Highest peak on each continent

Southern Alps

Highest versus tallest

A mountain's height is measured from sea level. Everest is indisputably the highest mountain on Earth. Mauna Kea, in Hawaii, is nowhere near as high as Everest, but it is a volcano rising from the deep ocean floor. If measured from its base to its peak, Mauna Kea is Earth's tallest mountain.

Mount Everest
8,848 m (29,028 ft) high
(above sea level)

4,207 m (13,803 ft) above sea level

Mauna Kea
10,200 m (33,500 ft) tall

6,000 m (19,685 ft) below sea level

A VOLCANO ON MARS THAT IS NEARLY 22 KM (14 MILES) HIGH.

Active Iceland
Iceland has many active volcanes, since it sits on top of the Mid-Atlantic Ridge, where magma wells up as the sea bed splits apart.

Alaska
Alaska and the Aleutian islands are located on the Pacific Ring of Fire.

Hawaii
This chain of island volcanoes has formed as Earth's crust passes over a "hot spot" in the mantle below.

How volcanoes form
Molten rock (magma) from Earth's interior may erupt where plates pull apart, or force its way to the surface where plates collide.

Plates collide and one is pushed beneath the other

Magma forms and pushes upwards

Mid-Atlantic Ridge
Volcanoes dot the sea floor in the middle of the Atlantic Ocean, where two plates are moving away from each other.

Volcanoes

Earth's crust is made up of plates of rock that fit together like a jigsaw. Most volcanoes occur where the plates meet, but some erupt in hot spots in the middle of the plates.

Largest eruptions since 1800

1. **Tambora, Indonesia, 1815**
   Tambora threw so much ash into the atmosphere that global weather was disrupted and temperatures fell.

2. **Krakatau, Indonesia, 1883**
   The explosion was heard 4,600 km (2,850 miles) away. It destroyed two-thirds of the island of Krakatau.

3. **Novarupta, Alaska, 1912**
   The largest volcanic blast of the 20th century marked the formation of this new volcano on the Pacific Ring of Fire.

4. **Mount Pinatubo, Philippines, 1991**
   A plume of ash 400 km (250 miles) wide rose 34 km (21 miles) into the sky, blocking out the Sun for days.

5. **Santa Maria, Guatemala, 1902**
   The explosion formed a 1 km (0.6 mile) wide crater. Ash fell in San Francisco, California, 4,000 km (2,500 miles) away.

KEY
The map shows volcanoes above sea level. Many more volcanoes erupt on the sea bed.

Most lethal

Largest since 1800

Recent volcano active 2006–2011

Other volcanoes, either single or in a cluster of up to six

Japan
Part of the Pacific Ring of Fire, Japan has more than 70 active volcanoes.

Europe
There are few volcanoes in Europe, which is on the Eurasian Plate.

There are around **1,500** known **active volcanoes** on Earth

East African Rift
Volcanoes occur here because the African Plate is slowly splitting in two.

Pacific Ring of Fire
Volcanoes are common along the edges of the plates forming the floor of the Pacific Ocean.

Inactive Australia
Australia lies in the middle of a plate and has no active volcanoes.

Most lethal volcanoes

① **Mount Tambora, Indonesia, 1815**
Falling volcanic ash destroyed plants and crops leading to famine. More than 71,000 Indonesians died, the majority from starvation.

② **Krakatau, Indonesia, 1883**
The official death toll was 36,417, most of whom died when tsunamis (tidal waves) created by the explosion swept through the region.

③ **Mont Pelée, Martinique, 1902**
A rapidly moving cloud of glowing gas, ash, and dust engulfed the town of St Pierre on the Caribbean island of Martinique, killing all but two of its inhabitants. In all, nearly 30,000 people lost their lives.

④ **Nevado Del Ruiz, Colombia, 1985**
The eruption melted snow and ice on the volcano, creating mudflows that killed around 25,000 people in surrounding valleys.

⑤ **Mount Unzen, Japan, 1792**
Some 14,300 people died when, about a month after lava stopped erupting, part of the volcano collapsed in a landslide, triggering a tsunami.

Trenches

Rifts in the ocean floor that form when Earth's tectonic plates meet. The deepest places in the ocean and the lowest points on Earth, about 8,000–10,000 m (26,000–33,000 ft) below the surface of the ocean.

● **Trenches**

Mid-ocean ridges

Underwater mountain ranges found at the boundary between two divergent (moving apart) tectonic plates. They are all linked, making them the world's longest mountain range at 65,000 km (40,000 miles).

● **Mid-ocean ridges**

Seamounts

Undersea mountains rising at least 1,000 m (3,300 ft) above the sea bed. They are volcanoes and many are hotspots of marine life. Flat-topped seamounts are called guyots, and smaller mounts are sea knolls.

○ **Seamounts**

Iceland
The largest of the islands created by the Mid-Atlantic Ridge, where the ridge's volcanoes have grown to break the ocean's surface.

East Greenland Basin

Aleutian Trench
This trench forms the border between the Altantic and Pacific plates. It reaches a depth of 7,679 m (25,194 ft).

Aleutian Trench

Tufts Plain

Abyssal plain
Abyssal plains are flat or very gently sloping areas of the deep ocean floor and are among the world's least explored regions. They make up about half of the Earth's surface.

Davidson Seamount

Labrador Basin

Reykjanes Ridge

Biscay Plain

Grand Banks of Newfoundland

Hatteras Abyssal Plain

Texas-Louisiana Shelf

Nares Plain

Mid-Atlantic Ridge

Great Meteor Seamount

Cape Verde Plain

Cape Verde Basin

Mid-Atlantic Ridge
A very long ridge that extends 16,000 km (10,000 miles) from the Arctic Ocean to the South Atlantic.

Hawaiian-Emperor Seamount Chain

Middle America Trench

Guatemala Basin

East Pacific Rise
This mid-ocean ridge winds under the Pacific from Mexico to the South Pacific. It is the fastest-spreading mid-ocean ridge in the world.

East Pacific Rise

Tuamotu Ridge

Sala y Gomez Ridge

Peru Basin

Peru-Chile Trench

Basin
Basins are vast underwater areas that cover about 75 per cent of Earth's surface. They contain ridges, trenches, and other features of the ocean floor.

Brazil Basin

Guinea Basin

Angola Basin

Namib Plain

Cape Basin

Peru-Chile Trench
Marks the point where the Pacific Plate is diving beneath South America – a movement that also caused the uplift of the Andes mountains.

Argentine Basin

Argentine Plain

Patagonian Shelf

Pacific-Antarctic Ridge

Mornington Abyssal Plain

Atlantic-Indian Ridge

Southeast Pacific Basin

Weddell Plain

IF MOUNT EVEREST WERE PLACED ON THE DEEPEST PART OF THE OCEAN

Fram Basin

Gakkel Ridge

Nansen Basin

Continental shelf
A continental shelf is the edge of a land mass that lies under the ocean. It slopes gently from the shore towards the continental slope, where the deep ocean truly begins.

Kara Shelf

Mendelev Ridge

Canada Basin

Barents Shelf

Laptev Shelf

East Siberian Shelf

Chukchi Shelf

Ocean floor

The enormous mountain ranges, vast plains, and deep trenches of the ocean floor were created by the constant shifting and colliding of the plates that make up Earth's crust.

Aleutian Basin

Kurile Trench

Northwest Pacific Basin

Emperor Seamounts
A chain of undersea volcanoes stretching from the seamounts at the end of the Hawaiian chain all the way to the Aleutian Islands.

Great Yangtze Bank

Makarov Seamount

Hawaiian Ridge

Arabian Basin

Philippine Basin

Mid-Pacific Seamounts

Somali Basin

Mid-Indian Ridge

Ninetyeast Ridge

Mariana Trench

Central Pacific Basin

Mid-Indian Basin

Muirfield Seamount

Christmas Island Seamounts

Arafura Shelf

Mariana Trench
The deepest part of the world's oceans. Its lowest point, the Challenger Deep valley, is 11,033 m (36,201 ft) below the surface.

Tonga Trench

Southwest Indian Ridge

Crozet Basin

Kerguelen Plateau

Southeast Indian Ridge

Campbell Plateau

Enderby Plain

South Indian Basin

SURFACE CURRENTS
Surface currents are driven by the winds. They carry cold water to the tropics and warm water to the poles.

→ **Warm current**

→ **Cold current**

North Atlantic
Warm water is cooled by the ice of the Arctic and begins to sink.

Gyre
Surface currents, driven by winds and by the spin of planet Earth, often form circular patterns called gyres. Gyres north of the equator move clockwise, while those in the south move anticlockwise.

Ocean in motion

Ocean waters are constantly moving. Their movements, called currents, are driven by wind and Earth's spin. But ocean currents are also affected by the water's temperature and saltiness, as well as sea depth.

OCEANIC CONVEYOR
Surface currents and deep ocean currents link up to form a planet-wide conveyor belt flowing at times across the ocean basins, then rising to the surface, before sinking again to the deep ocean floor.

Warm ——————— Cold

IT CAN TAKE UP TO 1,000 YEARS FOR OCEAN CURRENTS TO

Gulf Stream
The warm currents of the Gulf Stream make northern Europe's climate warmer than it would be otherwise.

How currents sink

When currents reach the cold polar oceans, some of the sea water freezes. When it does this, it leaves its salt behind. The salt mixes with the remaining water, making it saltier and heavier. This water then sinks towards the ocean floor and drives the currents that flow slowly through the ocean depths. Where these deep-water currents flow back up to the surface, scientists call it "upwelling".

Warm surface water flows in

Salt leaves the water when it freezes and makes the remaining water saltier and heavier

Cold, salty water sinks below the warm water and flows away slowly

Great Pacific Garbage Patch
Plastics and other rubbish carried by currents collect within this slow-moving zone in the centre of the North Pacific Gyre.

Deep water current
The deep current flowing across the basin of the Pacific begins to rise, warming up as it does so.

Friendly floaters
A cargo of plastic ducks lost in the Pacific in 1992 is still helping scientists to learn more about the speed and direction of ocean currents. So far, the ducks have drifted 27,500 km (17,000 miles).

Southern oceans
Cold, dense water flows east across the deep ocean floor in the Antarctic, then heads north.

CARRY WATER FROM THE NORTH ATLANTIC TO THE NORTH PACIFIC.

Rivers

Rivers help to shape Earth, wearing down mountains, carving valleys, and laying down soil and rocks to form new land. Lakes hold 20 times more of the planet's fresh water than rivers.

Thames
Although only 338 km (210 miles) long, it is England's most important waterway.

Mackenzie
The longest river in Canada, it freezes for about seven months of the year.

Loire
The longest river in France, it plays an important role in wine-growing in the area.

Great Lakes
The five lakes cover an area of about 245,000 sq km (95,000 sq miles), which is more than the entire UK.

Mississippi–Missouri
Supplies drinking water for more than 18 million people in the USA.

Amazon
The Amazon basin (the area containing the river and all its tributaries) covers about 7 million sq km (2.7 million sq miles) – almost as large as Australia.

Congo
One of the deepest rivers in the world, with depths of more than 220 m (720 ft).

Madeira
The biggest tributary of the Amazon.

Paraná
The Paraná's Itaipú Dam is the second-largest hydroelectric power station in the world.

River volume

A river's size is measured by its discharge, or volume flow rate. This is the amount of water that flows into the sea in a given time.

RIVER FLOW, IN MILLIONS OF LITRES PER SECOND (MILLIONS OF GALLONS PER SECOND)

Amazon 219 (57.9)

Congo–Chambeshi 41.8 (11)

Yangtze 31.9 (8.4)

Yenisei–Angara–Selenga 19.6 (5.2)

Rio de la Plata–Parana–Paranaiba 22 (5.8)

Mississippi–Missouri 16.8 (4.4)

Ob–Irtysh 12.5 (3.3)

Amur–Arqun 11.4 (3)

Nile 2.8 (0.7)

Yellow River 2.6 (0.7)

Longest rivers

Advances in GPS technology mean that scientists can now measure a river's length much more accurately than they could in the past.

LENGTH IN KILOMETRES 0   50

Nile
Amazon
Yangtze
Mississippi–Missouri
Yenisei–Angara–Selenga
Yellow River
Ob–Irtysh
Rio de la Plata–Paraná–Paranaíba
Congo–Chambeshi
Amur–Arqun

LENGTH IN MILES 0   3

RIVERS ARE EARTH'S MOST POWERFUL FORCE OF EROSION, CARRYING

Ob' Ends in the Arctic Ocean.

Yenisey
Freezes along its whole length by mid-November each year.

Danube
Flows through 10 countries on its way to the Black Sea.

Pechora

Yenisey

Olenëk

Kolyma

Northern Dvina

Lower Tunguska

Vilyuy

Lena

Lake Onega

Ob'

Lena

Aldan

Lake Ladoga

Volga

Ob'

Angara

Dnieper

Irtysh

Lake Baikal

Amur

Don

Volga

Aral Sea

Syr Darya

Lake Balkash

Amu Darya

Lake Baikal
At around 25 million years old, by far the oldest and deepest lake on Earth.

Amur
Part of the Amur provides a natural boundary between Russia and the People's Republic of China.

Tigris

Euphrates

Indus

Brahmaputra

Yangtze

Yellow River

anube

Ganges

Irrawaddy

Salween

Mekong

Yellow River (Huang He)
So-called because of the huge amounts of mineral-rich silt it carries downstream.

Nile

Yangtze (Chang Jiang)
One of the world's busiest rivers, it flows through the major Chinese cities of Shanghai, Nanjing, and Chengdu.

Nile

Nile
About 90 per cent of the people of Egypt live close to the banks of the Nile.

Seasonal rivers
Some rivers, shown in brown, flow only in the wet season. Some of these flow only in particularly wet years.

angi

Congo

Lake Victoria

Lake Tanganyika

Lake Victoria
The world's second-largest freshwater lake by area (after Lake Superior), it provides water for the Nile.

Ganges
Holy river to the world's 900 million Hindus.

Lake Nyasa

Zambezi

ge River

The **Amazon** carries **one-fifth** of all the **fresh water** emptied into the **oceans**

Darling

Murray

Murray–Darling
Crosses south-east Australia from the Snowy Mountains to the the Indian Ocean.

,000	1,500	2,000	2,500	3,000	3,500	4,000	4,500	5,000	5,500	6,000	6,500

620	930	1,240	1,550	1,860	2,170	2,480	2,790	3,100	3,410	3,720	4,030

20 BILLION TONNES OF LAND SURFACE TO THE OCEANS EACH YEAR.

Avak
USA. Discovered by scientists looking for oil, this crater has been buried during the last 3 million years by a thin layer of rock.

Haughton
Nunavut, Canada

Nicholson
Canada

Steen River
Canada

Clearwater East and West
Canada

Mistastin
Canada

Carswell
Canada

Deep Bay
Canada

Saint Martin
Canada

Manicouagan
Canada
The inner part of this 215-million-year-old crater now forms a striking ring-shaped lake 70 km (40 miles) across.

Nördlinger
Germany

Beaverhead
USA

Eagle Butte
Canada

Charlevoix
Canada

Rochechouart
France

IMPACT CRATERS
The largest objects that hit Earth – asteroids and comets – can make such a violent impact that they are destroyed. A crater is left behind, though, although over millions of years, it can be buried, worn away, and disorted by the Earth's crust moving. On the map are all the largest craters scientists know about.

Manson
USA

Montagnais
Canada

Guarda
Portugal

Ames
USA

2

4

Sudbury Basin
Canada

Chesapeake Bay
USA

Sierra Madera
USA

3

Largest known impact craters, by diameter in km (miles)				
8–10 (5.0–6.2)	10–20 (6.2–12.4)	20–50 (12.4–31.0)	50–100 (31–62)	100–300 (62–186)

Chicxulub
Mexico

Bosumtwi
Ghana

Sierra Madiera
Brazil

The Great Dying
An asteroid probably killed off the dinosaurs, but an even bigger impact may have almost wiped out life completely, 250 million years ago. Called the "Great Dying", this disaster may have been caused by an asteroid impact some scientists think they have discovered under the Antarctic ice sheet.

Araguainha
Brazil

Vista Alegre
Brazil

Vargeão Dome
Brazil

Craters and meteorites

Earth would be peppered with craters like the Moon if it weren't for wind, water, and Earth's moving crust covering them up or wearing them away. More craters can be seen in old, quiet parts of Earth's crust such as in Canada and Australia.

AN ASTEROID HITTING ANTARCTICA 250 MILLION YEARS AGO MAY HAVE

Mjølnir
Named after the hammer of Thor the thunder god, this 40-km (25-mile) crater is on the floor of the Barents Sea.

Siljan
Sweden

Keurusselkä
Finland

Lappajärvi
Finland

Kara
Russia

Popigai
Russia
This giant crater, 100 km (62 miles) across, formed about 36 million years ago when Earth was struck by an asteroid 5–8 km (3–5 miles) wide.

El'Gygytgyn
Russia

Loganchai
Russia

Puchezh-Katunki
Russia

Ragozinka
Russia

Karla
Russia

Tunguska Event
Before it hit the ground, a meteroid or comet exploded here in Russia in 1911 with the force of a nuclear bomb, flattening 80 million trees. Objects not quite large enough to get through Earth's atmosphere sometimes explode like this.

Kamensk
Russia

Zhamanshin
Kazakhstan

Boltysh
Ukraine

Karakul
Tajikistan

Tai
China

Oasis
Libya

Dhala
India

Aorounga
Chad

Gweni-Fada
Chad

Luizi
Democratic Republic of Congo

Morokweng
South Africa

Vredefort
South Africa

Fresh crater

Barringer Crater, also called Meteor Crater, in Arizona, USA, is well preserved because it is so young – only 50,000 years old. Most of Earth's craters have been covered by layers of younger rock or reshaped by wind, rain, and flowing water.

Greatest impacts

4 **Chesapeake Bay, USA**
A buried impact crater is at the heart of Chesapeake Bay on the US coast. The impact made a tsunami so enormous, it may have crossed the Blue Ridge Mountains.

3 **Chicxulub, Mexico**
Buried under the Gulf of Mexico and Yucatán Peninsula is a crater 180 km (110 miles) across, made 65 million years ago. Scientists blame it for the death of the dinosaurs.

2 **Sudbury Basin, Canada**
This is the second-biggest confirmed asteroid crater on Earth. The impact that created it was so massive, it scattered debris as far as Minnesota, USA.

1 **Vredefort impact structure, South Africa**
Made 1.8 billion years ago by a 15-km (9-mile) asteroid, this is Earth's largest definite impact crater.

Strangways
Spider
Lawn Hill
Connolly Basin
Amelia Creek
Glikson
Gosse's Bluff
Woodleigh
Shoemaker
Yarrabubba
Tookoonooka
Acraman
Flaxman
Crawford

Australia
Traces of many impacts dot Australia, because Earth's crust here is very old.

Earth's **biggest impact crater** is **300 km** (180 miles) wide

Prospect Creek, USA
At −62°C (−80°F), this is the seventh-coldest place on the planet.

Malgovik, Sweden
Its record of −53°C (−63.4°F) is Earth's ninth-lowest temperature.

North Ice Research Station, Greenland
Fifth-coldest spot on Earth, at −66.1°C. (−87°F).

Snag, Canada
Recorded temperature of −63°C (−81°F), to make it the coldest site in North America.

Kebili, Tunisia
Recorded temperature of 55°C (131°F) in 1931, tying for the third-hottest place ever.

Furnace Creek, USA
The world's highest ever air temperature, 56.7°C (134°F), was recorded here in 1913.

Illizi, Algeria
Earth's tenth-hottest spot, at 51°C (123.8°F).

Ciudad Obregón, Mexico
Recorded temperature of 53°C (127.4 °F), to make it the eighth hottest location on Earth.

Daily differences
Many deserts are hot during the day but drastically cooler at night. With no clouds or mist in the way of the Sun, the ground warms up fast during the day. With no blanketing cloud at night, the heat escapes quickly. In humid climates, daily temperatures vary a lot less.

Cold mountains
The higher up you are, the lower the air pressure – and the temperature. The Andes mountain range is much colder than the land that surrounds it.

Al 'Aziziyah, Libya
Lost its title as world's hottest place in 2012, when weather scientists found its 1922 record measurement was probably wrong.

◯ **Luxor, Egypt**
Luxor has a dry, desert climate. In June, the daily temperature varies hugely, from an average maximum of 41°C (105.8°F) down to 22°C (71.6°F) at night.

◯ **Singapore**
Singapore's climate is very warm and humid all year round. In June, the daily temperature varies from 31.3°C (88.3°F) to a sticky 24.7°C (76.5°F) at night.

Blazing summers, freezing winters
In the middle of large continents, it is often hot in summer and very cold in winter. In coastal areas, warm or cool winds and currents carried by the sea moderate temperatures. Without this balance, inland areas can become extremely hot or cold.

① **Verkhoyansk, Russia**
The world's biggest seasonal temperature differences are found in Verkhoyansk. The highest temperature ever recorded was 39.9°C (103.8°F) and the lowest was -67.8°C (−90°F).

② **Regina, Canada**
Regina's highest-ever temperature was 43.3°C (109.9°F) and the lowest was -50°C (-58°F).

In **1924**, the Australian town of **Marble Bar** reached 37.8°C (100°F) or above for **160 days in a row**

Amundsen–Scott Station, South Pole
The second-coldest point on Earth, at −82.8°C (−117°F).

Verkhoyansk, Russia
Shares the coldest recorded temperature outside Antarctica of −67.8°C (−90°F) with the nearby town of Oimyakon. These are the world's coldest permanently inhabited places.

st' Shchugor, Russia
urope's coldest spot, at −58.1°C (−72.6°F).

Verkhoyansk range
These mountains are probably even colder than the town of Verkhoyansk, but the weather is not monitored closely in these remote ranges.

Tirat Zvi, Israel
Fifth-hottest place on Earth, at 54°C (129.2°F).

Kuwait International Airport
Joint number six in the world hotspot table, at 53.5°C (128.3°F).

Mohenjo-daro, Pakistan
Ties for Earth's sixth hottest place, at 53.5°C (128.3°F).

Mohe County, China
The coldest place in China, at −52.3°C (−62.1°F).

Basra, Iraq
52.0°C (125.7°F) recorded in 2011 makes the city Earth's ninth-hottest place.

Berbera, Somalia
Earth's joint third-hottest spot at 55°C (131°F).

Songea, Tanzania
World's second-highest temperature, 56°C (132.8°F), was recorded here.

KEY
This map was made by calculating average temperatures, throughout the day and night, over a whole year. It averages out the huge differences in temperature that can occur in some locations, either in a single day or between the seasons. You can see clearly that the hottest zones, on average, are those around the equator. The zones get cooler the nearer they get to the polar regions.

32°C

0°C

−45°C

Hot and cold

Whether somewhere is hot or cold is mainly to do with how close it is to the equator, but other factors, such as sea currents and altitude, are also important.

Dome A, East Antarctica
Earth's third-coldest spot, at −82.5°C (−116.5 °F).

Vostok Research Station, Antarctica
Recorded temperature of −89.2°C (−128.6°F), Earth's coldest ever temperature.

Snowiest place contender
17 m (56.3 ft) yearly average; Mount Rainier, Washington, USA

Largest snowflake
38 cm (15 in) across; 1887, Fort Keogh, Montana, USA

Largest hailstone
20 cm (8 in) across, nearly 1 kg (2 lb) in weight; 2010, Vivian, South Dakota, USA

Greenland
About 80 per cent of the land is always covered by snow and ice.

Wettest place contender
11,500 mm (452 in) yearly average; Waialeale, Hawaii

Sahara Desert
Some places in the Sahara do not see rain for several years.

Heaviest snowfall (24 hours)
1,930 mm (76 in); 1921, Silver Lake, Colorado, USA

KEY
Scientists call rain and snow "precipitation". The bluest areas have the most precipitation.

Highest precipitation
Fairly high precipitation
Fairly low precipitation
Lowest precipitation

Wettest place contender
13,309 mm (524 in) yearly average; Lloro, Colombia

Driest place contender
0.76 mm (0.03 in) yearly average; Arica, Chile

Flash floods

If a lot of rain falls in a short time it can result in "flash" floods, when torrents of water suddenly run off hills into valleys.

① **Tehran, Iran, 1954**
A flash flood rushed through a gully killing around 2,000 people who had gathered for religious devotions.

② **Black Hills, South Dakota, USA, 1972**
There were 238 deaths in a matter of hours; total damage was $165 million.

③ **Darfur and South Sudan, 2007**
Flash floods left 750,000 homeless.

④ **Krasnodarskiy Kray, Russia, 2012**
150 were killed in the worst flooding and landslides for 70 years.

Too much rain

Nonstop rain can cause rivers to burst their banks and flood low-lying areas. Other floods can be caused by storm tides and dams bursting.

① **Yangtze River, China, 1931**
Caused by the Yangtze bursting its banks. Killed 3.7 million people directly as well as from disease and starvation. China's Yellow River also flooded disastrously.

② **African floods, 2007**
Some of the worst, most widespread flooding in history, affecting a belt of countries from Senegal eastwards to Ethiopia and as far south as Rwanda.

③ **Bangladesh, 1998**
Two-thirds of the country was covered with water, and 25–30 million people lost their homes. Many floods affect this low-lying country, which is mostly floodplain.

④ **Mississippi Flood, USA, 1927**
The most destructive river flood in the history of the United States, with 246 deaths reported.

⑤ **Rio de Janeiro, Brazil, 2011**
In 24 hours, the local weather service recorded more rainfall than was expected for the entire month; caused mud slides and 903 deaths.

⑥ **Haiti and the Dominican Republic, 2004**
Torrential rains made the Soliel River overflow, causing floods and mud slides that destroyed villages and killed more than 2,000 people.

Rain and snow

5,000 mm
(197 in) of rain may fall in one place during India's **monsoon** season

Rainfall varies dramatically from place. Torrential rain drenches southern Asia during the monsoon season, yet some desert regions have virtually no rain at all. Near the poles, very little snow falls, but the snow rarely melts, so some land is permanently under a layer of ice.

Heaviest rainfall (1 month, and 1 year)
9,300 mm (370 in) and 22,987 mm (905 in); both 1860–61, Cherrapunji, India

Arabian Peninsula
As in the Sahara, there is very little rain in this largely desert region.

Heaviest rainfall (24 hours)
1,825 mm (71.9 in); 1966, Foc-Foc, Réunion, during Tropical Cyclone Denise

Snowiest place contender
15 m (49.5 ft) yearly average; Niseko, Japan

Borneo
Many equatorial rainforests, such as those in Borneo, have no dry season, and it rains every day.

Australia
This is the driest inhabited continent.

New Zealand
Rainfall is fairly high and is spread evenly throughout the year.

Driest place on Earth
0 mm (0 in) yearly average; Antarctica's Dry Valleys, which are free of snow and ice.

Monsoon extremes

In the dry season, Chittagong, in Bangladesh, has almost no rain, but its monsoon rains are torrential. Paris, in France, has more even monthly rainfall.

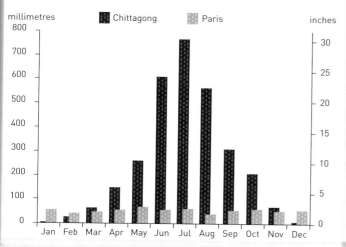

■ Chittagong ■ Paris

(Bar chart: millimetres (0–800) and inches (0–30) by month, Jan–Dec)

A cyclone may travel thousands of kilometres before it is completely spent.

Hurricane Iniki, 1992
Iniki, which reached Category 4, was the most powerful storm ever to strike Hawaii, where it caused six deaths and $1.8 billion of damage.

Hurricane Katrina, 2005
Over 1,800 people died when this Category 5 storm hit the USA's east coast, producing $106 billion of damage.

Hurricane Kenna, 2002
With wind speeds peaking at about 265 kph (165 mph), Kenna was a Category 5 storm. It hit San Blas, Mexico, killing four people and damaging 95 per cent of homes.

TROPICAL CYCLONE STRENGTH
Big storms that rotate around a core of low-pressure air are called tropical cyclones. The fiercest of these are hurricanes (also known as typhoons or just "cyclones"), with winds over 119 kph (74 mph). Their category number is linked to their intensity, or strength.

Category	Wind speed	Effects
5	Over 252 kph (157 mph)	Buildings destroyed; catastrophic flooding
4	209–252 kph (130–157 mph)	Roofs blown off; major coastal flooding
3	178–209 kph (111–130 mph)	Large trees uprooted; mobile homes wrecked
2	154–178 kph (96–111 mph)	Some roof, door, and window damage
1	119–154 kph (74–96 mph)	Minor building damage; branches snapped
Tropical storm	63–119 kph (38–74 mph)	No significant damage; some flood risk
Tropical depression	Under 63 kph (38 mph)	No significant damage; some flood risk
Unknown intensity	No recorded wind speed data	Various, sometimes catastrophic

STORM TRACKS
This map shows the paths of some tropical cyclones. When they move beyond the tropical regions, they become known as "extratropical" cyclones. By this time, they are much weaker.

●●● **Tropical cyclone**

▲▲▲ **Extratropical cyclone/ cyclone remnant**

Hurricanes

TROPICAL CYCLONES ROTATE ANTICLOCKWISE IN THE NORTHERN

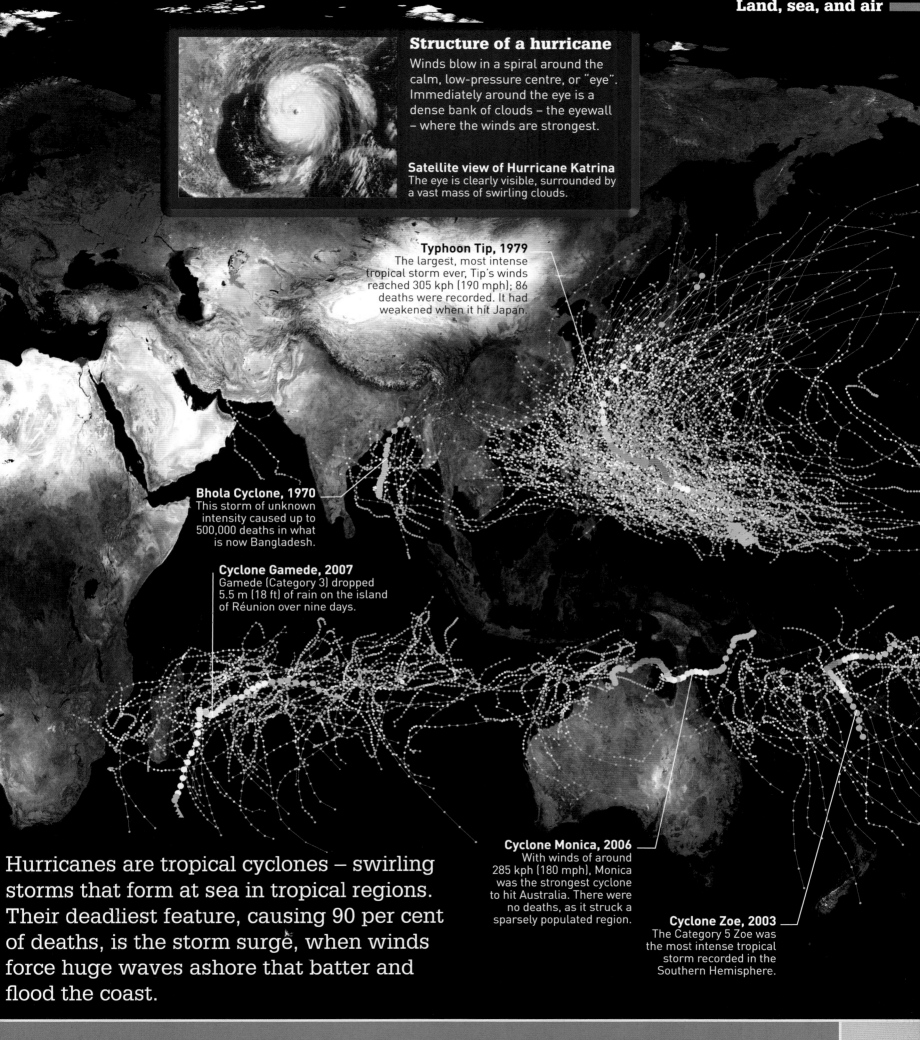

Structure of a hurricane

Winds blow in a spiral around the calm, low-pressure centre, or "eye". Immediately around the eye is a dense bank of clouds – the eyewall – where the winds are strongest.

Satellite view of Hurricane Katrina
The eye is clearly visible, surrounded by a vast mass of swirling clouds.

Typhoon Tip, 1979
The largest, most intense tropical storm ever, Tip's winds reached 305 kph (190 mph); 86 deaths were recorded. It had weakened when it hit Japan.

Bhola Cyclone, 1970
This storm of unknown intensity caused up to 500,000 deaths in what is now Bangladesh.

Cyclone Gamede, 2007
Gamede (Category 3) dropped 5.5 m (18 ft) of rain on the island of Réunion over nine days.

Cyclone Monica, 2006
With winds of around 285 kph (180 mph), Monica was the strongest cyclone to hit Australia. There were no deaths, as it struck a sparsely populated region.

Cyclone Zoe, 2003
The Category 5 Zoe was the most intense tropical storm recorded in the Southern Hemisphere.

Hurricanes are tropical cyclones – swirling storms that form at sea in tropical regions. Their deadliest feature, causing 90 per cent of deaths, is the storm surge, when winds force huge waves ashore that batter and flood the coast.

Tropical broadleaf moist forest
Also known as rainforest, these warm, wet woods support a huge variety of animal and plant life.

Tropical dry broadleaf forest
These areas are warm all year round but have a long dry season, and many trees lose their leaves.

Tropical coniferous forest
Many migrating birds and butterflies spend the winter in these warm, dense conifer forests.

Temperate broadleaf forest
The most common habitat of northern Europe and home to trees that lose their leaves in winter.

Temperate coniferous forest
Giant trees, such as the California redwood, thrive in these regions of warm summers and cool winters.

Boreal forest
Also called taiga, this is the largest biome on Earth. It is dominated by just a few types of coniferous tree.

Savanna
A long dry season, and short rainy periods results in a grassland studded with trees and herds of gazing animals.

Flooded savanna
Birds are attracted to these marshy, wetland areas that are flooded in the wet season but grassland at other times.

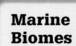

Temperate grassland
Also known as prairie, steppe, or pampas, many of these vast, fertile plains are now farmland.

Mountain grassland
The inhabitants of these remote, high habitats must adapt to the cold and the intense sunlight.

Coral reef
The warm, shallow waters of a reef support a huge variety of life, from sharks to tiny sea horses.

Marine Biomes

Sea biomes are as varied as those on land. From beaches to the darkest ocean depths, living things find ways to survive and thrive.

Mangrove
On the shore, the mangroves' thick, tangled roots slow the water's flow and create a swamp.

Mediterranean shrubland
Hot, dry summers can lead to fires that actually help the biome's typical shrubby plants sprout.

Desert and dry shrubland
Desert inhabitants have to be able to survive on less than 250 mm (10 in) of rainfall per year.

Arctic Tundra
A cold, dry biome where the soil stays frozen at depth. This permafrost stops trees from growing.

Polar desert
Too cold and dry for almost all plants. Only animals dependent on the sea, such as penguins, can live here.

A **biome's** plants and animals form a **complex** and interconnected community

Biomes

A biome is an area that we define according to the animals and plants that live there. They have to adapt to the biome's specific conditions such as temperature, type of soil, and the amount of light and water.

Pacific coast temperate rainforest
Stretching from Alaska to California, this coniferous forest is wet and relatively cool all year round.

Białowieża Forest
Located in Poland and Belarus, this is one of the largest existing parts of an ancient temperate broadleaf forest that covered much of Europe.

Deforestation in Europe
Europe lost most of its forest cover to crop-growing and pasture long ago. Between 1100 and 1500, many trees were cut down to provide timber for ship-building.

Amazon rainforest
The Amazon forest produces about 20 per cent of Earth's oxygen. Only the remote central and northern parts are untouched forest. Much of the rest has been logged (cut down for timber) and regrown or turned into palm oil and rubber plantations.

Congo rainforest
This is the second-largest tropical rainforest, home to gorillas, chimpanzees, and bonobos.

Atlantic rainforest
Just 7 per cent of this tropical rainforest in Brazil remains, and much of what is left is in small fragments.

KEY

- **Boreal forest**
  Cool northern (boreal) regions
- **Tropical rainforest**
  Warm and wet climates
- **Temperate broadleaf forest**
  Mild (temperate) climates
- **Temperate coniferous forest**
  Mild (temperate) climates
- **Original forest cover**
  Red areas show the full extent of the world's forest cover in the past, before the effects of human activity

Forests

Forests are vital to life on Earth. They make the air breathable, protect the soil, and preserve fresh water supplies. But they are disappearing fast – by 2011, about half of the world's original forests had been cut down by humans.

Types of forest

Forests differ according to climate. Each type of forest has its own distinct collection of trees, forest-floor plants, and animal life. Tropical rainforests are the most diverse – 30 per cent all plant and animal species live in the Amazon alone. Some tropical forests are evergreen, but the trees in some others lose their leaves in the dry season.

Temperate broadleaf
Deciduous trees, such as oak and beech. Herbs, ferns, and shrubs on the forest floor.

WORLDWIDE, AN AREA OF TROPICAL RAINFOREST ABOUT THE SIZE OF

Taiga
This vast belt of boreal forest stretches right across northern Europe and Asia. In the east, it is wilderness, but much in the west is working forest, managed for timber and paper production.

Disappearing forests
With the world's population growing, demand for timber and land for farming and towns has increased the rate of forest clearance. Here you can see the decline in Borneo's forests since 1950.

Borneo, 1950   **1985**   **2010**

Japan
Japan retains a lot of its original woodland and is the most thickly forested industrialized country.

Borneo
Home of most of the world's orangutans, Borneo's rainforest has declined by more than 50 per cent since the mid-20th century (see above).

New Guinea
Two-thirds of New Guinea is largely unspoiled rainforest, with many unique species. It is at risk from logging, mining, and agriculture.

At current rates of **logging**, in **100 years** we will **no longer** have any **rainforests**

New Zealand
The remote southwest of New Zealand is home to unique temperate rainforests full of lush tree ferns.

Australia
About 38 per cent of Australia's forests have been lost since European settlers arrived around 200 years ago.

Tropical rainforest
As many as 300 tree species per hectare (2.5 acres). Often rich in forest-floor plants.

Boreal forest
Hardy conifers, such as larch, spruce, fir, and pine. Mosses dominate the forest floor.

Desert tortoise
Has shovel-shaped forefeet that help it dig burrows, where it shelters from the extreme heat of the day and the cold of the night.

Mesquite
Tree with a long taproot that can grow up to 60 m (190 ft) long, as it searches for water deep underground.

Caribou
A deer specialized in living in the cold, high Arctic. Although it experiences the low rainfall of a desert, there is rarely a water shortage, because water collects in pools above the deeply frozen soil. There is no hot Sun to dry it up.

Greenland ice sheet
This region experiences the coldest and driest conditions in the Arctic. Nothing can live on top of the ice.

Great Basin
USA

Chihuahuan Desert
Northern Mexico

Almería, Spain
Europe's driest region is true desert in parts.

Syrian Desert

Negev Desert

Mojave Desert
USA

Sonoran Desert
USA and Mexico

Spadefoot toad
Digs a burrow with spadelike ridges on its back feet. It then makes a watertight cocoon of shed skin and waits – sometimes for months – for the next rains to fall.

Saguaro cactus
Tall, treelike cactus that grows in the Sonoran Desert. Survives by storing water in its fleshy trunk and stems when it rains. It lives off this water until the rains come again.

Sechura Desert
Peru

Dromedary camel
Native to Arabia but lives throughout deserts of north Africa. Can live on fat stored in its hump and survives for 2 weeks without a drink.

Sahel
A belt of semidesert, also known as arid savanna, or dry grassland.

Atacama Desert, Chile
Like the Namib, this is a coastal desert, kept dry by a cold ocean current nearby.

Tsamma watermelon
Wild ancestor of the watermelon. Grows in the Kalahari Desert and stores water in its big, round fruits.

Patagonian Desert, Argentina
Some experts call this a dry grassland rather than a desert.

Lithops, or "living stones"
Plants also known as pebble plants, because their single pair of round leaves looks like stones, camouflaging them against grazers. The leaves also help the plants to save and store water.

Namib desert beetle
Collects minute droplets of water from early-morning fog on its legs and hard wing cases. When enough water forms, a droplet rolls down the beetle's body into its mouth.

Namib Desert
Namibia

Kalahari Desert
Botswana and South Africa

Deserts

Deserts are found from the icy poles to the tropics. So while all deserts have low rainfall – less than 250 mm (10 in) a year, and often much less – they are not always hot. Even in hot deserts, the nights are often cold.

Antarctica
One of the most arid parts of Earth's largest desert is its Dry Valleys region (right), the only area of Antarctica not covered in thick ice, and where there is almost no snowfall. Cold, dry winds blast down from mountain peaks and turn all moisture to water vapour.

THE SAHARA TAKES UP 8 PER CENT OF THE EARTH'S LAND

Desert terrain

Deserts range widely in how they look. Soil forms only very slowly and the land is often bare rock or gravel. Any loose sandy soil may be blown into dunes. Sometimes, though, tough grasses or fleshy plants bind the soil together.

Dunes, or "sand seas"
Shifting mountains of sand can prevent plant growth.

Rock and gravel
Where no plants grow, the bedrock is often visible.

Dry grassland
Desert grasses can form soil and provide food for grazers.

Fleshy plants
Fleshy, water-storing plants may form thick vegetation.

Saxaul
Short, shrubby tree that grows in the deserts of Asia. Its spongy bark stores water, and it holds on to its water supply, because its tiny leaves lose very little water by evaporation.

Central Asia
The deserts and semideserts here are so dry simply because they are so far from the ocean.

Turpan Depression, China
Low-lying area hotter than the surrounding regions.

Kyzyl Kum
Kazakhstan, Uzbekistan, and Turkmenistan

Karakum
Turkmenistan

Dasht-e Lut
Iran

Takla Makan
China

Gobi Desert
Mongolia and China

Arabian Desert

Thar Desert
Pakistan and India

Thorny devil
This lizard of Australian deserts collects dew on its body at night, then microscopic grooves on its skin channel the water to its mouth.

The whole of the **Antarctic** continent is a desert – the **largest** on **Earth**

Great Sandy Desert

Gibson Desert

Simpson Desert

Great Victoria Desert

TYPES OF DESERT

Hot desert
Tends to lie in two bands, 15–35 degrees north and south of the equator, where the atmosphere tends to create weather systems that produce no rainfall.

Semidesert
This dry land type often lies at the edges of deserts and ranges from dry grassland to shrubland. Some has short periods of rain, but no more than 500 mm (20 in) a year.

Cold desert
Includes the Gobi in Asia and the Atacama in South America. In these deserts, temperatures are low, and the main form of moisture may be fog or snow.

Tundra
Treeless region of low-growing shrubs. Qualifies as a desert due to rainfall of less than 250 mm (10 in) a year, but low evaporation means there is no lack of water.

Polar desert
Includes the driest, coldest parts of the Arctic where few tundra plants can live, and the ice sheets on Greenland and Antarctica, where almost nothing lives at all.

AND IS AROUND THE SAME SIZE AS THE ENTIRE UNITED STATES!

Ice

Ice covers one-tenth of Earth's surface, mostly in the polar regions. At earlier times in Earth's history, when the climate was much cooler, ice covered an area up to three times larger than it does today.

Sea ice

Sea ice is frozen sea. It forms when the ocean's surface freezes in winter. Where it lasts year round, it may be 6 m (20 ft) thick – elsewhere it is thinner. "Pancake ice" (right) is discs of sea ice up to 10 cm (4 in) thick.

Summer ice The polar sea ice cover shrinks in summer, but some sea always remains under a layer of ice.

Winter ice As the weather gets colder, the polar sea ice spreads far beyond its summer limits.

Sea of Okhotsk

Siberia

ASIA

Arctic Circle

EUROPE

Kara Sea

Laptev Sea

Severnaya Zemlya

Novosibirskiye Ostrova

Franz Josef Land

Novaya Zemlya

Barents Sea

Svalbard

Norwegian Sea

East Siberian Sea

PACIFIC OCEAN

Greenland Sea

North Pole

Wrangel Island

Wandel Sea

Chukchi Sea

ARCTIC OCEAN

Iceland

Bering Sea

Bering Strait

Greenland

Denmark Strait

ATLANTIC OCEAN

Beaufort Sea

Queen Elizabeth Islands

Amundsen Gulf

Baffin Bay

Davis Strait

0 km   500   1000   150

0 miles   500

Ice sheet A vast layer of land ice that has formed over thousands or even millions of years.

Ice shelf A floating extension of an ice sheet or glacier, usually hundreds of metres thick.

Baffin Island

Labrador Sea

Arctic Circle

Land ice

Thick ice gradually builds up on land as old, unmelted snow is compacted by layers of fresh snow and turned into ice. Antarctica's ice sheet is up to 4.8 km (3 miles) thick.

Hudson Bay

NORTH AMERICA

THE LARGEST ICEBERG EVER SEEN IN THE NORTH ATLANTIC ROSE 168 M

Prince
Edward
Islands

Crozet
Islands

SOUTHERN

OCEAN

Antarctic Circle

Kerguelen

South
Georgia

South
Sandwich
Islands

*Scotia
Sea*

SOUTH
AMERICA

Falkland
Islands

South
Orkney
Islands

Drake Passage

*Weddell
Sea*

Fimbul
Ice Shelf

Riiser-Larsen
Ice Shelf

Brunt
Ice Shelf

*Larsen
Ice Shelf*

Berkner
Island

Filchner
Ice Shelf

*Ronne
Ice Shelf*

ANTARCTICA

Heard and
McDonald
Islands

*Amery
Ice Shelf*

Davis Sea

+ **South Pole**

*West
Ice Shelf*

INDIAN

OCEAN

*Bellingshausen
Sea*

*Shackleton
Ice Shelf*

*Amundsen
Sea*

| 0 km | 500 | 1000 | 1500 |

| 0 miles | 500 | 1000 |

*Ross
Ice Shelf*

*Ross
Sea*

PACIFIC

OCEAN

Antarctic Circle

Icebergs

At the coast, waves, currents, and tides break chunks off ice sheets and glaciers, which float away as icebergs. Only about 12 per cent of an iceberg is visible above the water.

Iceberg tracks The arrows show paths of two satellite-tracked icebergs as they drifted on the ocean currents.

Glaciers and ice sheets

Glaciers are permanent bodies of land ice that form on high mountains in many parts of the world. These "rivers of ice" flow slowly downhill until the end melts or meets the ocean. As they flow, they dramatically shape the landscape by carving deep valleys in the rock over which they pass. The largest glaciers are the ice sheets that cover land in polar regions such as the Greenland and Antarctic ice sheets.

■ GLACIERS

The map shows the time of day at 12 noon Coordinated Universal Time (UTC), the base from which all times are set. The columns are time zones labelled with the number of hours they are ahead or behind UTC. If you stood halfway between the boundaries of a time zone with your watch set to the correct time, at 12 noon the Sun would be at its highest point.

Time zones

As Earth rotates, some of the it faces the Sun and the rest is in darkness. Since the Sun is high in the sky at noon, noon is at different times in different places. We adjust by splitting Earth into time zones.

Day and night

On the globe of Earth, we can see day and night divided by a straight line from north to south. When Earth is laid flat as on the map here, the light and dark areas form a bell shape.

Northern summer

Earth is tilted. When the North Pole tilts towards the Sun and the South Pole leans away, it is summer in the northern hemisphere (northern half of the world) and winter in the southern hemisphere, as on the main map.

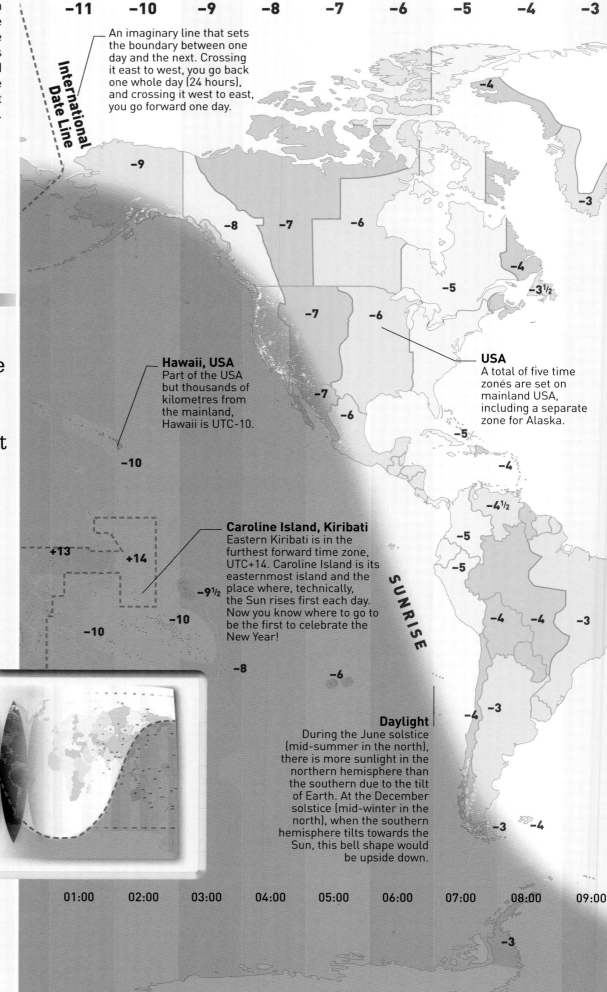

International Date Line
An imaginary line that sets the boundary between one day and the next. Crossing it east to west, you go back one whole day (24 hours), and crossing it west to east, you go forward one day.

Hawaii, USA
Part of the USA but thousands of kilometres from the mainland, Hawaii is UTC-10.

USA
A total of five time zones are set on mainland USA, including a separate zone for Alaska.

Caroline Island, Kiribati
Eastern Kiribati is in the furthest forward time zone, UTC+14. Caroline Island is its easternmost island and the place where, technically, the Sun rises first each day. Now you know where to go to be the first to celebrate the New Year!

Daylight
During the June solstice (mid-summer in the north), there is more sunlight in the northern hemisphere than the southern hemisphere due to the tilt of Earth. At the December solstice (mid-winter in the north), when the southern hemisphere tilts towards the Sun, this bell shape would be upside down.

SUNRISE

−11 −10 −9 −8 −7 −6 −5 −4 −3

01:00 02:00 03:00 04:00 05:00 06:00 07:00 08:00 09:00

BEFORE TIME ZONES, LOCAL TIME WAS DECIDED BY THE TOWN TIME-

−1 0 +1 +2 +3 +4 +5 +6 +7 +8 +9 +10 +11 +12 −12

International Date Line

Norway–Russia border
You can be in three time zones at once at this border. The time moves a full 3 hours forward when crossing from Norway to Russia.

Russia
As the country that spans the greatest distance west to east, Russia has the most time zones – 11.

Greenwich, London, UK
Where global standard time was first agreed.

China
Some countries prefer not to be divided by different time zones, even if they cross more than one. Though it spans five time zones, all of China is at UTC+8 hours.

India
Some nations set their clocks to half- or even quarter-hour time zones, so they can be as close to the worldwide time zone as possible.

SUNSET

Prime Meridian

The Prime Meridian is a line of longitude running from the North to the South Pole and through Greenwich, UK. It is the origin of worldwide time and given a longitude value of 0°. All time zones are measured from this, according to 24 other lines of longitude corresponding to the 24 hours in the day.

These are the worldwide times according to the position of the Sun in the sky. Artificial time zones often differ according to political borders, in order to unite an area or an entire nation under one time.

11:00 12:00 13:00 14:00 15:00 16:00 17:00 18:00 19:00 20:00 21:00 22:00 23:00 24:00

//night at 12:00 UTC on June 20th, 2012

KEEPER, WHO RECORDED 12 PM WHEN THE SUN WAS DIRECTLY OVERHEAD.

Living world

Humpback whales
Two humpbacks "breach" (leap out of the water) off the coast of Alaska, USA. During winter, humpbacks move south to warmer waters.

Introduction

Life exists in every corner of the planet – from high mountains to deep oceans, and from blazing deserts to the freezing polar regions. Each animal's body, life cycle, and behaviour is adapted to its particular habitat, because this maximizes its chances of survival. Plant species, too, have their own adaptations that help them thrive.

Birds

The power of flight allows birds to reach the remotest islands, and some to live in different parts of the world in summer and winter, migrating between the two. There is almost nowhere on Earth that lacks birdlife. Here are their secrets.

● **Lightweight bones**
Most bird bones are hollow, reinforced by bony struts.

● **Flight feathers**
Wing and tail feathers provide lift and steer the bird in fight.

● **Warming feathers**
Two layers of body feathers keep the bird's skin warm.

● **Efficient lungs**
Bird lungs are far more efficient than mammals', giving them the oxygen they need for energetic flight.

Bald eagle
A North American bird of prey, the bald eagle snatches fish from lakes.

Marine animals

Living in water gives more support than living on land, so many sea creatures survive without strong skeletons. Sea water carries clouds of microscopic life-forms and dead matter, and many sea animals can afford to give up moving from place to place, fix themselves to the sea bed, and "filter feed" by grabbing these passing pieces of food.

Coral
Tropical coral reefs are giant growths of filter-feeding life forms on the sea bed.

● **Gills**
Sea mammals must surface to breathe, but fish take oxygen directly from the water using their gills.

● **Smooth shape**
Fast-moving marine animals have a streamlined body, which helps them move through the water easily.

● **Buoyancy aid**
Some fish have an air-filled "swim bladder" to help control buoyancy.

● **Bioluminescence**
It is dark in the ocean depths. Many deep-sea animals produce light by chemical reactions in their bodies.

Desert cacti
The waxy, fleshy bodies of these desert plants store water. The leaves are reduced to spines, which lose less water to the air. The roots of a cactus may spread out over a wide area, to absorb as much water as possible.

Spineless cactus
A spineless variety of the prickly pear.

Polar regions

The sea in the Arctic and Antarctic is so cold, fish are in danger of freezing. Above the water, it is even colder, and no large, cold-blooded animals exist. Warm-blooded animals – those able to retain body heat – predominate. Polar mammals often have two layers of fur: an underlayer of soft hairs that trap air warmed by the animal's body close to the skin, and an outer coat of coarse hairs that keeps out the fiercest gales.

Polar bear
This Arctic mammal has a bulky, rounded body surrounded by fat and fur that keep it warm.

● **Natural antifreeze**
Most polar fish have a chemical in their blood that prevents ice crystals forming in the body.

● **Small extremities**
Polar bears and Arctic foxes have small, rounded ears and muzzles that reduce heat loss.

● **Legs and feet**
Some animals have long legs that wade through snow or broad feet that act like snowshoes.

Western brown snake
A venomous Australian desert species.

Desert regions

The driest parts of the world challenge plants and animals, and desert wildlife is not as abundant as in wetter regions. Desert life-forms must get enough water – and keep what they have. Some desert animals get all the water they need from their food.

● **Nocturnal lifestyle**
Many animals are active only at night. Gerbils and jerboas retreat into daytime burrows to stay cool.

● **Large extremities**
Fennec foxes have huge ears that radiate heat away from the body.

● **Drinking dew**
Insects and lizards drink dewdrops. Larger desert animals that feed at dawn take in dew as they eat plants.

Plant adaptations

In rainforests, plants are in strong competition to reach sunlight. They all grow as fast as possible whenever there is an opening allowing in the Sun. In deserts, plants get plenty of light, but they struggle to get enough water from the soil.

Bo tree leaves
This fig tree with drip-tip leaves grows in the rainforests of southern Asia.

Rainforest plants
To reach the Sun, many rainforest plants are specialist climbers, and others are epiphytes, which grow on top of other plants. Many rainforest leaves taper to a long point, a "drip tip", to help excess rainwater run off.

Dinosaur fossils

Dinosaur fossils occur in layers of rock that formed millions of years ago. Scientists excavate (dig up) the fossils in places where the movement of Earth's tectonic plates has forced these layers to the surface.

Ornithomimus ⑥

⑦ *Tyrannosaurus*

Barosaurus ③

● *Coelophysis*

● *Eoraptor*

Zhucheng, or **Dinosaur City**, in China has yielded more than **7,600** fossils

Major fossil sites

Triassic

KEY
The dinosaur age spanned three geological periods. Fossil sites are coloured according to period (mya = million years ago).

- ○ **Triassic (251–200 mya)**
- ● **Jurassic (200–145 mya)**
- ○ **Cretaceous (145–65 mya)**

● **Ghost Ranch, USA**
Thousands of *Coelophysis* found here in 1947. They died when caught in a flash flood about 215 mya.

② **Valle de la Luna, Argentina**
Eoraptor – perhaps the first true dinosaur, from about 230 mya – was discovered here in 1993.

Jurassic

③ **Dinosaur National Monument, US**
Famed for long-necked sauropod dinosaurs, such as *Barosaurus*.

④ **Solnhofen, Germany**
Discovered here in 1861, *Archaeopteryx* was an ancestor of modern birds. It lived 150 mya.

⑤ **Liaoning, China**
Many birdlike dinosaur fossils have been unearthed here, including the turkey-sized *Caudipteryx*.

AS WELL AS BONES, NESTS, EGGS, AND TRACKS, FOSSILS INCLUDE

Dinosaur footprints

Fossil-hunters have found tracks preserved in mud and sand that later turned into rock. These tracks can tell us how dinosaurs walked, and whether they lived alone or in groups. The sites shown here are all in the USA.

Dinosaur Ridge
Dakota. Hundreds of prints unearthed when building a road.

Dinosaur State Park
Connecticut. One of the largest track sites in North America.

Purgatoire River site
Colorado. Giant sauropod prints left on a lake shore.

Archaeopteryx

⑤ *Caudipteryx*

⑨ *Hadrosaurus*

⑧

Protoceratops

⑩

Leaellynasaura

Cretaceous

⑥ **Dinosaur Provincial Park, Canada**
An entire *Ornithomimus*, from 75 mya, was discovered here in 1995.

⑦ **Hell Creek, USA**
Ancient rocks here have yielded a range of dinosaur fossils – among them, *Tyrannosaurus*.

⑧ **Flaming Cliffs, Mongolia**
The first *Protoceratops* fossils and dinosaur nest were found here.

⑨ **Zhucheng, China**
Since the 1960s, over 50 tonnes of fossils have been found here. Rich in remains of "duck-billed" dinosaurs such as *Hadrosaurus*.

⑩ **Dinosaur Cove, Australia**
About 105 mya this was near the South Pole. Until the discovery of *Leaellynasaura* here in 1989, no one knew dinosaurs could live through cold, long, dark winters.

TRACES OF SKIN AND FEATHERS, AND EVEN DINOSAUR POO!

Americas

1. Bald eagle
Stabs its sharp talons into prey and rips open the body with its hooked bill.

2. Wolverine
Preys on rodents, other small mammals, and even weakened reindeer.

3. Coyote
Eats almost anything, from insects, and frogs to calves and lambs.

4. Boa constrictor
A large snake, the boa coils around its prey and squeezes until the victim suffocates.

5. Jaguar
Unable to run fast for very long, the jaguar relies on stealth to creep up on prey.

6. Piranha
Using razor-sharp teeth, a shoal can reduce a deer to bones in minutes.

Africa

7. African rock python
Growing up to 8.5 m (28 ft) long, preys on monkeys, pigs, and birds.

8. African lion
The females do most of the hunting. The male defends the pride's territory.

9. African wild dog
Can chase down prey at 40 kph (25 mph) for 5 km (3 miles) or more.

Eurasia

10. Polar bear
Can kill with a single swipe from one of its 18-kg (40-lb) front paws.

11. Golden eagle
With its amazing eyesight, can spot prey 2 km (1.25 miles) away.

12. Grey wolf
Packs can bring down animals as large as reindeer or musk ox.

10. Polar bear
On land and sea ice within the Arctic Circle

11. Golden eagle
Europe, North America, northern Asia, and Africa

1. Bald eagle
Throughout North America

2. Wolverine
Canada and northern USA; Scandinavia and Siberia

3. Coyote
From Alaska to Central America

19. Killer whale (orca)
Oceans worldwide

4. Boa constrictor
From Mexico to Argentina

20. Common dolphin
Cool and warm oceans worldwide

21. Sperm whale
Worldwide, to the edge of the polar ice

7. African rock python
Africa, south of the Sahara

18. California sea lion
Pacific coast of North America and the Galápagos Islands

5. Jaguar
Southwestern USA to northern Argentina

3,000–4,000:
the number of **tigers** left in the wild

Predators

Found on every continent and in every ocean, predators are animals that kill and eat other creatures. With their incredible array of hunting strategies and body parts adapted for killing, they include some of the most fascinating species on the planet.

22. Tuna
Cool and warm oceans worldwide

6. Piranha
North, central, and eastern South America

23. Great white shark
Cool and warm oceans worldwide

WHEN A PEREGRINE FALCON DIVES ON A PIGEON AT FULL SPEED,

13. Eurasian lynx
Furry ear tufts gather prey noises in the dense forest, where sounds are muffled.

14. Peregrine falcon
Dives onto prey at 200 kph (125 mph), making it the fastest animal on Earth.

15. Eurasian badger
Eats worms, insects, birds, frogs, lizards, and small mammals, plus plants.

16. Tiger
Camouflaged by its stripes, stalks its prey and kills with a bite to the neck.

17. Sunda clouded leopard
For its size, this shy forest-dweller has longer canine teeth than any other cat.

Oceans

18. California sea lion
May hunt nonstop for 30 hours, diving for up to 5 minutes at a time.

19. Killer whale (orca)
Many hunt sea loins, dolphins, and even whales. Can snatch seals off the ice.

20. Common dolphin
Together, dolphins can herd fish to the surface, where they are easier to catch.

21. Sperm whale
May dive to 1,200 m (4,000 ft) deep in search of giant squid.

22. Tuna
Able to swim at 80 kph (50 mph), hunts fish and squid near the surface.

23. Great white shark
Kills dolphins, seals, and big fish, including sharks, with its jagged teeth.

12. Grey wolf
Much of Asia, parts of Europe, and northern North America

13. Eurasian lynx
Europe (mainly northern and eastern parts) to northern and central Asia

14. Peregrine falcon
Lives on every continent except Antarctica

15. Eurasian badger
Europe and Asia below the Arctic Circle

16. Tiger
Parts of India, China, Siberia, and southeast Asia

Australasia

24. Saltwater crocodile
Preys on water buffalo and cattle on land. Spends much of its life at sea, catching fish.

25. Tasmanian devil
This marsupial's strong jaws can crush the bones of birds, fish, and small mammals.

8. African lion
Africa, south of the Sahara

17. Sunda clouded leopard
Sumatra and Borneo in southeast Asia

9. African wild dog
Africa, south of the Sahara

Food chains
A food chain shows how food energy passes from one living thing to the next. Food chains start with plants, which use sunlight to make their own food. Plants are eaten by herbivores. Predators eat herbivores and smaller predators.

Martial eagle (top predator)

Meerkat (predator)

Imperial scorpion (predator)

Grasshopper (herbivore)

Grass

A FOOD CHAIN IN THE AFRICAN SAVANNA

24. Saltwater crocodile
Southeast Asia and Northern Australia

25. Tasmanian devil
Tasmania, an island off the southeastern tip of Australia

THE FORCE OF THE IMPACT MAY DECAPITATE (BEHEAD) ITS PREY!

Deadly creatures

Very few wild animals hunt people for food, but many pose a danger when they feel threatened – especially those armed with venom.

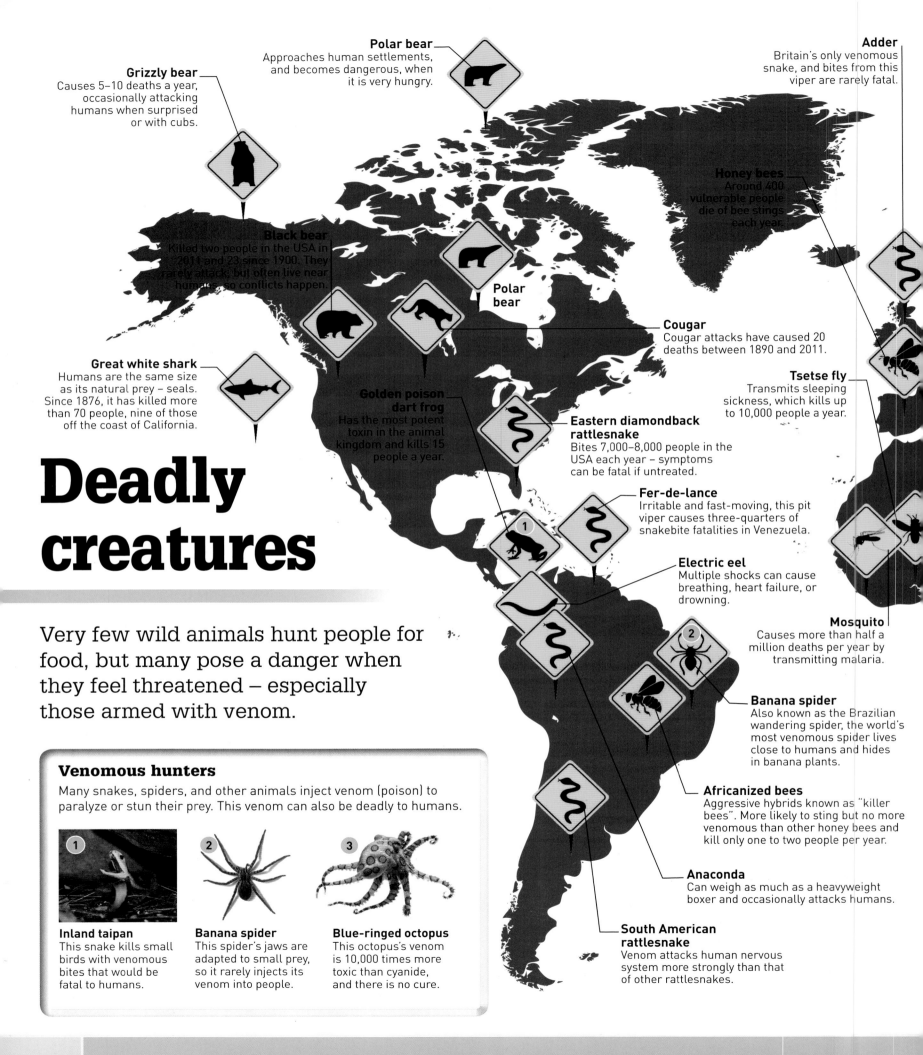

Grizzly bear
Causes 5–10 deaths a year, occasionally attacking humans when surprised or with cubs.

Polar bear
Approaches human settlements, and becomes dangerous, when it is very hungry.

Adder
Britain's only venomous snake, and bites from this viper are rarely fatal.

Honey bees
Around 400 vulnerable people die of bee stings each year.

Black bear
Killed two people in the USA in 2011 and 23 since 1900. They rarely attack, but often live near humans so conflicts happen.

Polar bear

Cougar
Cougar attacks have caused 20 deaths between 1890 and 2011.

Tsetse fly
Transmits sleeping sickness, which kills up to 10,000 people a year.

Great white shark
Humans are the same size as its natural prey – seals. Since 1876, it has killed more than 70 people, nine of those off the coast of California.

Golden poison dart frog
Has the most potent toxin in the animal kingdom and kills 15 people a year.

Eastern diamondback rattlesnake
Bites 7,000–8,000 people in the USA each year – symptoms can be fatal if untreated.

Fer-de-lance
Irritable and fast-moving, this pit viper causes three-quarters of snakebite fatalities in Venezuela.

Electric eel
Multiple shocks can cause breathing, heart failure, or drowning.

Mosquito
Causes more than half a million deaths per year by transmitting malaria.

Banana spider
Also known as the Brazilian wandering spider, the world's most venomous spider lives close to humans and hides in banana plants.

Africanized bees
Aggressive hybrids known as "killer bees". More likely to sting but no more venomous than other honey bees and kill only one to two people per year.

Anaconda
Can weigh as much as a heavyweight boxer and occasionally attacks humans.

South American rattlesnake
Venom attacks human nervous system more strongly than that of other rattlesnakes.

Venomous hunters

Many snakes, spiders, and other animals inject venom (poison) to paralyze or stun their prey. This venom can also be deadly to humans.

1 Inland taipan
This snake kills small birds with venomous bites that would be fatal to humans.

2 Banana spider
This spider's jaws are adapted to small prey, so it rarely injects its venom into people.

3 Blue-ringed octopus
This octopus's venom is 10,000 times more toxic than cyanide, and there is no cure.

ANIMAL TOXINS ARE USEFUL. SCIENTISTS HAVE ADAPTED THE

Some victims of **stonefish venom** say it's good for their **arthritis**

Defensive poisons

Many animals use toxins (poisons) against predators. The poisons may be in spines or stings, or they may ooze from the skin.

Golden poison dart frog
The skin has enough toxin to kill 10 people. It is effective against its snake predators.

Pufferfish
The poison in puffers' skin and liver could kill a human, but these fish make a prized dish in Japan.

Stonefish
This fish's spines stop predators, but also endanger humans who are pricked by accident.

Asp viper
Causes about 90 per cent of all snake bites in Italy, but only 4 per cent of bites are fatal.

Pallas's viper
0.1 gram (0.004 oz) of venom can kill a human, but only strikes if threatened.

European black widow spider
Venom is 15 times stronger than a rattlesnake's.

Fat-tailed scorpion
Most dangerous scorpion in North Africa and the Middle East.

Tiger
Until recent improvements in tiger management, hunted and killed around 50 people every year in the Sundarbans mangroves of India.

Pufferfish
Eaten as *fugu* in Japan and *bok-uh* in Korea, but some parts highly poisonous. Accidents happen when untrained people catch and eat the fish.

Common krait
Most venomous land snake in Asia.

Malayan pit viper
Responsible for 700 snakebites annually in Malaysia.

Box jellyfish
Has enough toxin to kill 60 humans, and in the Philippines, 20–40 people die each year from stings.

Puff adder
Lives in heavily populated areas and is the most dangerous snake in Africa.

Lionfish
Its venomous spines can cause severe injuries, breathing difficulties, and temporary paralysis.

Saltwater crocodile
Causes hundreds of deaths a year in New Guinea, the Solomon Islands, and Indonesia.

Elephant
Attacks people when threatened and kills nearly 300 people a year.

African lion
Kills 70 people a year in Tanzania, either by hunting them for food, or in defence.

Asian cobra
Responsible for most deaths by snakebite (of the 50,000 per year).

Stonefish
Venom injected by spines causes unbearable pain and death in a few hours if not treated.

Hippopotamus
Causes more than 300 deaths a year, sometimes by upturning boats.

Komodo dragon
Giant lizard that grows up to 3 m (10 ft) long and may, very rarely, attack and eat humans.

Cape buffalo
Attacks when defending itself and kills more than 200 people a year.

Blue-ringed octopus
Enough toxin in its body to kill 26 adult humans. It can cause respiratory failure.

Tiger snake
In humans, 60 per cent of untreated bites result in serious poisoning or death.

Black mamba
Fastest snake on Earth kills any human it bites unless the victim takes antivenom.

Redback spider
Also known as the Australian black widow. Deaths are rare, but bites can result in fatal complications.

Six-eyed sand spider
There is no antivenom for its bite but (luckily) it is shy and has little contact with people.

Inland taipan
Deadliest venom of any land snake, but snake scientists are almost the only known victims. They recovered after treatment with antivenom.

Funnel-web spider
Its extremely toxic venom could kill a small child in 15 minutes.

TOXIN FROM POISON DART FROGS TO PRODUCE A POTENT PAINKILLER.

How the aliens invade

Stowaways
Fleas and other parasites can hitch a ride via animal or human hosts. Rats, mice, and insects can travel hidden in ships' cargo. Some species sneak in when empty cargo ships take on local sea water as ballast, then pump it out at their destination. Every day, 3,000 marine organisms are transported around the globe in this way.

Black rat

Introduced by humans
Some species are deliberately introduced by humans. This can be by hunters, for meat, fur, or sport, by farmers, or for biological control, where a new species is introduced to control native pests. Some invaders are escaped pets, or plants washed out of home aquariums. A few have even been released by immigrants who introduce familiar wildlife to remind them of home!

Cane toad

Racoon
Since its introduction, has devastated the seabird population of Canada's Scott Islands.

Zebra mussel
Travelled from the Caspian Sea to the Great Lakes of North America in the ballast water of ships.

Common starling
European native bird released in New York City in 1890 by homesick English settler Eugene Schieffelin.

Stoat
Introduced to islands off Denmark and the Netherlands, it eradicated the native water voles.

Grey squirrel
This US import to Britain competes for habitat with the native red squirrel.

Rainbow trout
In California, this fish has wiped out the Sierra Nevada yellow-legged frog.

Gypsy moth
This French native costs about $870 million each year in damage to US trees.

Japanese knotweed
Dense thickets of this weed crowd out native plant life on riverbanks and roadsides in Europe.

Velvet tree
Known as the "purple plague of Hawaii", it threatens native rainforest plant species.

Flowerpot snake
Emigrated to the USA from Africa and Asia by stowing away in the soil of exported pot plants.

Chinese mitten crab
A migrating species that threatens the US fishery industry by eating bait and trapped fish.

Feral pig
In Mexico's Revillagigedo Islands, this former farm animal preys on the endangered Townsend's shearwater bird.

American bullfrog
Native to North America, it is now a resident of more than 40 countries.

Fire ant
Threatens tortoises on the Galápagos Islands by eating hatchlings and attacking adults.

Red-vented bulbul
A major agricultural pest in Tahiti, it feeds on fruit and vegetable crops.

Feral goat
Has caused serious damage to native vegetation on the Galápagos Islands.

Africanized honey bee
Specially bred for survival in the tropics, this "killer bee" turned out to be too aggressive and unpredictable for beekeepers.

About 90 per cent of the world's islands have now been invaded by rats

Red Deer
Introduced from Europe to provide sportspeople with game.

House mouse
With no predators on Gough Island, non-native mice have grown to three times their usual size.

Alien invasion

Invasive species are animals or plants that enter and thrive in an environment where they are not native. Native species (plants and animals already living there) usually have no defence. The invading aliens can wipe out native species by preying on them or out-competing them.

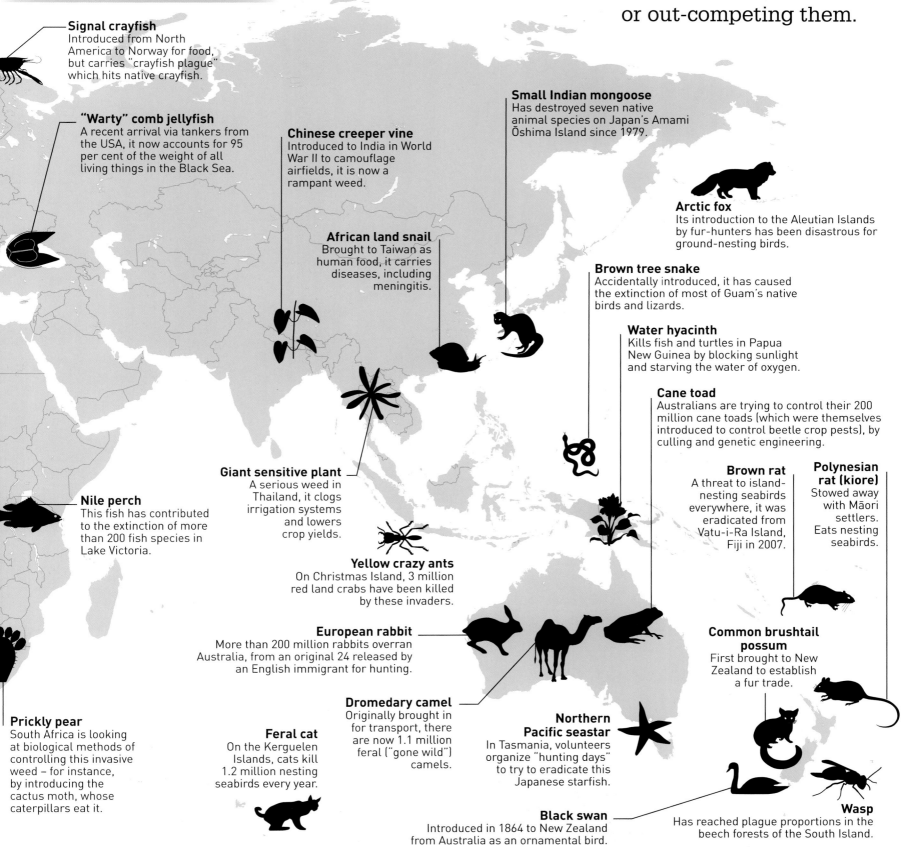

Signal crayfish
Introduced from North America to Norway for food, but carries "crayfish plague" which hits native crayfish.

"Warty" comb jellyfish
A recent arrival via tankers from the USA, it now accounts for 95 per cent of the weight of all living things in the Black Sea.

Chinese creeper vine
Introduced to India in World War II to camouflage airfields, it is now a rampant weed.

Small Indian mongoose
Has destroyed seven native animal species on Japan's Amami Ōshima Island since 1979.

African land snail
Brought to Taiwan as human food, it carries diseases, including meningitis.

Arctic fox
Its introduction to the Aleutian Islands by fur-hunters has been disastrous for ground-nesting birds.

Brown tree snake
Accidentally introduced, it has caused the extinction of most of Guam's native birds and lizards.

Water hyacinth
Kills fish and turtles in Papua New Guinea by blocking sunlight and starving the water of oxygen.

Cane toad
Australians are trying to control their 200 million cane toads (which were themselves introduced to control beetle crop pests), by culling and genetic engineering.

Brown rat
A threat to island-nesting seabirds everywhere, it was eradicated from Vatu-i-Ra Island, Fiji in 2007.

Polynesian rat (kiore)
Stowed away with Māori settlers. Eats nesting seabirds.

Nile perch
This fish has contributed to the extinction of more than 200 fish species in Lake Victoria.

Giant sensitive plant
A serious weed in Thailand, it clogs irrigation systems and lowers crop yields.

Yellow crazy ants
On Christmas Island, 3 million red land crabs have been killed by these invaders.

European rabbit
More than 200 million rabbits overran Australia, from an original 24 released by an English immigrant for hunting.

Common brushtail possum
First brought to New Zealand to establish a fur trade.

Prickly pear
South Africa is looking at biological methods of controlling this invasive weed – for instance, by introducing the cactus moth, whose caterpillars eat it.

Feral cat
On the Kerguelen Islands, cats kill 1.2 million nesting seabirds every year.

Dromedary camel
Originally brought in for transport, there are now 1.1 million feral ("gone wild") camels.

Northern Pacific seastar
In Tasmania, volunteers organize "hunting days" to try to eradicate this Japanese starfish.

Black swan
Introduced in 1864 to New Zealand from Australia as an ornamental bird.

Wasp
Has reached plague proportions in the beech forests of the South Island.

ANIMAL EXTINCTIONS THAT HAVE OCCURRED IN THE LAST 400 YEARS.

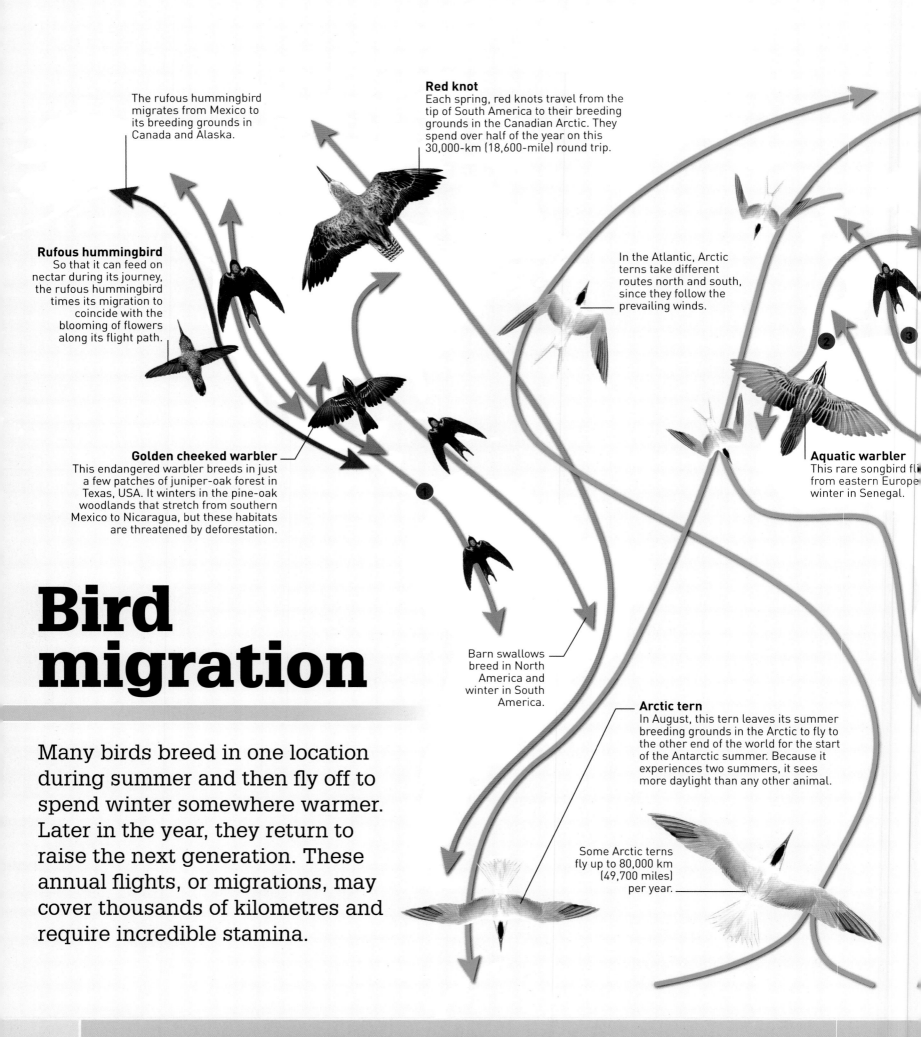

The rufous hummingbird migrates from Mexico to its breeding grounds in Canada and Alaska.

Red knot
Each spring, red knots travel from the tip of South America to their breeding grounds in the Canadian Arctic. They spend over half of the year on this 30,000-km (18,600-mile) round trip.

Rufous hummingbird
So that it can feed on nectar during its journey, the rufous hummingbird times its migration to coincide with the blooming of flowers along its flight path.

In the Atlantic, Arctic terns take different routes north and south, since they follow the prevailing winds.

Golden cheeked warbler
This endangered warbler breeds in just a few patches of juniper-oak forest in Texas, USA. It winters in the pine-oak woodlands that stretch from southern Mexico to Nicaragua, but these habitats are threatened by deforestation.

Aquatic warbler
This rare songbird fl[...] from eastern Europe [...] winter in Senegal.

Bird migration

Barn swallows breed in North America and winter in South America.

Arctic tern
In August, this tern leaves its summer breeding grounds in the Arctic to fly to the other end of the world for the start of the Antarctic summer. Because it experiences two summers, it sees more daylight than any other animal.

Many birds breed in one location during summer and then fly off to spend winter somewhere warmer. Later in the year, they return to raise the next generation. These annual flights, or migrations, may cover thousands of kilometres and require incredible stamina.

Some Arctic terns fly up to 80,000 km (49,700 miles) per year.

Red-breasted goose
After wintering on the Black Sea coast, the red-breasted goose heads north to raise chicks on the Russian tundra.

Swallows that spend winter in India fly north to nest in northern Asia.

Barn swallows of southern Africa fly to Europe to breed.

Ferruginous duck
This widespread duck breeds on marshes and lakes and makes relatively short migrations. Ferruginous ducks that breed in western China and Mongolia winter in India and Pakistan.

A bar-tailed godwit may travel up to 460,000 km (286,000 miles) during the course of its life.

Sociable lapwing
In 2007, the sociable lapwing's migration route from east Africa to Kazakhstan and Russia was revealed for the first time by satellite-tracking.

Barn swallow
Each year, huge flocks migrate between northern Australia and eastern Russia. These birds can catch insects on the wing and drink by scooping water from lakes.

Arctic terns fly from the **Antarctic** to **Greenland** in **40 days**

Aided by strong tailwinds at high altitude, the godwits can make the return journey to New Zealand in just over eight days.

Migration bottlenecks
Places that lie on the flight paths of many birds are known as migration bottlenecks. They are especially important for soaring birds such as storks and birds of prey. These birds can't fly far over water, so they rely on routes with the shortest sea crossings. Millions of birds may pass at these favourite spots.

1 Panama
About 3 million birds of prey use this land bridge between North and South America.

2 Strait of Gibraltar
Soaring birds fly to Europe from Africa on this sea crossing of only 14 km (9 miles).

3 Sicily and Malta
These islands are "stepping stones" for birds flying from Italy to Tunisia and Libya.

4 Egypt
Egypt has several bottlenecks – such as Suez, Hurghada, and Zaranik – for birds flying between Africa and Europe or Asia.

Bar-tailed godwit
Bar-tailed godwits fly from New Zealand to breed in Alaska. On the return trip, one was tracked flying 11,680 km (7,258 miles) nonstop over the Pacific Ocean – the longest continuous journey ever recorded for a bird.

This flock of white storks flying over Spain reached Europe via the Strait of Gibraltar.

1. Alaska
Humpbacks make "bubblenets". They blow a curtain of bubbles around a shoal of fish. This causes the fish to cluster tightly, making them easier to catch.

2. Sea of Cortez
Humpback whales in the Sea of Cortez can often be seen breaching (launching out of the water) and slapping their fins and tails on the surface. Whales are social animals, and this behaviour may be a form of communication.

4. North Atlantic right whale
There are only about 450 North Atlantic right whales left. Most spend the summer feeding in the waters from New York to Nova Scotia. They head south in winter to breed in the warmer waters off Georgia and Florida.

3. Baja California, Mexico
The grey whales here are exceptionally friendly, approaching boats to let whale-watchers touch them and even scratch their tongues. The whales migrate between Baja California and Alaska.

5. Brazil
From June to November each year, more than 300 southern right whales gather off the state of Santa Catarina to mate, calve, and nurse their young.

Whales

Graceful swimmers, superb divers, and powerful predators, whales and orcas (a type of dolphin) are among the most impressive ocean creatures. They were once hunted near to extinction. Today, thousands of people take whale-watching trips to see these majestic marine mammals in the wild.

7. South Africa
Each June, southern right whales arrive off the coast of South Africa from their Antarctic breeding grounds, giving whale-watchers a chance to enjoy their spectacular acrobatic displays.

6. Patagonia, Argentina
Orcas snatch elephant seals and sea lions from their colonies. They surge ashore on the surf and grab prey in their jaws as they land on the beach, before manoeuvring back into the water with the next wave. If they misjudged the attack, they would become fatally stranded on the beach.

Migration

Whales travel to cold waters near the poles to feed, then move to warmer waters closer to the equator to breed. Few species migrate across the equator, so there can be separate populations in the northern and southern hemispheres.

KEY

- **Breeding areas** Warmer waters for giving birth
- **Feeding areas** Cooler waters that are rich in food
- ←‑→ **Migration routes** Breeding-to-feeding areas and back
- **Site of spectacular whale behaviour**

1 million sperm whales were killed before hunting them was banned in 1981

10. Migration of humpback whales
In winter, the humpbacks of the western Pacific mate and calve in warm, subtropical waters from the Philippines to Japan. Summer sees them travelling to feed in the extreme north of the Pacific, around the Aleutian Islands.

8. Sri Lanka
Between December and April, Dondra Point, on Sri Lanka's southern tip, is the best place to see blue whales. Unlike most populations of blue whales, this one does not migrate to polar waters to feed. These northern Indian Ocean blue whales both breed and feed year round in tropical waters.

9. Antarctica
Antarctic orcas often hunt in teams, herding their prey together before attacking from different angles. They will also tip over ice floes to knock penguins and seals into the water.

11. Kaikoura, New Zealand
This one of few places in the world where sperm whales can be seen year round. They are attracted by an underwater canyon close to the shore that has abundant marine life, including the giant squid that the whales hunt.

Some **sharks** grow up to **30,000** teeth in their **lifetime**

Freshwater sharks
Some shark species are found in freshwater habitats. The bull shark, for example, lives in warm coastal waters worldwide, but it sometimes swims up larger rivers and into lakes. Bull sharks are very territorial, so if they find humans swimming in their river, they may attack them.

Mississippi River
One bull shark reached Alton, Illinois, 1,850 km (1,150 miles) upstream.

Potomac River
Bull sharks up to 2.4 m (8 ft) long have been caught in the Potomac.

Lake Nicaragua
Bull sharks reach the lake via the San Juan River.

Amazon River
There have been sightings of bull sharks 2,000 km (1,200 miles) from the sea.

Nicole
In 2003–04, a female great white shark, nicknamed Nicole, made the longest known migration by a shark. Nicole swam from Africa to Australia and back – more than 20,000 km (12,400 miles) – in 9 months. She mostly swam at the surface, but at times she reached depths of up to 980 m (3,200 ft).

Nicole's route was tracked using an electronic tag fitted to her fin.

DISTRIBUTION OF SHARKS WORLDWIDE
Some shark species cruise almost all the world's oceans, while others have a more limited range, preferring either cooler or warmer seas.

Whale shark
The largest fish in the sea, reaching lengths of 12 m (40 ft) or more, the whale shark prefers warm waters. It feeds mainly on plankton.

Basking shark
At 10 m (30 ft) long, this is the second-largest fish. Found in temperate seas, it swims open-mouthed, filtering plankton from the water.

Great white shark
Found in the majority of the world's seas, the great white has made the most recorded attacks on humans. It can swim at over 40 kph (25 mph).

Great hammerhead shark
Often found near tropical reefs, the great hammerhead preys on stingrays, using its hammer to pin down the fish before biting them.

Port Jackson
A reef-dweller from around southern Australia, this shark has wide, flat teeth that crush hard-shelled prey such as oysters, snails, and crab

Pygmy shark
At 20–25 cm (8–10 in) long, this is one the smallest sharks. It hunts squid at depths of up 1,800 m (6,000 ft) in subtropical and temperate seas

Sharks

Fast, powerful, and armed with razor-sharp teeth, sharks are superb predators. They are much feared, but attacks on people are relatively rare. Humans, in contrast, kill 100 million sharks per year.

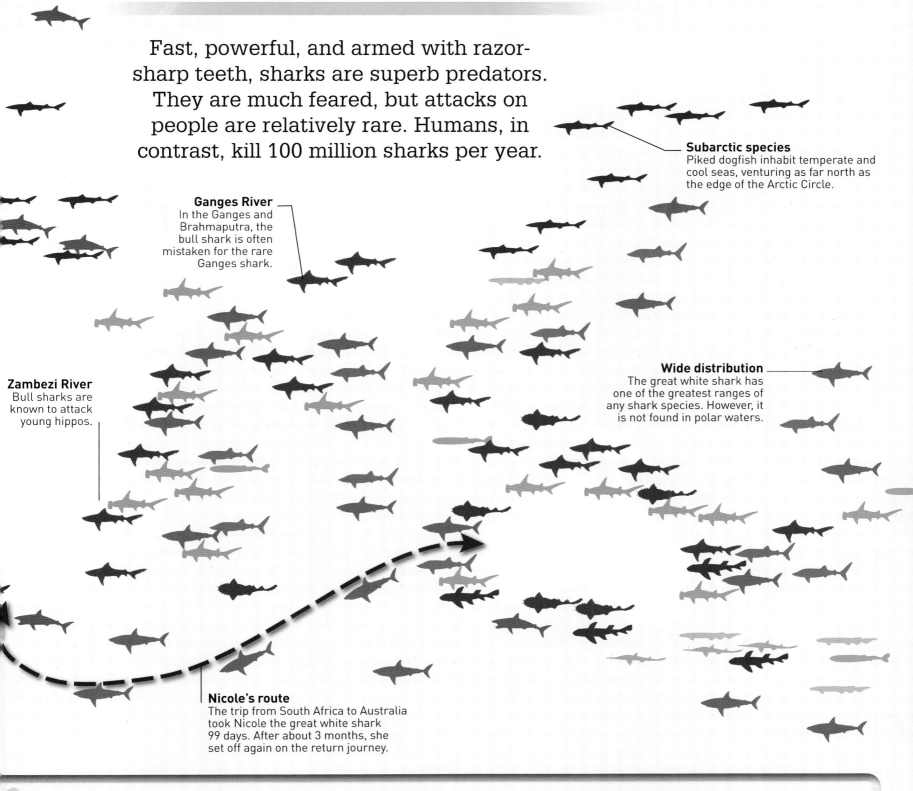

Subarctic species
Piked dogfish inhabit temperate and cool seas, venturing as far north as the edge of the Arctic Circle.

Ganges River
In the Ganges and Brahmaputra, the bull shark is often mistaken for the rare Ganges shark.

Wide distribution
The great white shark has one of the greatest ranges of any shark species. However, it is not found in polar waters.

Zambezi River
Bull sharks are known to attack young hippos.

Nicole's route
The trip from South Africa to Australia took Nicole the great white shark 99 days. After about 3 months, she set off again on the return journey.

Pacific angel shark
This shark of the eastern Pacific lies on the sea bed and ambushes passing fish. It is superbly camouflaged by its mottled, sandy back.

Ornate wobbegong
Elaborately patterned and with fleshy projections around its jaws, this shark inhabits tropical waters, mainly around the Australian coast.

Frilled shark
With its flat head and eel-like body, this frilled shark looks very different to other sharks. It lives near the sea bed in deep water.

Longnose sawshark
The longnose lives off southern Australia. Its snout is a long, sawlike projection edged with rows of large, sharp teeth.

Bull shark
This shark is one of the most dangerous to humans. It preys on sharks, rays, and other fish, as well as squid, turtles, and crustaceans.

Piked dogfish
Once among the most abundant sharks, the piked dogfish is now threatened as a result of overfishing. It gathers in shoals by the thousand.

DROPS OF BLOOD IN THE WATER FROM 5 KM (3 MILES) AWAY.

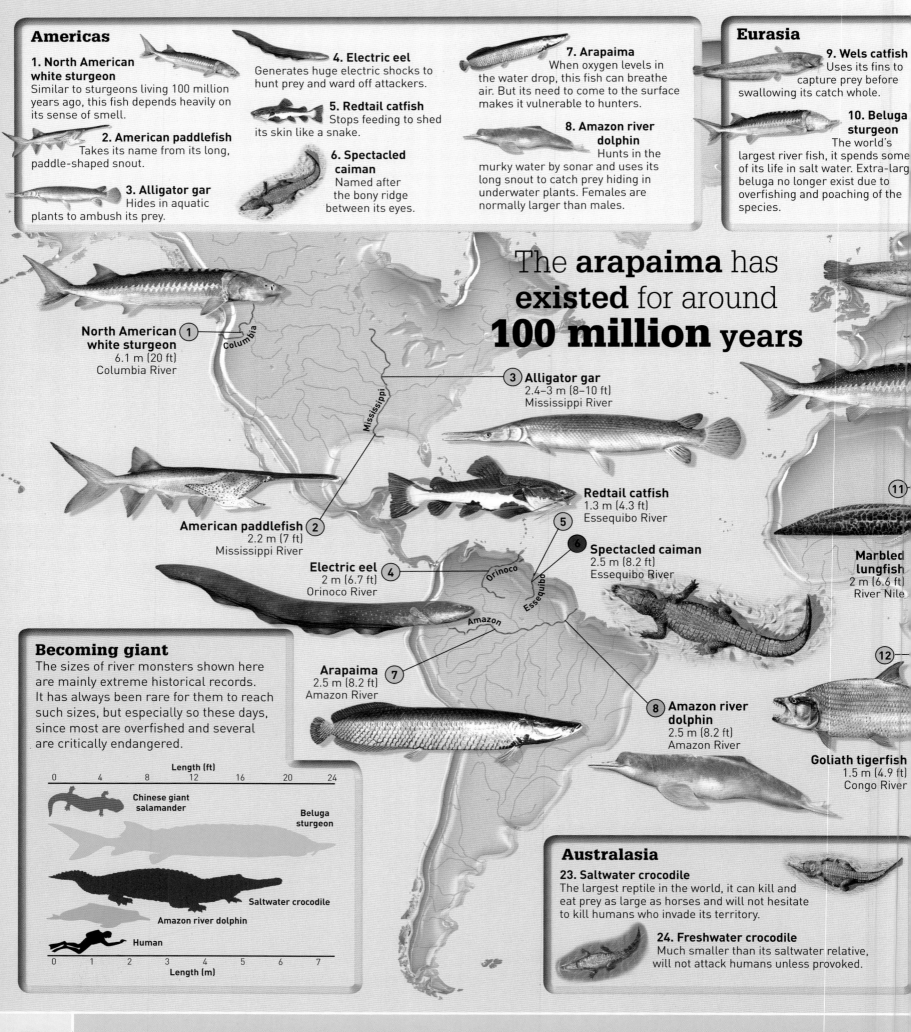

Americas

1. North American white sturgeon
Similar to sturgeons living 100 million years ago, this fish depends heavily on its sense of smell.

2. American paddlefish
Takes its name from its long, paddle-shaped snout.

3. Alligator gar
Hides in aquatic plants to ambush its prey.

4. Electric eel
Generates huge electric shocks to hunt prey and ward off attackers.

5. Redtail catfish
Stops feeding to shed its skin like a snake.

6. Spectacled caiman
Named after the bony ridge between its eyes.

7. Arapaima
When oxygen levels in the water drop, this fish can breathe air. But its need to come to the surface makes it vulnerable to hunters.

8. Amazon river dolphin
Hunts in the murky water by sonar and uses its long snout to catch prey hiding in underwater plants. Females are normally larger than males.

Eurasia

9. Wels catfish
Uses its fins to capture prey before swallowing its catch whole.

10. Beluga sturgeon
The world's largest river fish, it spends some of its life in salt water. Extra-large beluga no longer exist due to overfishing and poaching of the species.

The **arapaima** has **existed** for around **100 million** years

North American white sturgeon ①
6.1 m (20 ft)
Columbia River

Columbia

Mississippi

③ Alligator gar
2.4–3 m (8–10 ft)
Mississippi River

American paddlefish ②
2.2 m (7 ft)
Mississippi River

Redtail catfish
1.3 m (4.3 ft)
Essequibo River

Electric eel ④
2 m (6.7 ft)
Orinoco River

Orinoco

Essequibo

⑤

⑥ Spectacled caiman
2.5 m (8.2 ft)
Essequibo River

⑪ Marbled lungfish
2 m (6.6 ft)
River Nile

Amazon

Arapaima ⑦
2.5 m (8.2 ft)
Amazon River

⑧ Amazon river dolphin
2.5 m (8.2 ft)
Amazon River

⑫

Goliath tigerfish
1.5 m (4.9 ft)
Congo River

Becoming giant
The sizes of river monsters shown here are mainly extreme historical records. It has always been rare for them to reach such sizes, but especially so these days, since most are overfished and several are critically endangered.

Length (ft)
0   4   8   12   16   20   24

Chinese giant salamander

Beluga sturgeon

Saltwater crocodile

Amazon river dolphin

Human

0   1   2   3   4   5   6   7
Length (m)

Australasia

23. Saltwater crocodile
The largest reptile in the world, it can kill and eat prey as large as horses and will not hesitate to kill humans who invade its territory.

24. Freshwater crocodile
Much smaller than its saltwater relative, will not attack humans unless provoked.

IN ANCIENT JAPANESE FOLKLORE, A GIANT CATFISH, NAMAZU,

Africa

11. Marbled lungfish
In the dry season, digs itself into a mud cocoon for up to 2 years.

12. Goliath tigerfish
Fierce fish known to attack humans.

13. Nile perch
When brought to live in new rivers and lakes, can kill so many fish that it causes the extinction of native fish species.

Asia

14. Giant Devil catfish
This rare species has sharp teeth similar to a shark's.

15. Wallago
Human remains have been found inside its stomach.

16. Gavial
An endangered crocodilian with a long, thin snout, good for catching fish. Rarely grows to 7 m (23 ft).

17. Chinese giant salamander
The world's largest living amphibian.

18. Giant freshwater stingray
Finds its prey using an electric field sensor.

19. Kaluga
Cannabalism is common among these sturgeons of the Russian Far East.

20. Taiman
The largest of the salmon family, called the "Mongolian terror trout".

21. Chinese paddlefish
Verging on extinction – none has been seen in the wild since 2003.

22. Giant pangasius
Also known as the "dog-eating catfish". Another critically endangered fish.

Wels catfish
3 m (9.8 ft)
River Danube

Kaluga
5.6 m (18.6 ft)
Amur River

Chinese giant salamander
2 m (6.6 ft)
Mekong River

Taiman
2.1 m (6.9 ft)
Amur River

Giant devil catfish
2 m (6.6 ft)
Great Kali River

Kaluga sturgeon
7.2 m (24 ft)
Black Sea

Wallago
2.4 m (7.9 ft)
Rivers of Southeast Asia

Chinese paddlefish
3 m (9.8 ft)
Yangtze River

Giant pangasius
3 m (9.8 ft)
Mekong River

Gavial
7 m (23 ft)
Chambal River

Saltwater crocodile
6 m (20 ft)
Northern Australia

Nile perch
1.8 m (6 ft)
River Nile

Giant freshwater stingray
4.88 m (16 ft)
Chao Phraya

Freshwater crocodile
4 m (13 ft)
Northern Australia

Black Sea

Caspian Sea

Amur

Nile

Chambal

Great Kali

Yangtze

Mekong

Chao Phraya

River monsters

KEY
River monsters belong to different groups.
○ Fish
○ Mammal
● Reptile
○ Amphibian

Hiding in the muddy waters of the world's greatest rivers are some of the largest and most ferocious freshwater creatures in existence. Many can become larger than a fully grown human, and some are man-eaters.

LIVES IN THE MUD UNDER THE SEA AND CAUSES EARTHQUAKES.

59

KEY

Some insects are found the world over, and some survive only in specific habitats and locations. The insects shown in this map are in locations where they are frequently found.

- Insect swarms
- Insect record-breakers

Types of swarms

When insects form a large group that moves as a single unit, it is called a swarm. Insects sometimes migrate in swarms, or they swarm when looking for a new home, a mate, or for food.

Rhyniognatha
Earliest.
A 400-million-year-old fossil was found in Scotland in 1919. Scientists believe it may have been winged.

Mayflies
Shortest adult life.
Mayflies spend most of their lives as water-living nymphs. They transform into winged adults that live just long enough to mate and lay eggs. The most extreme example is the American sand-burrowing mayfly whose adult life lasts just a few minutes.

Maricopa harvester ant
Most venomous.
12 stings can kill a rat.

Fairy wasp
Smallest.
0.14 mm (0.006 in) long. Only visible under a powerful microscope.

Termite queen
Longest life.
Can live up to 45 years.

Goliath Beetle
Heaviest larva.
Weighs up to 100 g (3.5 oz).

Swarming insects

1 Asian ladybird
Swarm through Oregon, USA, every autumn looking for somewhere to hibernate for the winter.

2 Miller moths
Six- to eight-week migration from eastern plains of Colorado, USA, to the mountains.

3 Monarch butterfly
The long migration from the northern USA to Mexico lasts generations – no one butterfly makes the whole journey.

4 Termites
In New Orleans, Louisiana, USA, termites build colonies by invading people's homes.

5 Cicadas
In the eastern states of the USA, cicada swarms have 13- or 17-year cycles. Young cicadas, known as nymphs, mature, mate, and then die.

6 Mayflies
Annual mass hatching from Lake Erie, Ohio, USA. They mate, reproduce, then die.

7 Army ants
Found in Central and South America, swarms are called "raids" made up of 100,000– 2,000,000 adults.

8 Africanized bees
Aggressive hybrid first released in São Paulo, Brazil. Swarm in groups of up to 100,000 bees.

9 Dragonflies
A single swarm in Argentina in 1991 was estimated to contain 4–6 billion migrating dragonflies.

10 Flying ants
Swarm annually in Britain as part of a mating ritual.

11 Driver ants
Found in central and east Africa, vast swarms kill animals in their path. People who cannot move out the way, such as the sick or injured, can be killed.

12 Mosquito swarms
In May 2012, immense swarms of mosquitoes hatched from a lake near Mikoltsy, Belarus.

13 Locusts
The largest swarm recorded was in Kenya in 1954. It covered 200 sq km (77 sq miles) and involved an estimated 10 billion locusts.

14 Midges
The midges that form mating swarms start out as underwater larvae in lakes. Once they can fly, they take off and try to find a mate.

AT ANY ONE TIME, THERE ARE AN ESTIMATED 10 QUINTILLION

Honey bees
Bees swarm when they leave their hive to find a new home. Once a small number of special "scouts" have agreed on the most suitable site, the queen and the main cluster of bees fly to the new location.

Monarch migration
By instinct alone, every year millions of monarch butterflies travel up to 4,000 km (2,500 miles) from northern parts of America to warmer climates as far south as Mexico, before they return north in spring.

Midges
Huge swarms appear over Lake Victoria in Africa during the annual mating season, as thousands of dancing male midges try to attract females. Swarms are so big, they look like giant brown clouds.

Froghopper
Highest jumper.
Jumps 71 cm (28 in) – 150 times its own height – comparable to a human jumping over a 60-storey building!

12

Stink bug
Smelliest.
Toxic odour can be smelled by humans about 1–1.5 m (3.3–5 ft) away.

Himalayan cicada
Loudest.
Calls at up to 120 decibels – as loud as an ambulance siren.

Flea
Longest jumper.
Can jump over 200 times its body length.

Scientists estimate **4–20 million** types of **insect** have yet to be **discovered**

13

14

Dung beetle
Strongest.
Can pull 1,141 times its own body weight – the equivalent to an average human pulling six double-decker buses full of people.

Chan's megastick
Longest.
56.7 cm (22.3 in).
Only six specimens have ever been found, all on the island of Borneo.

Australian tiger beetle
Fastest runner.
9 kph (5.6 mph). Equivalent to a human running at 770 kph (480 mph).

Giant weta
Heaviest.
Weighs up to 70 g (2.5 oz) – heavier than a sparrow.

Insects

Horse fly
Fastest flyer.
Maximum speed recorded briefly on take-off at 145 kph (90 mph). The next fastest are dragonflies and hawk moths, at around 50–55 kph (30–35 mph).

We know of more than 1 million different types of insect, and more are identified every year. They have fascinating habits, and their strange appearances can be seen with the help of microscopes and special cameras.

(10,000,000,000,000,000,000) INDIVIDUAL INSECTS ALIVE.

European yew
Europe. All parts are poisonous, apart from the bright red, berrylike cones.

White snakeroot
Eastern North America. Poisons can travel in the food chain through cattle to humans, causing "milk sickness".

Water hemlock
North America and Europe. One of North America's most toxic plants.

Aloe vera
North Africa. Long valued for its medicinal properties, has a gel in its leaves that is said to help heal damaged skin and aid digestion.

Cobra lily
Northern California and Oregon, USA. Like other pitcher plants, it attracts insects into its pitchers – jug-shaped body parts full of digestive juices.

Venus flytrap
North and South Carolina, USA. Closes its jawlike traps on prey in 0.1 seconds.

Trumpet pitcher
Southeast USA. Uses a drug in its nectar to make insects slip into its pitchers.

Resurrection fern
Southeast USA. Can survive for 100 years without water. Appears to die but is quickly revived by moisture.

The six floral kingdoms

Plant geographers divide the world into six "kingdoms". Each kingdom has its own unique collection of native plant life. Some kingdoms span more than one continent. The Cape kingdom, however, covers just the southern tip of Africa.

Manchineel
Florida (USA), Central America, and the Caribbean. Milky-white sap causes blisters on human skin.

Boreal kingdom
North America and Eurasia. Native plant families include rose (above), birch, brassica, primrose, saxifrage, and buttercup.

Neotropical kingdom
Mexico to southern South America. Characteristic native plant families include bromeliads and cacti.

Palaeotropical kingdom
Most of Africa, southern Asia, and Polynesia. Umbrella thorn acacias (above) and baobab trees are native plants.

Sensitive plant
Central and South America. A type of *Mimosa* and one of the few plants capable of rapid movement. The leaves fold and droop when touched. They re-open after a few minutes.

Australian kingdom
Australia. Many Australian plants are completely unlike those elsewhere in the world. Bottlebrushes (above) are an example.

Antarctic kingdom
Southern South America, New Zealand, and Antarctica. *Francoa* herbs (above) form one of the few uniquely Antarctic families.

Cape kingdom
A small yet highly diverse region around the Cape of South Africa, with around 9,000 plant types, including the king protea (above).

Genlisea
Africa and Central and South America. Traps prey in the soil with its strange underground leaves.

Butterwort
Boggy parts of Europe, North and South America, and Asia. Sticky hairs on its leaves trap insects.

Monkshood
Mountains of the northern hemisphere. Also known as aconite, it is a source of a deadly poison contained in the seeds.

KEY

 Poisonous plants
Some plants contain toxic chemicals. The map shows ten of the most poisonous.

 Carnivorous plants
These plants trap and consume insects and other small creatures.

 Incredible plants
Four amazing plants are highlighted on the map, but there are many thousands more worldwide.

Sundew
Worldwide in boggy places. Traps insects with droplets of glue coating its leaves.

Waterwheel plant
Africa, Asia, Australia, and Europe. Freshwater plant a little like an underwater Venus flytrap.

Deadly nightshade
Europe, north Africa, and west Asia

Castor oil plant
East Africa, Mediterranean, and India. Origin of the poison ricin.

Nepenthes rajah
Borneo. This giant pitcher plant may sometimes catch rats or lizards to eat.

Rosary pea
Indonesia. Toxins are used in herbal medicines of southern India.

Welwitschia
Namib Desert. Has just two strap-like leaves. They can grow up to 6.2 m (20 ft) long over several centuries.

Rainbow plant
Western Australia. Catches insects on its sticky leaves.

Terrestrial bladderwort
Africa. Grows on wet, rocky surfaces and catches tiny prey in bladderlike traps.

World of plants

Scientists estimate there are at least 400,000 species of plant on Earth — and possibly many thousands more. Some parts of the world have a rich diversity of plant life; in others, such as Antarctica, plants are scarce.

Total number of life-forms

There are many thousands of species of vertebrate animals, such as birds and reptiles. But these numbers are dwarfed by the amazing number of other life-forms, particularly insects.

NUMBER OF SPECIES IN EACH GROUP	
13,000	Algae
74,000	Fungi
17,000	Lichens
320,000	Plants
85,000	Molluscs (squid, clams, snails, and relatives)
47,000	Crustaceans (crabs, shrimps, and relatives)
102,000	Arachnids (spiders, scorpions, and relatives)
1,000,000	Insects
71,000	Other invertebrates (without backbones)
62,000	Vertebrates (animals with backbones)

70,000 weevils
Weevils form only one family of beetles, yet there are more different types than all the world's vertebrates.

Giraffe-necked weevil

Cratosomus roddami, a weevil

Eupholus linnei, a weevil

Barren Arctic
Plants grow very slowly in the cold Canadian Arctic, so there is not a lot of food to go round. Vegetation is ground-hugging, with little variety of homes for small animals – unlike forests. Biodiversity is low.

Rich Amazon
The Amazon is the largest and oldest tropical forest on Earth. In general, large, continuous areas of habitat support the greatest diversity of species.

Deserted Sahara
There are hardly any amphibians in this dry environment, but the few that survive here are uniquely adapted to the conditions. Preserving areas of pristine Sahara would ensure the survival of some rare creatures.

Unique Atlantic Forest
This small coastal strip of rainforest in Brazil is not only rich in species. Because it is isolated from other rainforests, many of its species are also found nowhere else.

KEY
This map shows the pattern of biodiversity across the world's land, combining measures of 5,700 mammal species, 7,000 amphibians, and 10,000 species of bird. This gives an overall measure, because the variety of these three groups usually mirrors the total biodiversity, including the numbers of different insects and plants. Scientists know biodiversity in the oceans is lower than on land, but it is not shown on the map.

Lowest   Highest

BIODIVERSITY (SPECIES RICHNESS)

Biodiversity

Richness of different life-forms, or species, is called biodiversity. Places such as tropical rainforests are naturally high in biodiversity. Harsh environments have fewer species, but those species might be unique and equally precious.

IN BORNEO'S TROPICAL RAINFOREST, SCIENTISTS ONCE FOUND 1,200

A few tough species
Only a few animal species have what it takes to survive in cold habitats such as the Russian Arctic.

Diverse tropical Asian forests
Tropical rainforest is the most biodiverse habitat. It has abundant water and no shortage of food. The trees provide a multitude of animal homes, from their roots up to their crowns. The climate changes little. All these things allow plants and animals to diversify by evolution into thousands of species.

Borneo
Scientists found an amazing 1,200 tree species here within a tiny plot of rainforest.

Himalayas and Hundu Kush
This mountainous region is home to 25,000 plant species, or 10 per cent of the world's total.

Varied African highlands
Mountains are diverse places because they contain a range of different conditions at different heights. At each height lives a different community of plants and animals adapted to those conditions.

Life on land is as much as **25 times** as varied as **life in the sea**

POISON-DART FROGS
There are 175 species in the poison-dart frog family, which lives in the tropical rainforests of Central and South America. They are all related, but each has evolved slightly differently.

Mimic poison-dart frog   Granular poison-dart frog

Three-striped poison-dart frog

Yellow-banded poison-dart frog

Brazil-nut poison-dart frog

Golden poison-dart frog

DIFFERENT TYPES OF TREE WITHIN AN AREA THE SIZE OF A VILLAGE.

Unique wildlife

Some parts of the world are home to animals and plants that live nowhere else. These places are often remote islands, where life is cut off. In other cases, they are patches of unusual habitat, complete with the unique wildlife that depends on it.

California
A Mediterranean-type climate results in some unique forests featuring the world's largest living organism – the giant sequoia, a gigantic species of coniferous tree.

Mexican pine-oak forests
These forests on Mexican mountain ridges are patches of habitat not found anywhere else nearby. There are nearly 4,000 endemic plants and unique birds such as the Montezuma quail.

Hawaii and Polynesia
Only certain life-forms have reached these remote islands. Hawaii has no ants, but has 500 species of unique fruit fly, all evolved from a single species blown ashore 8 million years ago. Some of them are flightless and have taken up antlike lifestyles. Hawaii also has many unique plants, including the strange Hawaiian silversword, endemic to its mountain tops.

Galápagos Islands
These islands were made famous by Charles Darwin for their unique wildlife, including their giant tortoises.

Tropical Andes
Perhaps the richest region on Earth, these mountains are home to 664 species of amphibian, 450 of which are in danger of dying out. Of 1,700 bird species, 600, including this fiery-throated fruiteater, are found nowhere else.

Western Mediterranean
Europe's hot spot of unique wildlife. One species of midwife toad lives only on Majorca, and Barbary macaques live only on Gibraltar and in patches of habitat in Morocco and Algeria.

Canary Islands
Rich in endemic plants, the Canary Islands off Africa are named after their unique bird, the canary.

Caribbean Islands
Each island has its own versions of many plants and animals. This Cuban knight anole lives only on Cuba.

Atlantic Forest
This thin strip of rainforest is cut off from the Amazon rainforest, so it has its own set of wildlife, including the endangered golden lion tamarin.

75 per cent of the unique plants of the Canary Islands are endangered

ENDEMIC HOT SPOTS
Scientists have shown that these regions have the greatest number of plant species living only within a small area. They call these species "endemic" to that area. In these hot spots of unique plants, scientists tend to find lots of endemic animals, too.

■ Region rich in endemic species

BIOMES

- Tropical dry broadleaf forest
- Tropical coniferous forest
- Temperate broadleaf forest
- Temperate coniferous forest
- Tropical moist broadleaf forest
- Boreal forest
- Savanna
- Flooded savanna
- Steppe
- Mountain grasslands and shrublands
- Mediterranean shrublands
- Desert and dry shrublands
- Arctic tundra
- Polar desert
- Mangroves

Mountains of southwest China
Each ridge of mountains has its own distinct wildlife. Endangered species, such as the Yunnan snub-nosed monkey, live only here.

Philippines
Of this country's 1,000 types of orchid, 70 per cent grow nowhere else.

Wallacea
This region is named after 19th-century naturalist Alfred Russell-Wallace, who noticed its unique wildlife such as the piglike babirusa.

New Guinea
This large island is home to many unique birds of paradise and several endemic tree kangaroos, including this species, the ursine tree kangaroo.

East Melanesia
This string of islands has 3,000 endemic plant species and unique insects such as this Ulysses swallowtail butterfly.

Eastern Mediterranean
The Cedar of Lebanon lives only in a small area, including Lebanon, Israel, Palestine, and parts of Syria, Jordan, and Turkey.

Ethiopian Highlands
These highlands are home to 30 endemic bird species and the endangered Ethiopian wolf.

Madagascar
Ninety-eight per cent of Madagascar's land mammals, 92 per cent of its reptiles, 68 per cent of its plants, and 41 per cent of its breeding bird species exist nowhere else on Earth. All 16 mantella frogs are also endemic to the island.

Sri lanka and Western Ghats
This hot spot is home to 5,000 species of flowering plant, 139 mammal species, 508 birds, and 179 amphibian species.

Sundaland
Naturalists outline this region because its wildlife is distinct from next-door regions. One bizarre plant unique to Sundaland is *Rafflesia*, the stinking corpse lily.

East African Highlands
These islands of high ground in a sea of savanna support unusual plants such as the giant lobelia that grows on the slopes of Mount Kenya and Kilimanjaro.

Cape region
This is a small area of amazingly distinctive plantlife, including 6,000 endemic species such as this pincushion protea.

Western Australia
Like the South African Cape region, this is a "habitat island" of Mediterranean-type shrubland, full of plants found nowhere else, including the odd kangaroo paw.

New Caledonia
Nothing like the strange, flightless kagu bird is found anywhere else in the world.

Kittlitz's murrelet
Alaska and Russian Far East

Maui parrotbill
Hawaii, USA

Vaquita
Gulf of California

Hawaiian monk seal
Hawaii, USA

Iberian lynx
Spain

Blue iguana
Grand Cayman
Island, Caribbean

Lamotte's roundleaf bat
Mount Nimba (border area of Guinea, Liberia, and Côte d'Ivoire)

Variable harlequin frog
Costa Rica

Short-tailed chinchilla
Mountains on the Bolivia–Chile border

Western gorilla
Congo rainforest

Glaucous macaw
Argentina, Uruguay, Paraguay, and Brazil

Blue-eyed black lemur
Madagascar

Maui parrotbill
In danger because of the loss of its forest habitat, only around 500 now survive.

Hawaiian monk seal
Once hunted for its skin and oil, today many become tangled in fishing nets or die because of pollution.

Over **4,000** species may soon be **extinct**

Critically endangered

All these animals are classed as "critically endangered" on the Red List – a list kept by the IUCN (International Union for the Conservation of Nature). This means they may soon die out completely in the wild.

Vaquita
This porpoise is the most endangered sea mammal in the world. Only 100–300 now remain.

Kittlitz's murrelet
Thousands of these seabirds have been killed by sticky oil, spilled from giant tankers.

Blue iguana
This lizard lives only on Grand Cayman Island. Fewer than five may now exist in the wild.

Variable harlequin frog
One of several harlequin frog species critically endangered due to a fungal disease.

Short-tailed chinchilla
Hunted for its soft grey fur, this small rodent is now almost extinct in the wild.

Glaucous macaw
Became rare because so many were caught and sold as pets. Only sighted twice in 100 years.

Iberian lynx
If it dies out, it will be the first big cat species to go extinct for 10,000 years.

Western gorilla
Many of these apes are killed for their meat, or have died from disease.

Lamotte's roundleaf bat
This African mammal has become endangered mainly through the loss of its habitat.

Greater bamboo lemur
Less than 100 have been spotted in 20 years of surveys.

Blue-eyed black lemur
Like many other lemurs, this one could soon die out due to loss of its forest habitat.

Russian sturgeon
This fish has been killed for its roe (eggs), known as caviar.

Indian vulture
Many of these birds died afte[r] feeding on cattle that had been given medicine to h[elp] them work longer.

Bactrian camel
Fewer than 1,000 survive in the wild.

Irrawaddy river shark
As no one has seen this spec[ies] for many years, it may be extinct in the wild.

Sumatran orang-utan
Just 7,000 of this species are left, since their forest is being cut down.

PEOPLE ARE WORKING HARD TO SAVE THE WORLD'S FEW REMAINING

Endangered animals

Our world has thousands of species, or kinds, of animal. Many are in danger of dying out, mainly because humans are destroying their habitats, or homes. Some animals have not been seen in their habitats for 50 years or more and can be declared "extinct in the wild".

Russian sturgeon
Caspian, Black, and Azov seas; Ural, Volga, and Danube rivers

Bactrian camel
Gobi Desert of Mongolia and China

Indian vulture
Pakistan and India

Sumatran orangutan
Sumatra, Indonesia

Southern bluefin tuna
These large, bony fish are dying out because too many have been caught by humans for food.

Kakapo (owl parrot)
These birds were hunted by the first humans to settle in New Zealand. Today, only 100 survive.

David's tiger butterfly
Philippines

Greater bamboo lemur
Madagascar

Attenborough's long-beaked echidna
New Guinea

Irrawaddy River shark
Around the mouth of the Irrawaddy River, Myanmar

Javan rhinoceros
Java, Indonesia

Javan rhinoceros
Today, only around 50 adults survive in the remaining rainforest on Java.

David's tiger butterfly
One of the world's most endangered butterflies, found only in the Philippines.

Attenborough's long-beaked echidna
One of three critically endangered echidna (spiny anteater) species.

Woylie
Only 1,000 of these marsupials survive. The species has declined, mainly because of habitat loss.

Woylie
Western Australia

Southern bluefin tuna
Throughout southern oceans

Kakapo
Islands off the coast of New Zealand

KAKAPO – EVERY BIRD IS PROTECTED, AND EACH ONE HAS A NAME!

69

Americas

Passenger pigeon
A flock of this once-common species could contain 2 million birds.

Laysan rail
This bird's Hawaiian habitat was taken over by non-native rats and rabbits.

Xerces blue butterfly
Its habitat of sand dunes in California was replaced by growing cities.

Golden toad
Its extinction may have been caused by habitat loss or a fungal disease.

Labrador duck
Its extinction was not caused by hunting, as its flesh reportedly tasted horrible!

Pinta Island tortoise
The last living member of the species, Lonesome George, died in 2012.

Red-bellied gracile opossum
Its Argentinian forest habitat was turned into grazing land for cattle.

Falkland Island wolf
Hunted to extinction by human settlers.

Eurasia

Great auk
Hunted by humans mainly for its meat and feathers.

Eurasian aurochs
Massive cattle species wiped out by overhunting.

Yunnan lake newt
Became extinct due to the introduction of exotic fish and frogs.

Baiji
Died out when its river habitat was taken over by industry.

Japanese sea lion
Killed by fishermen to prevent them competing for fish.

Woolly mammoth
Lost much of its habitat when the Ice Age ended.

Passenger pigeon
Extinct by 1914

Xerces blue butterfly
Extinct by 1943

Laysan rail
Extinct by 1944

Pinta Island tortoise
Extinct in 2012

Golden toad
Last seen in 1989

Red-bellied gracile opossum
Last seen in 1962

Labrador duck
Extinct by 1878

Great auk
Last one killed in 1852

Quagga
Extinct by 1883

Elephant bird
(Madagascar)
Extinct since 17th century

Falkland Island wolf
Presumed extinct in 1876

Extinct animals

The animal species on this map died out, or became extinct, quite recently and probably as a result of the actions of humans. But extinction has been happening naturally in the animal kingdom for millions of years.

ANIMALS ARE GOING EXTINCT AT UP TO 1,000 TIMES FASTER THAN

Africa

Quagga
Its very distinctive markings made it an easy target for hunters.

Aldabra banded snail
A sudden decrease in rainfall, possibly caused by climate change, spelled extinction for this species.

Large sloth lemur
Gorilla-sized species that died out in Madagascar around 400 years ago.

Elephant bird
Huge flightless bird that was wiped out by hunting.

Dodo
This flightless bird became extinct within only 100 years of humans and their farm animals arriving on the island of Mauritius.

Australasia

Lesser bilby
Probably wiped out by cats and foxes.

Eastern hare wallaby
Extinction was partly due to the introduction of cats, which hunted them.

Desert-rat kangaroo
Thought extinct, recovered, then declared extinct again in 1994.

King Island emu
Wiped out by settlers and their hunting dogs.

Tasmanian wolf
Possibly lost the competition for prey to the dingo.

Moa
Victims of overhunting and loss of habitat.

Woolly mammoth
Extinct by c. 1700 BCE

Eurasian aurochs
Extinct by 1627

Baiji
Last confirmed sighting in 2004

Yunnan lake newt
Last seen in 1979

Japanese sea lion
Last confirmed sighting in 1951

Aldabra banded snail
(Aldabra Island, Indian Ocean)
Last seen in 1997

Desert-rat kangaroo
Last confirmed sighting in 1935, although sightings reported until the 1980s

Eastern hare wallaby
Extinct by around 1890

Large sloth lemur
Extinct by around 1600

Dodo
(Mauritius, Indian Ocean)
Extinct by 1690

Lesser bilby
Reported sightings until the 1960s

Moa
Extinct by around 1400

About **23 per cent** of all **mammals** are in danger of **extinction**

King Island emu
Extinct by around 1802

Tasmanian wolf
Presumed extinct in 1936

THE NATURAL RATE, WHICH IS ABOUT 25 SPECIES PER YEAR.

People and planet

Sprawling city
Los Angeles, California, USA, stretches as far as the horizon in this photo taken from Mount Hollywood. The skyscrapers of downtown LA can be seen on the left.

Introduction

Humans, together with animals and other living things, form what is called the biosphere – the living part of the world. Since modern humans first appeared in Africa about 200,000 years ago, we have colonized virtually the entire world – even hot deserts and the ice-cold Arctic. As we have done so, our impact on the biosphere has been far-reaching.

Human impact

The human "footprint" on planet Earth is deep and broad. We have transformed the landscape – clearing forests to produce food, digging minerals and ores from the ground, and channelling and storing water to meet our needs. Our living space is concentrated into larger and larger cities, but these cities are hungry for food and energy taken from the surrounding land.

Energy
New ways of harnessing the energy of sunlight and wind are reducing our use of fossil fuels. Unlike fossil fuels, these energy sources will never run out.

Natural resources
Buried within Earth's crust there are limited supplies of minerals, metal ores, and fossil fuels (coal, oil, and gas). Once these reserves are exhausted, we will not be able to replace them. Recycling materials and renewable energy will become ever more important.

Population
For most of humanity's existence, the human population grew relatively slowly. In 10,000 BCE, there were only 1–5 million people on Earth. By 1000 BCE, after farming was invented, the population had increased to about 50 million. Since reaching the 1 billion mark in 1804, during the early Industrial Revolution, the population has expanded much more quickly than ever before.

Growing bigger, fast
The period since the late 1950s has seen the human population more than double.

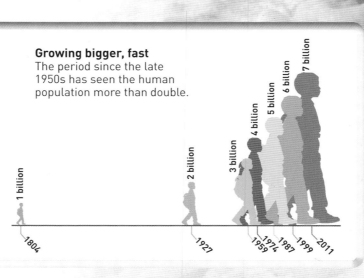

1 billion — 1804
2 billion — 1927
3 billion — 1959
4 billion — 1974
5 billion — 1987
6 billion — 1999
7 billion — 2011

SINCE 1965, THE WORLD'S POPULATION HAS

Agriculture
In 1700 CE, about 7 per cent of Earth's land area was used for growing crops and raising farm animals. Today, that figure has risen to around 40 per cent.

Pollution
Vehicle exhaust gases, smoke and waste chemicals from factories, and oil spills all poison the environment, threatening plant and animal life.

Conservation
To protect the plant and animal life of unique habitats, many countries set up conservation areas, where no farming, industry, or new settlement can occur.

Using water
We build dams and reservoirs to store water. We need it for drinking, for use in industrial processes, and to irrigate crops and generate electricity.

Successful species

Part of the success of humans is down to our ability to use the materials around us to give us protection and shelter. This ability opens up nearly every part of the globe for human living space, no matter how harsh the environment. Even thousands of years ago, the Inuit of the North American Arctic made coats from the fur of caribou (reindeer) and waterproof boots from seal skin. They found a way to live on the meagre resources of the high Arctic.

Inuit boat
The *umiak* is a type of traditional open boat used by Inuit people. The frame is made of driftwood or whalebone, with a walrus- or seal-skin covering. These boats are still used, since the law allows whale hunting only with traditional Inuit tools.

DOUBLED, BUT ITS WEALTH HAS MULIPLIED BY SEVEN.

Canada
Most of the 34.3 million Canadians live below the Arctic Circle.

Iceland
Glaciers, mountains, and volcanoes make much of Iceland uninhabitable.

4

Mexico City, Mexico
North America's largest city.

New York City, USA
Largest population in the Americas. Over half of the USA's 313 million people live in the eastern states.

United Kingdom
About 80 per cent of the UK's 62.4 million people live in urban areas.

Spain
Population has risen by 50 per cent in the last 50 years.

Suriname
Dense jungle covers most of this country.

5

Cairo, Egypt
Africa's largest city, with 6.8 million people.

Colombia
Second-most populous country in South America, with 46.9 million people.

Sahara
Almost deserted, since there is not enough water for crops or pasture.

Nigerian cities
These spikes highlight that Nigeria has the largest population in Africa, at 162.4 million.

Santiago, Chile
About 30 per cent of Chile's 17 million people live here.

Coastal Brazil
Contains most of the region's large cities. To the north is the Amazon Rainforest, with few roads and almost no towns.

Namibia
The very dry conditions in the Namib and Kalahari deserts make human life difficult.

2

Patagonia, Argentina
This cold, dry region is sparsely populated and largely grazing land for sheep.

São Paulo, Brazil
Largest city in South America, home to 11.2 million people.

South Africa
The population of 50.5 million people is mainly concentrated in the east.

Biggest cities

More than half the world's people now live in towns and cities, rather than in the countryside. Many cities have grown quickly and there are now more than 25 continuously built-up areas of more than 20 million people. Below are the 10 largest.

- Tokyo 37,220,000
- Delhi 22,650,000
- Mexico City 20,450,000
- New York City 20,350,000
- Shanghai 20,210,000
- São Paulo 19,920,000
- Mumbai 19,740,000
- Beijing 15,590,000
- Dhaka 15,390,000
- Kolkata 14,400,000

KEY

The map shows population density, or how closely people are packed together. Denser places, such as cities, appear as red mountains.

Low ———— High

Density of people

IN 1800, THE WORLD'S POPULATION WAS LESS THAN 1 BILLION PEOPLE.

Where people live

Siberia, Russia
Few people live here, since the climate is too cold to grow crops. Some spikes show the location of cities based around extracting oil and gas from under the frozen tundra.

Moscow, Russia
Home to 11 million people.

The world's 7 billion people are not spread evenly across the globe: most live where there are natural resources and fertile land for farming. Some places are too hostile for humans to thrive in.

Kolkata, India
Centre of eastern India.

Mongolia
Little of the land is good for growing crops and many people are scattered in small communities of nomadic herdspeople.

Shanghai, China
China's largest city.

Beijing
The capital of China.

Tokyo, Japan
The largest city in the world since the 1960s.

Delhi, India
India's capital sits in the densely populated Ganges River basin, home to 400 million people packed in at nearly 400 per sq km (1,000 per sq mile).

Eastern China
Most of China's 1.3 billion people live here.

Dhaka, Bangladesh
The world's most densely populated, continuously built-up area.

Manila, Philippines
Discounting its outlying districts, this is the world's most densely populated city.

In **Manila**, Philippines, on average **215 people live** in an area the size of a **football pitch**

Mumbai, India
Fast-growing entertainment hub of India.

Jakarta, Indonesia
Of all Indonesia's islands, Java is by far the most crowded and contains the booming capital, Jakarta.

Australia
Australia's centre is too dry to support farming and very few people live here.

Auckland, New Zealand
Almost one in three New Zealanders live here.

Melbourne, Australia
Most of Australia's population lives on the southeastern coast, in cities including Melbourne.

Most sparsely populated countries

		total population	people per sq km	people per sq mile
1	Mongolia	2,671,000	1.7	4.4
2	Namibia	2,171,000	2.6	6.7
3	Australia	23,238,688	3.0	7.8
4	Iceland	319,575	3.1	8.0
5	Suriname	520,000	3.2	8.3

Inuit
Arctic parts of Alaska, Canada, and Greenland, beyond the northernmost trees.

Sami
Northern Scandinavia

Pavee
Ireland

Beja
Sudan, Eritrea, and Egypt

Awá
Rainforests of northern Ecuador and southern Colombia

Nukak-Maku
Tropical forests of the Amazon Basin

Ayoreo
Dry lowlands of Bolivia and Paraguay

Tuareg
Sahara Desert

Fulani
West Africa

Toubou
Tibesti mountains, Chad

Karamojong
Northern Uganda

San
Kalahari Desert – Botswana, Namibia, and South Africa

There are up to
40 million
nomads around the world

Americas

Inuit
For 4,000 years, the Inuit have roamed the region they call Nunavut, "our land".

Awá
The Awá speak their own ancient language called Awa Pit.

Nukak-Maku
The Nukak people are expert hunters who were entirely isolated until 1988.

Ayoreo
The Ayoreo mix a hunter-gatherer lifestyle with agriculture.

Europe

Pavee, or Irish Travellers
The Pavee have strict moral beliefs laid out in "The Travellers' Code".

Sami
The Sami reindeer herders and fur trappers have existed for over 5,000 years.

Roma
There are 8–10 million Roma worldwide, mostly in Europe.

Nenets
Annually, Nenets move huge herds of reindeer up to 1,000 km (620 miles).

Africa

Beja
Only some Beja clans are nomadic.

Tuareg
In Tuareg culture, men rather than women wear the veil.

Toubou
The Toubou are divided into two peoples, the Teda and the Daza.

Fulani
The Fulani traditionally herd goats, sheep and cattle across large areas of west Africa.

Gabra
These herders make their dome-shaped houses out of acacia roots and cloth.

Afar
The Afar live by rivers in the dry season and head for higher ground in the wet season.

Karamojong
This name means "the old men can walk no further".

San
The San are famous for being excellent trackers and hunters.

Roma
Central and eastern Europe

Kazakhs
Kazhakstan and other parts of northern central Asia

Nenets
Arctic Russia

Bakhtiari
Southwestern Iran

Qashqai
Southwestern Iran

Bedouin
The Middle East, predominantly Saudi Arabia

Afar
The Horn of Africa

Gabra
Chalbi Desert of Kenya and highlands of southern Ethiopia

Evenks
Southern Siberia, Mongolia, and northeasternmost China

Moken
Southern Burma and the west coast of Thailand

Yakut
The Yakutia Republic, Russia

Chukchi
The Bering Strait region of Siberia

Penan
Sarawak, Malaysia

Aboriginal peoples
Australia

Asia

Bakhtiari
Bakhtiari means "bearer of good luck". Some still move pastures with the seasons.

Kazakhs
There are still many nomadic Kazakhs left in Xinjiang, China.

Bedouin
Bedouin are desert-dwelling wanderers known for their hospitality.

Qashqai
Qashqai are traditionally farmers known for their beautiful wool products.

Yakut
The Yakut are semi-nomadic reindeer herders.

Evenks
The Evenks kept small herds of domesticated reindeer, which helped the people move around easily.

Chukchi
The word "chukchi" means "rich in reindeer".

Moken
Moken children have extremely good underwater vision due to diving for food.

Penan
In Penan society everything is shared.

Nomads

Nomads move home every year to find fresh pasture or hunting grounds. Some are herders, some hunter-gatherers, and others are wandering traders. Their nomadic lifestyle is quickly dying out as many of them are settling in villages and towns.

Australasia

Aboriginal peoples
Groups of Aboriginals have lived all over Australia for about 60,000 years.

ON'T PROVIDE ENOUGH FOOD FOR PEOPLE TO STAY ALL YEAR ROUND.

MEDIAN AGES AROUND THE WORLD
The median age is the age that divides a population into two equal groups, so that half the people are younger than this age and half are older. The lower the median age, the younger the population. The median age for the whole world is 28.4 years.

Years

14–20	30–35
20–25	35–40
25–30	40+

No data

Greenland
The median age here is 33.5. Over 70 per cent of people are aged 15–64. Population growth is just 0.4 per cent.

Population pyramids
A population pyramid plots the sizes of age groups within a population. A pyramid showing a young population often shows a country where families are large but where the death rate has recently gone down, possibly due to improved health care. Populations age when people begin to have smaller families.

Canada
Canada's population – median age 40.7 – is ageing, with around 16 per cent over the age of 64.

United Kingdom
With a median age of 40.5 years, the UK has an ageing, but still-growing, population.

United States of America
The US population's median age is 36.9 years. About 20 per cent of people are aged 0–14. The population grows by 0.9 per cent each year.

Morocco
This African country has the third-highest median age, at 26.5, after Tunisia (29.7) and Algeria (27.1).

Mexico
In Mexico, where 28.2 per cent of the population is aged 0–14, the median age is 26.7 years.

Guatemala
This is the youngest population in Central America, with a median age of 19.7.

Africa
This is the continent with the youngest population, with a median age of 19.7.

Young and old

Guyana
Guyana's median age of 23.6 years is the lowest in South America. About 32 per cent of Guyanese are aged 0–14.

Poorer developing nations tend to have younger, faster-growing populations than wealthier developed countries, whose populations are ageing and sometimes even declining.

Uruguay
This is the country with the highest median age in South America, at 33.7 years.

BY 2100, ABOUT 22 PER CENT OF THE WORLD'S POPULATION WILL

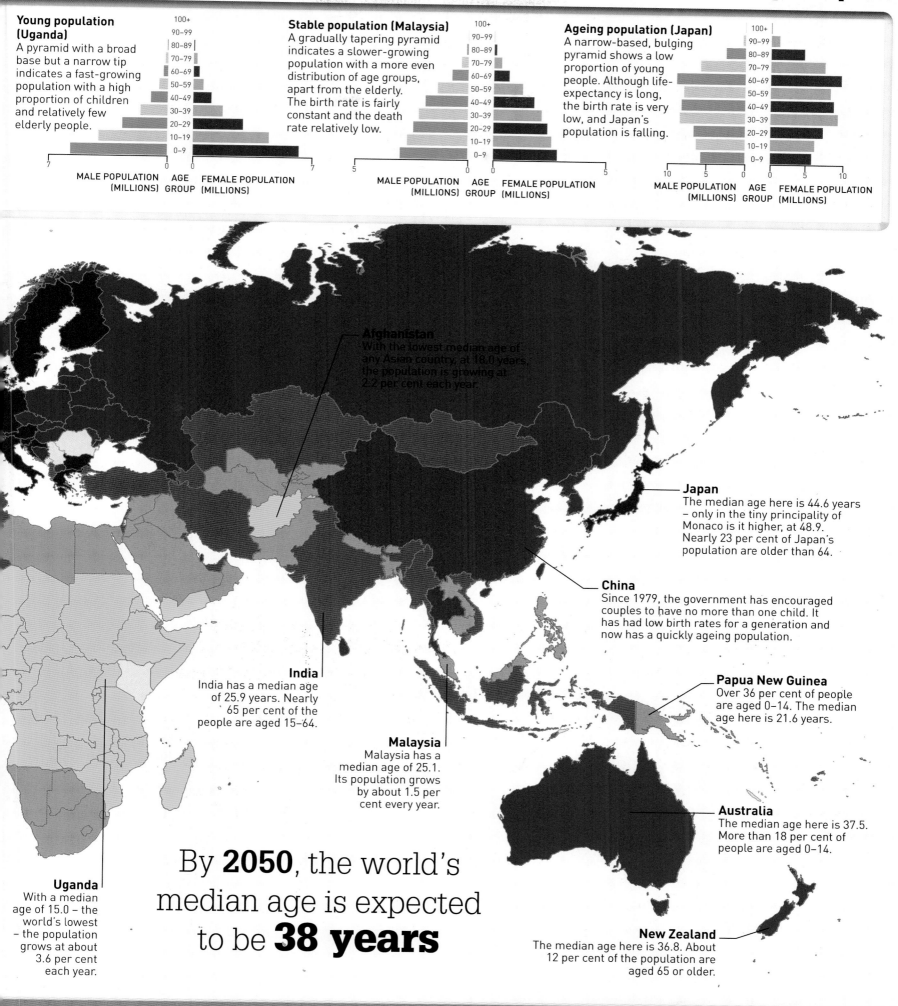

Young population (Uganda)
A pyramid with a broad base but a narrow tip indicates a fast-growing population with a high proportion of children and relatively few elderly people.

100+
90–99
80–89
70–79
60–69
50–59
40–49
30–39
20–29
10–19
0–9

7 0 0 7
MALE POPULATION (MILLIONS) — AGE GROUP — FEMALE POPULATION (MILLIONS)

Stable population (Malaysia)
A gradually tapering pyramid indicates a slower-growing population with a more even distribution of age groups, apart from the elderly. The birth rate is fairly constant and the death rate relatively low.

100+
90–99
80–89
70–79
60–69
50–59
40–49
30–39
20–29
10–19
0–9

5 0 0 5
MALE POPULATION (MILLIONS) — AGE GROUP — FEMALE POPULATION (MILLIONS)

Ageing population (Japan)
A narrow-based, bulging pyramid shows a low proportion of young people. Although life-expectancy is long, the birth rate is very low, and Japan's population is falling.

100+
90–99
80–89
70–79
60–69
50–59
40–49
30–39
20–29
10–19
0–9

10 5 0 0 5 10
MALE POPULATION (MILLIONS) — AGE GROUP — FEMALE POPULATION (MILLIONS)

Afghanistan
With the lowest median age of any Asian country, at 18.0 years, the population is growing at 2.2 per cent each year.

Japan
The median age here is 44.6 years – only in the tiny principality of Monaco is it higher, at 48.9. Nearly 23 per cent of Japan's population are older than 64.

China
Since 1979, the government has encouraged couples to have no more than one child. It has had low birth rates for a generation and now has a quickly ageing population.

India
India has a median age of 25.9 years. Nearly 65 per cent of the people are aged 15–64.

Papua New Guinea
Over 36 per cent of people are aged 0–14. The median age here is 21.6 years.

Malaysia
Malaysia has a median age of 25.1. Its population grows by about 1.5 per cent every year.

Australia
The median age here is 37.5. More than 18 per cent of people are aged 0–14.

Uganda
With a median age of 15.0 – the world's lowest – the population grows at about 3.6 per cent each year.

By **2050**, the world's median age is expected to be **38 years**

New Zealand
The median age here is 36.8. About 12 per cent of the population are aged 65 or older.

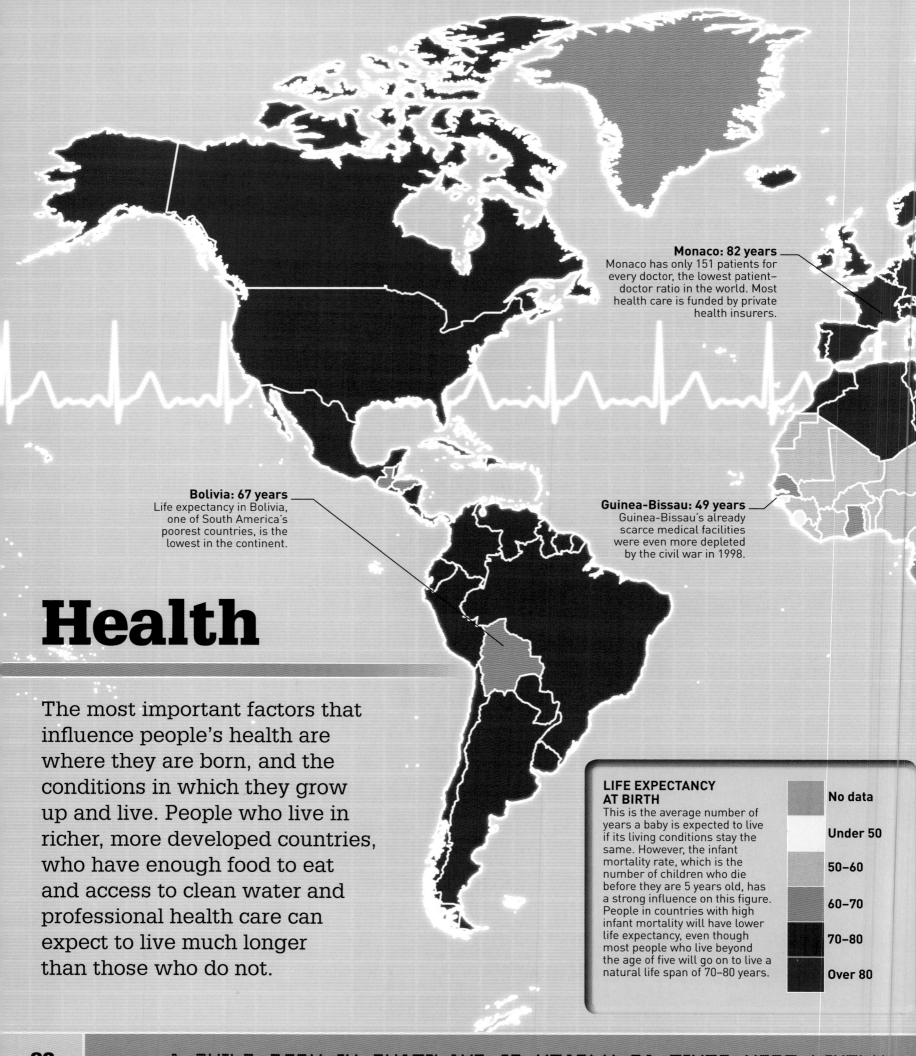

Health

Monaco: 82 years
Monaco has only 151 patients for every doctor, the lowest patient–doctor ratio in the world. Most health care is funded by private health insurers.

Bolivia: 67 years
Life expectancy in Bolivia, one of South America's poorest countries, is the lowest in the continent.

Guinea-Bissau: 49 years
Guinea-Bissau's already scarce medical facilities were even more depleted by the civil war in 1998.

The most important factors that influence people's health are where they are born, and the conditions in which they grow up and live. People who live in richer, more developed countries, who have enough food to eat and access to clean water and professional health care can expect to live much longer than those who do not.

LIFE EXPECTANCY AT BIRTH
This is the average number of years a baby is expected to live if its living conditions stay the same. However, the infant mortality rate, which is the number of children who die before they are 5 years old, has a strong influence on this figure. People in countries with high infant mortality will have lower life expectancy, even though most people who live beyond the age of five will go on to live a natural life span of 70–80 years.

	No data
	Under 50
	50–60
	60–70
	70–80
	Over 80

A CHILD BORN IN SWAZILAND IS NEARLY 30 TIMES MORE LIKELY

Afghanistan: 48
About one in 23 Afghan mothers die in childbirth or from pregnancy-related causes – the highest rate in the world.

Japan: 83 years
Japan's health care system has been ranked by the World Health Organization (WHO) as the best in the world.

South Sudan: 42 years
A long-term shortage of food in South Sudan means that one-third of all its children are underweight.

In **1900**, world **life expectancy** was **30 years**. Today it is **67 years**

Access to medical help

Having good access to doctors and other health care workers is essential in helping people to stay healthy, recover from illness, and live longer. The number of doctors per person in the population has an important effect on life expectancy, but other factors influence people's life span. Bhutan, for instance, has roughly the same number of doctors per head as Malawi, but life expectancy in Bhutan is 63, compared to 47 in Malawi.

PEOPLE PER DOCTOR

Monaco	151
Cuba	170
St Lucia	204
Belarus	209
Georgia	214
Liberia	34,014
Mozambique	37,313
Niger	41,841
Bhutan	44,248
Malawi	46,296

Australia: 82 years
Life expectancy among the Aboriginal population of Australia is only 70 years, much lower than the national average.

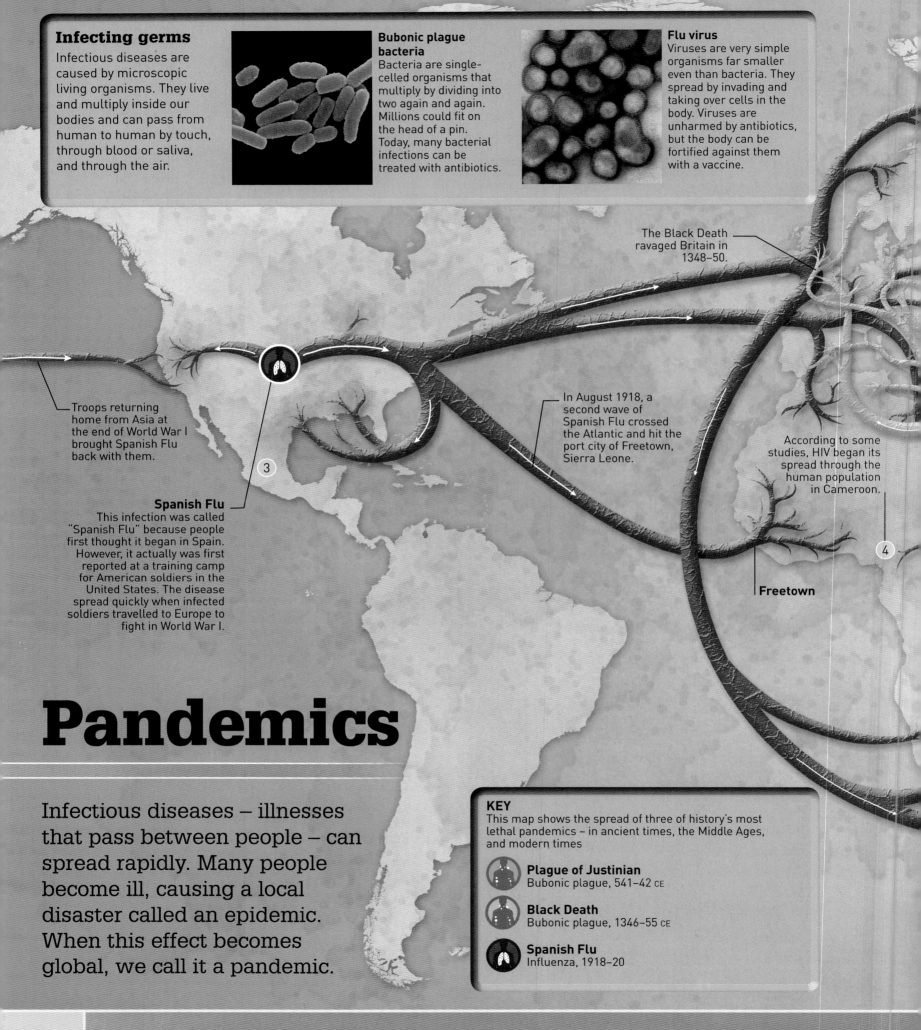

Infecting germs
Infectious diseases are caused by microscopic living organisms. They live and multiply inside our bodies and can pass from human to human by touch, through blood or saliva, and through the air.

Bubonic plague bacteria
Bacteria are single-celled organisms that multiply by dividing into two again and again. Millions could fit on the head of a pin. Today, many bacterial infections can be treated with antibiotics.

Flu virus
Viruses are very simple organisms far smaller even than bacteria. They spread by invading and taking over cells in the body. Viruses are unharmed by antibiotics, but the body can be fortified against them with a vaccine.

The Black Death ravaged Britain in 1348–50.

Troops returning home from Asia at the end of World War I brought Spanish Flu back with them.

③

In August 1918, a second wave of Spanish Flu crossed the Atlantic and hit the port city of Freetown, Sierra Leone.

According to some studies, HIV began its spread through the human population in Cameroon.

④

Freetown

Spanish Flu
This infection was called "Spanish Flu" because people first thought it began in Spain. However, it actually was first reported at a training camp for American soldiers in the United States. The disease spread quickly when infected soldiers travelled to Europe to fight in World War I.

Pandemics

Infectious diseases – illnesses that pass between people – can spread rapidly. Many people become ill, causing a local disaster called an epidemic. When this effect becomes global, we call it a pandemic.

KEY
This map shows the spread of three of history's most lethal pandemics – in ancient times, the Middle Ages, and modern times

Plague of Justinian
Bubonic plague, 541–42 CE

Black Death
Bubonic plague, 1346–55 CE

Spanish Flu
Influenza, 1918–20

SPANISH FLU MAY HAVE KILLED UP TO 100 MILLION PEOPLE.

Superbugs and air travel

Bacteria and viruses change fast. "Superbug" bacteria become immune to antibiotics, while scientists try to develop vaccines against new viruses. Today, air travel can spread infection worldwide in days, so the fear of a fast-spreading pandemic is greater than ever. Here are four recent cases of new viruses.

1. **Hong Kong Flu, 1968–69**
In 2 years, Hong Kong Flu caused about 1 million deaths. The virus killed around 34,000 people in the United States alone.

2. **Avian (Bird) Flu, Hong Kong, 1997–2003**
This virus first appeared in humans in Hong Kong, through contact with infected poultry. It killed 352 people in 15 countries.

3. **H1N1 ("Swine Flu"), Mexico City, 2009–10**
This new flu developed from viruses of birds, pigs, and humans. Total deaths will number many more than the 18,500 so far confirmed.

4. **HIV, west–central Africa, 1981–present**
This virus causes AIDS – an often-fatal disease of the body's defences. It now infects more than 30 million people worldwide.

Black Death
In the 14th century, an outbreak of bubonic plague spread from Asia across Europe, causing devastation along the way. In just four years, the disease killed 45–50 per cent of Europe's population.

Constantinople (Istanbul)

Some experts think the Plague of Justinian began not in Ethiopia, but in Central Asia.

The Black Death passed along sea trade routes, since the bacteria that caused the disease lived in fleas, which lived on ships' rats.

Plague of Justinian
At its height, during the rule of the Emperor Justinian (ruler of the Byzantine, or Eastern Roman, Empire), this disease killed at least 25 million people. It may have started in Ethiopia, then spread along trade routes through northern Egypt and Constantinople (modern-day Istanbul) into Europe.

Local outbreaks

The ebola virus (above) is not a pandemic, but causes such shocking symptoms, including internal bleeding, that local outbreaks in Africa have caused worldwide concern.

Around **3,000 people** still die from **bubonic plague** each year

Spanish Flu was brought to New Zealand in 1918 by soldiers returning home from fighting in World War I in Europe.

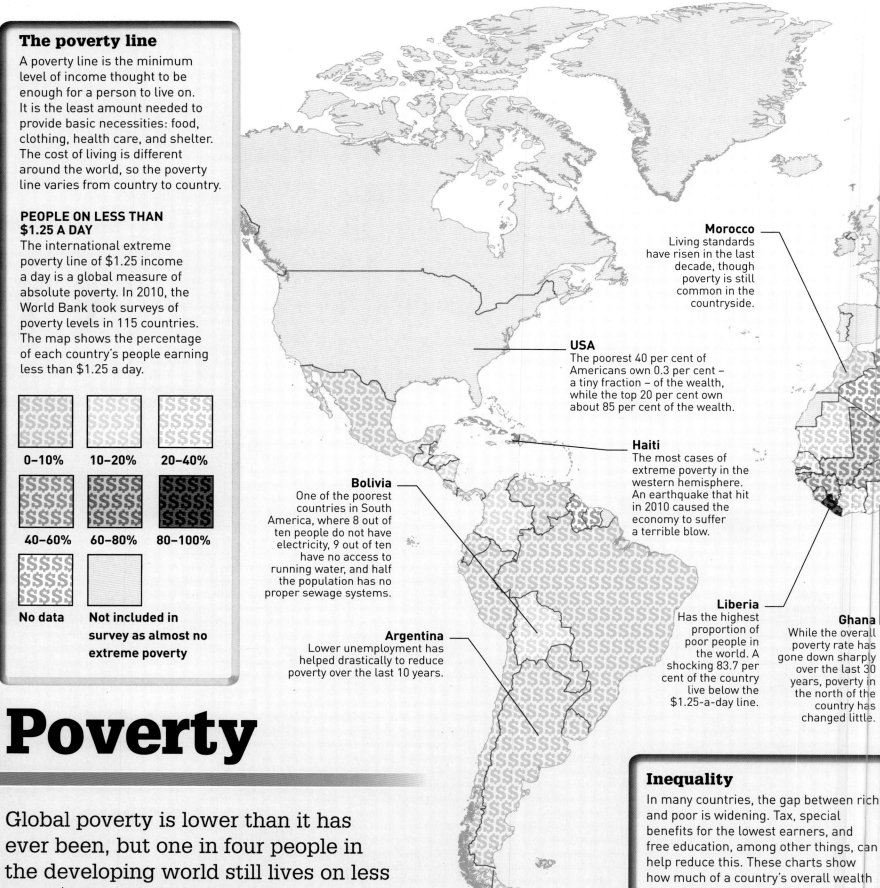

The poverty line

A poverty line is the minimum level of income thought to be enough for a person to live on. It is the least amount needed to provide basic necessities: food, clothing, health care, and shelter. The cost of living is different around the world, so the poverty line varies from country to country.

PEOPLE ON LESS THAN $1.25 A DAY

The international extreme poverty line of $1.25 income a day is a global measure of absolute poverty. In 2010, the World Bank took surveys of poverty levels in 115 countries. The map shows the percentage of each country's people earning less than $1.25 a day.

0–10%	10–20%	20–40%
40–60%	60–80%	80–100%
No data	Not included in survey as almost no extreme poverty	

Poverty

Global poverty is lower than it has ever been, but one in four people in the developing world still lives on less than $1.25 a day. Sub-Saharan Africa has by far the most cases of extreme poverty – almost half the people cannot afford basic necessities.

Morocco
Living standards have risen in the last decade, though poverty is still common in the countryside.

USA
The poorest 40 per cent of Americans own 0.3 per cent – a tiny fraction – of the wealth, while the top 20 per cent own about 85 per cent of the wealth.

Haiti
The most cases of extreme poverty in the western hemisphere. An earthquake that hit in 2010 caused the economy to suffer a terrible blow.

Bolivia
One of the poorest countries in South America, where 8 out of ten people do not have electricity, 9 out of ten have no access to running water, and half the population has no proper sewage systems.

Liberia
Has the highest proportion of poor people in the world. A shocking 83.7 per cent of the country live below the $1.25-a-day line.

Ghana
While the overall poverty rate has gone down sharply over the last 30 years, poverty in the north of the country has changed little.

Argentina
Lower unemployment has helped drastically to reduce poverty over the last 10 years.

Inequality

In many countries, the gap between rich and poor is widening. Tax, special benefits for the lowest earners, and free education, among other things, can help reduce this. These charts show how much of a country's overall wealth the richest people own. The countries shown here are those with a very large gap between rich and poor, and those where the gap is less noticeable.

OVER 3 BILLION PEOPLE LIVE ON LESS THAN $2.50 A DAY, AND

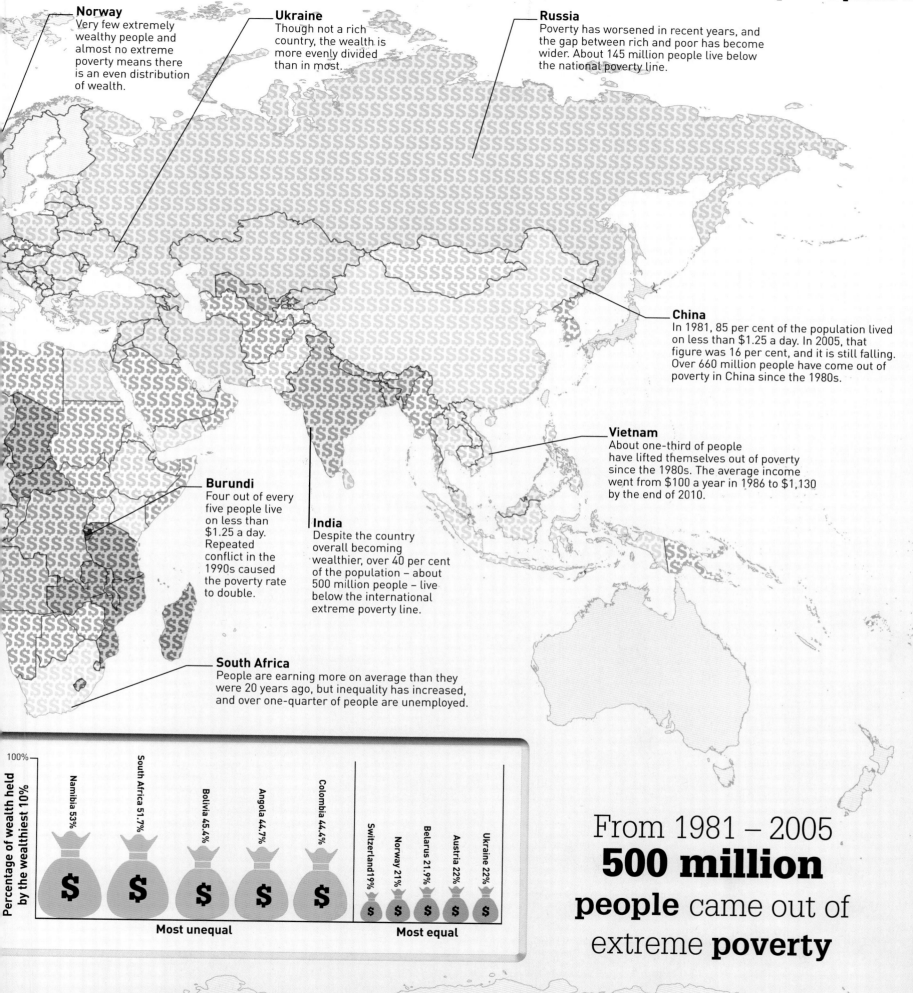

Norway
Very few extremely wealthy people and almost no extreme poverty means there is an even distribution of wealth.

Ukraine
Though not a rich country, the wealth is more evenly divided than in most.

Russia
Poverty has worsened in recent years, and the gap between rich and poor has become wider. About 145 million people live below the national poverty line.

China
In 1981, 85 per cent of the population lived on less than $1.25 a day. In 2005, that figure was 16 per cent, and it is still falling. Over 660 million people have come out of poverty in China since the 1980s.

Vietnam
About one-third of people have lifted themselves out of poverty since the 1980s. The average income went from $100 a year in 1986 to $1,130 by the end of 2010.

Burundi
Four out of every five people live on less than $1.25 a day. Repeated conflict in the 1990s caused the poverty rate to double.

India
Despite the country overall becoming wealthier, over 40 per cent of the population – about 500 million people – live below the international extreme poverty line.

South Africa
People are earning more on average than they were 20 years ago, but inequality has increased, and over one-quarter of people are unemployed.

Percentage of wealth held by the wealthiest 10%

100%

Namibia 53%
South Africa 51.7%
Bolivia 45.4%
Angola 44.7%
Colombia 44.4%

Switzerland 19%
Norway 21%
Belarus 21.9%
Austria 22%
Ukraine 22%

Most unequal

Most equal

From 1981 – 2005
500 million
people came out of extreme **poverty**

FOUR OUT OF EVERY FIVE PEOPLE LIVE ON LESS THAN $10 A DAY.

The world's gold

Beautiful, rare, and highly prized, gold has been mined since ancient Egyptian times. Sometimes a discovery of gold led to a "gold rush", with thousands of people flocking to the site in the hope of making their fortune.

Klondike gold rush, Canada, 1897–99
100,000 prospectors headed for Klondike. About 4,000 found gold.

California gold rush, USA, 1848–55
300,000 people flocked to California, aiming to strike gold.

Canada
Four per cent of the world's gold comes from Canada.

United States
This is the third-largest gold producer, mining 237 tonnes annually (9 per cent of the global total).

Ghana
Ghana is Africa's second-largest gold producer, supplying 4 per cent of the world's gold. South Africa supplies 7 per cent.

Peru
Peru is the largest gold producer in South America, and the world's sixth largest (6 per cent of all gold)

Top 10 gold mines
Figures show gold mined in 2011.

1. **Grasberg , Indonesia**
   63 tonnes
2. **Muruntau, Uzbekistan**
   56 tonnes
3. **Carlin-Nevada, Nevada, USA**
   54 tonnes
4. **Yanacocha, Peru**
   45.4 tonnes
5. **Goldstrike, Nevada, USA**
   38.6 tonnes
6. **Cortez, Nevada, USA**
   35.5 tonnes
7. **Veladero, Argentina**
   34.8 tonnes
8. **Lagunas Norte, Peru**
   25 tonnes
9. **Lihir, Papua New Guinea**
   24.6 tonnes
10. **Super Pit, Kalgoorlie, Australia**
    24.5 tonnes

All the **gold** that has ever been **mined** would make a cube **20.5 m** (67 ft) along each side.

FOUND IN AUSTRALIA IN 1869, "WELCOME STRANGER" WAS THE BIGGEST

Gold reserves

The central banks of the world's nations store gold to back up their currencies. The Federal Reserve in the USA has the largest gold reserves. There are also international gold reserves, such as those held by the International Monetary Fund.

THOUSANDS OF TONNES

8
7
6
5
4
3
2
1
0

United States | Germany | Italy | France | China | Switzerland | Russia | Japan | Netherlands | India

Russia
The world's fourth-largest gold producer, Russia extracted 200 tonnes in 2011 (8 per cent of the global total).

China
China is the world's largest gold producer, extracting 355 tonnes in 2011 (14 per cent of the global total).

Indonesia
Much of Indonesia's gold production – about 4 per cent of the world total – is a by-product of copper mining.

Africa
The continent is responsible for about one-fifth of the world's gold production.

KEY
Circles show locations of the world's gold mines.

⬤ Top-10 gold mine

• Other gold mine

World gold holdings

Of the 165,000 tonnes of gold now above ground, more than half is now jewellery. One-fifth is stored as reserves in central banks (see above). Some of the rest exists as parts in engineering such as electric cables and protective coatings on spacecraft. Still more is in the hands of investors, waiting for the right time to sell.

Witwatersrand gold rush, South Africa, 1886
Triggered by the discovery of the "Golden Arc" – an ancient lake bed rich in gold deposits that stretches from Johannesburg to Welkom.

Jewellery 52% | Central banks 18% | Investment 16% | Industrial 12% | Other 2%

WORLD'S GOLD HOLDINGS

Australia
With 270 tonnes mined in 2011 (10 per cent of the global total), Australia is the second-largest gold-producing nation.

GOLD NUGGET EVER FOUND. IT CONTAINED 71 KG (156 LB) OF GOLD.

Most billionaires
The USA has over 400 billionaires – more than any other country.

Sweden

61 Bill Gates
44 Warren Buffett
36 Larry Ellison
25.3 Christy Walton and family
25 Charles Koch
25 David Koch
24.9 Sheldon Adelson
23.7 Jim Walton
23.4 Alice Walton
23.1 S. Robson Walton
22 Michael Bloomberg
20 George Soros
18.7 Sergey Brin
18.7 Larry Page
18.4 Jeff Bezos
17.5 Mark Zuckerberg
17.5 David Thomson and family
15.9 Michael Dell
15.7 Steve Ballmer
14.4 Phil Knight

USA

41 Bernard Arnault
24 Liliane Bettencourt
37.5 Amancio Ortega Gaona

France

Spain

United States
The USA has the world's largest economy, worth around US$15.5 trillion, and the world's third-largest population.

19 Michele Ferrero and family

Italy

69 Carlos Slim Helu and family
17.4 Ricardo Salinas Pliego and family
16.5 Alberto Baillleres Gonzalez and family
14.2 German Larrea Mota Velasco and family

Mexico

Africa
In 2011, Africa was the continent with the fewest billionaires – just 14.

17.8 Iris Fontbana and family

Chile

30 Eike Batista

Brazil

WORLD'S WEALTHIEST
The map shows the citizenship of the world's richest people, and the value of their fortunes in billions of US dollars.

▭ = Approximately US$1.6 billion

Billionaires

Some billionaires inherit wealth. Others get rich through banking, making or trading goods, or inventing new things. Not surprisingly, billionaires tend to be concentrated in more prosperous nations.

● **Bill Gates**
Founded Microsoft software firm in 1975. Now devotes himself to charity work.

● **Liliane Bettencourt**
A principal shareholder in the cosmetics and beauty company L'Oréal.

Russia
Rich in natural resources, such as metals, minerals, and oil, Russia had around 100 billionaires in 2011.

Germany

Karl Albrecht 25.4
Berthold and Theo, Junior, Albrecht 17.8
Michael Otto and family 17.6

Ukraine

Rinat Akhmetov 16

Russia

Alisher Usmanov 18
Alexey Mordashov 15.3
Vladimir Lisin 15.9
Vladimir Potanin 14.5

Saudi Arabia

Prince Alwaleed Bin Talal Alsaud 18

India

Mukesh Ambani 22.3
Lakshmi Mittal 20.7
Azim Premji 15.9

Hong Kong

Li Ka-shing 25.5
Thomas and Raymond Kwok and family 18.3
Lee Shau Kee 18
Cheng Yu-tang 16

Australia

Georgina Rinehart 18

Facebook's
Mark Zuckerberg
was a billionaire by
the age of **23**

● Sergey Brin and Larry Page
Founders of Google, which provides Internet-related products and services.

●Amancio Ortega Gaona
Founder of fashion group Inditex, which owns the clothing store chain Zara.

Jeff Bezos
In 1994, Bezos founded Amazon – now the world's largest online store.

● **Mark Zuckerberg**
Cofounded Facebook social networking site in 2004, while at university.

● **Carlos Slim Helu**
Telecommunications tycoon, and the richest person in the world.

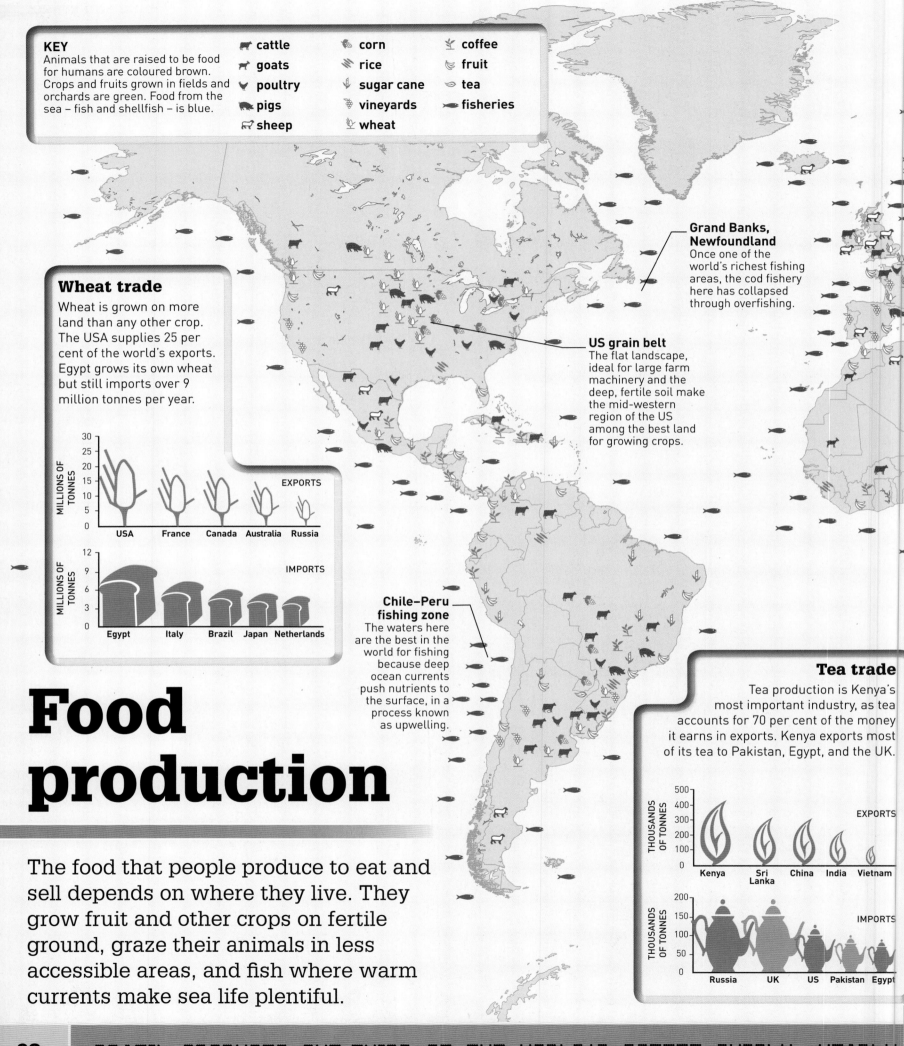

KEY

Animals that are raised to be food for humans are coloured brown. Crops and fruits grown in fields and orchards are green. Food from the sea – fish and shellfish – is blue.

- cattle
- goats
- poultry
- pigs
- sheep
- corn
- rice
- sugar cane
- vineyards
- wheat
- coffee
- fruit
- tea
- fisheries

Wheat trade

Wheat is grown on more land than any other crop. The USA supplies 25 per cent of the world's exports. Egypt grows its own wheat but still imports over 9 million tonnes per year.

MILLIONS OF TONNES

EXPORTS

30 / 25 / 20 / 15 / 10 / 5 / 0

USA France Canada Australia Russia

MILLIONS OF TONNES

IMPORTS

12 / 9 / 6 / 3 / 0

Egypt Italy Brazil Japan Netherlands

Food production

The food that people produce to eat and sell depends on where they live. They grow fruit and other crops on fertile ground, graze their animals in less accessible areas, and fish where warm currents make sea life plentiful.

Grand Banks, Newfoundland

Once one of the world's richest fishing areas, the cod fishery here has collapsed through overfishing.

US grain belt

The flat landscape, ideal for large farm machinery and the deep, fertile soil make the mid-western region of the US among the best land for growing crops.

Chile–Peru fishing zone

The waters here are the best in the world for fishing because deep ocean currents push nutrients to the surface, in a process known as upwelling.

Tea trade

Tea production is Kenya's most important industry, as tea accounts for 70 per cent of the money it earns in exports. Kenya exports most of its tea to Pakistan, Egypt, and the UK.

THOUSANDS OF TONNES

EXPORTS

500 / 400 / 300 / 200 / 100 / 0

Kenya Sri Lanka China India Vietnam

THOUSANDS OF TONNES

IMPORTS

200 / 150 / 100 / 50 / 0

Russia UK US Pakistan Egypt

Rice production in India
Rice can grow in many places, as long as it has plenty of water. But cultivating rice takes a lot of human labour, so it is often grown in countries with a large and low-cost workforce, such as India.

China and Japan
China and Japan are the two nations that catch – and eat – the most fish. Making fish the main part of their diet has been central to both Japanese and Chinese cultures for centuries.

To feed the rising world **population, the UN** says **food production** must increase by **70 per cent** before **2050**

Sheep meat trade

With 4 million people and over 31 million sheep, it is not surprising that New Zealand exports 90 per cent of the meat produced there. Its best customer is the UK, which buys about one-fifth of New Zealand's sheep meat.

EXPORTS

THOUSANDS OF TONNES

400 / 350 / 300 / 250 / 200 / 150 / 100 / 50 / 0

New Zealand — Australia — UK — Ireland — Spain

IMPORTS

THOUSANDS OF TONNES

120 / 105 / 90 / 75 / 60 / 45 / 30 / 15 / 0

France — UK — China — USA — Belgium

Canada
Canada has a lower adult obesity rate than the United States, at about 24 per cent. Daily calorie intake is around 3,400 kcal.

United Kingdom
Obesity in the UK is estimated to add an extra £5.1 billion each year to the country's health-care costs.

Africa
Africa is the continent with the lowest calorie intake, at 2,550 kcal per day. The global average is 2,830 kcal.

United States
Larger portions and cheap, high-calorie, high-fat fast foods and ready meals have helped raise daily intake levels to 3,700 kcal. Adult obesity is now around 35 per cent.

Cuba
Although Cuba is not a rich country, its citizens are well fed, with a daily intake of about 3,250 kcal.

Bolivia
Daily calorie intake for the average adult in Bolivia is around 2,200 kcal.

Weight around the world

Pacific island nations such as Nauru, Tonga, and French Polynesia have among the highest obesity levels. This is partly because the islanders now eat mainly cheap, fatty, imported foods, and partly because plumpness traditionally signifies wealth and fertility.

PERCENTAGE OF THE POPULATION CLASSED AS OBESE

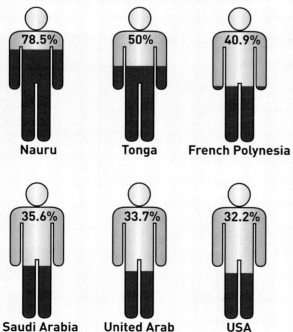

78.5%	50%	40.9%
Nauru	**Tonga**	**French Polynesia**

35.6%	33.7%	32.2%
Saudi Arabia	**United Arab Emirates**	**USA**

Food intake

Food and the energy it contains is the fuel for our bodies. Overeating and unhealthy diets can lead to obesity – when a person gains so much weight that it can cause illness and disease.

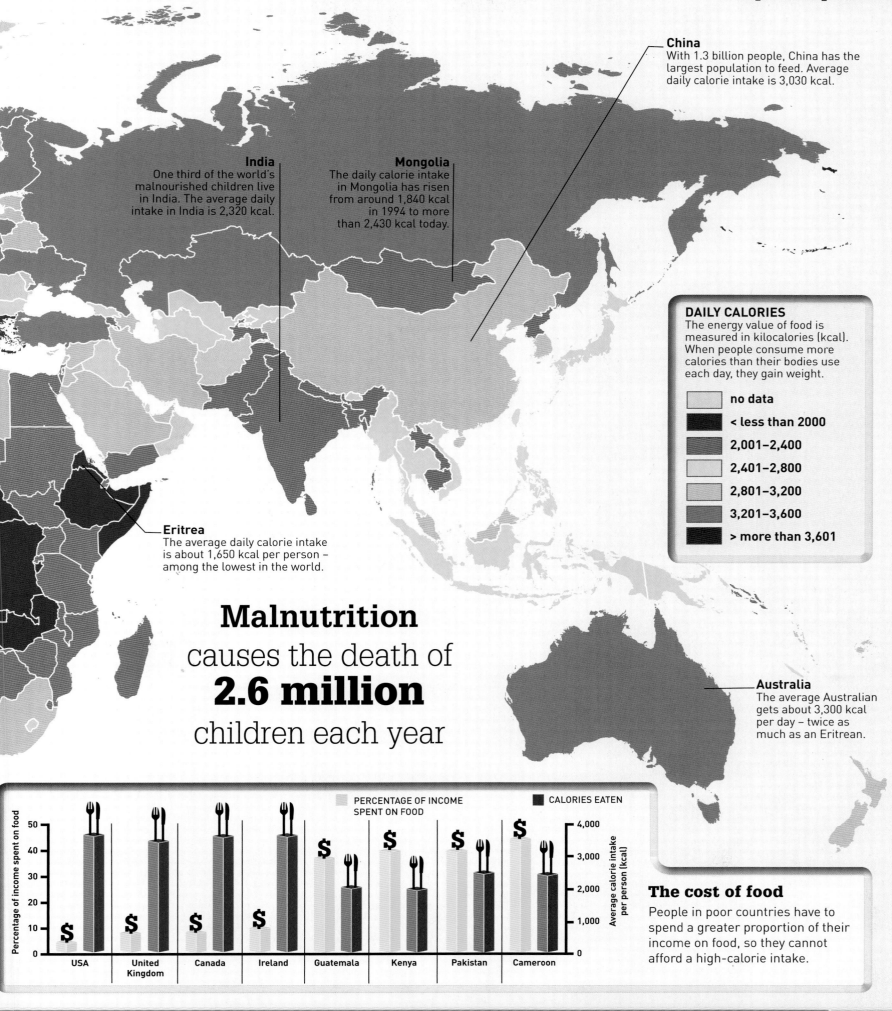

China
With 1.3 billion people, China has the largest population to feed. Average daily calorie intake is 3,030 kcal.

India
One third of the world's malnourished children live in India. The average daily intake in India is 2,320 kcal.

Mongolia
The daily calorie intake in Mongolia has risen from around 1,840 kcal in 1994 to more than 2,430 kcal today.

DAILY CALORIES
The energy value of food is measured in kilocalories (kcal). When people consume more calories than their bodies use each day, they gain weight.

	no data
	< less than 2000
	2,001–2,400
	2,401–2,800
	2,801–3,200
	3,201–3,600
	> more than 3,601

Eritrea
The average daily calorie intake is about 1,650 kcal per person – among the lowest in the world.

Malnutrition
causes the death of
2.6 million
children each year

Australia
The average Australian gets about 3,300 kcal per day – twice as much as an Eritrean.

PERCENTAGE OF INCOME SPENT ON FOOD   CALORIES EATEN

Percentage of income spent on food

50
40
30
20
10
0

Average calorie intake per person (kcal)

4,000
3,000
2,000
1,000
0

USA | United Kingdom | Canada | Ireland | Guatemala | Kenya | Pakistan | Cameroon

The cost of food

People in poor countries have to spend a greater proportion of their income on food, so they cannot afford a high-calorie intake.

Canada
As in the USA, only 1 per cent of people are illiterate.

Europe
Although most countries in Europe have very high literacy rates, over 76 million adults classed as "literate" still lack basic reading and writing skills.

United States
The literacy rate in the USA is 99 per cent.

Mauritania
Little more than half of Mauritania's population – 57.5 per cent – can read and write.

Mali
Just 26.2 per cent of people in Mali are literate – the world's lowest literacy rate.

Brazil
Nine out of every ten Brazilians are literate.

Going to secondary school

Wealthy nations can afford to provide secondary education for all children, but governments in poorer countries cannot offer every child a place. This is particularly true in Africa south of the Sahara. In Burundi, for example, only 9 per cent of children go to secondary school.

PERCENTAGE OF SECONDARY-SCHOOL-AGE CHILDREN GOING TO SCHOOL FULL-TIME

100%
80%
60%
40%
20%
0%

France | Japan | Sweden | Seychelles | New Zealand | Burkina Faso | Mozambique | Central African Republic | Niger | Burundi

Literacy

Literacy – being able to read and write – is an essential life skill. Being literate makes it easier for people to learn, make the most of their abilities, and get better jobs. High levels of illiteracy make it difficult for nations to develop and become wealthier.

In developing countries, **200 million** people aged **15–24** have not completed **primary school**

Georgia
Georgia has the world's highest literacy rate, at 100 per cent.

Russia
This vast country has one of the highest literacy rates, at 99.5 per cent.

KEY
People more than 15 years old in each country who can read and write:

- >97%
- 90–97%
- 80–90%
- 70–80%
- 60–70%
- 50–60%
- 35–50%
- <35%
- Data not available

China
The literacy rate in China is 95.9 per cent.

Somalia
With literacy at only 36 per cent, nearly two-thirds of Somalis cannot read and write.

Indonesia
Around 60 per cent of children attend secondary school. Literacy is 92 per cent.

Madagascar
Over two-thirds of all Madagascans – 70.7 per cent – are literate.

Papua New Guinea
Literacy is around 60 per cent.

Australia
While the literacy rate for Australia as a whole is 99 per cent, it is much lower among the country's Aboriginal population.

New Zealand
Ninety-nine per cent of New Zealanders are literate.

Percentage of adults who can read and write

■ Male   ■ Female

- Afghanistan: 43% / 13%
- Guinea-Bissau: 58% / 27%
- Central African Republic: 65% / 34%
- Mozambique: 65% / 33%
- Yemen: 71% / 30%

100%
80%
60%
40%
20%
0%

Male–female differences
Of the 774 million illiterate adults around the world in 2010, two-thirds were women. In some countries, girls are discouraged from attending school, leading to wide differences in literacy rates between men and women.

NO SCHOOLING IN 2009 - NEARLY HALF WERE IN SUB-SAHARAN AFRICA.

Biggest oil spills

Oil spills – when oil escapes into the environment – cause devastation to wildlife and are difficult and costly to clean up.

1. Gulf War oil spill, Persian Gulf, 1991
300,000–1,200,000 tonnes
Iraqi forces opened valves on Kuwaiti oil wells and pipes, causing a 250-km (100-mile) slick.

2. Lakeview gusher, California, USA, 1910-11
1,100,000 tonnes
An oil well erupted like a geyser, spilling out oil for over a year until it naturally died down.

3. Deepwater Horizon, Gulf of Mexico, 2010
671,000 tonnes
A deep-sea oil spill occurred when an explosion destroyed the Deepwater Horizon drillling rig.

4. Ixtoc 1 oil spill, Gulf of Mexico, USA, 1979–80
412,000–435,000 tonnes
The Ixtoc 1 drilling platform collapsed after an explosion. The spill continued for 9 months.

5. *Atlantic Empress*, Trinidad and Tobago, 1979
260,000 tonnes
The largest oil spill from a ship. The tanker *Atlantic Empress* hit another ship, killing 26 crew.

Pollution

Oil spills, industrial waste, and radiation leaks from nuclear power stations cause harm to people and the environment. Carbon dioxide gas (CO_2) produced by transport and industry is adding to global warming.

Persistent organic pollutants (POPs): Canadian Arctic
These pollutants include industrial products and pesticides. They travel on the world's oceans and air currents, accumulate in the Arctic regions, and contaminate the foods that Inuit people eat.

Lead: Haina, Dominican Republic
Located near an abandoned recycling centre for lead-acid batteries, Haina has the world's highest level of lead contamination. All its inhabitants show signs of lead poisoning.

Lead: La Oroya, Peru
A metal smelting plant has emitted toxic lead since 1922. This has led to contaminated water supplies, dangerously polluted air, and unsafe levels of lead in the blood of local residents.

The 1991 **Gulf War** oil slick was up to **13 cm (5 in)** thick

Nuclear accidents
Splitting atoms in nuclear reactors produces energy for generating electricity. Accidents at reactors may lead to radioactive material escaping, which can cause illness such as cancer for many years.

 Chernobyl, Ukraine 26 April 1986
A reactor explosion released radioactive material. Radiation-related illnesses may have caused thousands of deaths.

Chemical waste: Dzerzhinsk, Russia
Chemical weapons were made here until 1998. The town's water contains extreme levels of toxic chemicals. Average life expectancy for the area in 2007 was 45.

Organic chemicals, Sumgayit, Azerbaijan
A town once home to chemical plants that released 109,000 tonnes of toxic chemicals per year. Cancer rates are up to 51 per cent higher than elsewhere in the country.

Nickel ore: Norilsk, Russia
Few trees grow within 48 km (30 miles) of a massive metal-smelting complex in this industrial town, due to acid rain and smog.

Industrial chemicals: Bhopal, India
In 1984, poisonous gas escaped from a pesticide factory, killing 4,000–15,000 people. Thousands continue to suffer and die from illnesses related to the accident.

Air pollution: Linfen, China
Among the world's most polluted cities, Linfen is at the heart of China's coal industry. Soot and coal dust fill the air, raising the risk of bronchitis, pneumonia, and lung cancer in the people.

Mercury: Central Kalimantan, Indonesia
Toxic mercury is used to extract gold from mines in Kalimantan, with about 45 tonnes of mercury released into the air each year.

Pesticides: Kasaragod, India
20 years of pesticide use on cashew-nut plantations have caused disease and mental illness for a generation of residents.

Tanning wastes: Ranipet, India
Water polluted by waste from a leather-tanning factory stings the skin and causes ulcers.

Lead: Kabwe, Zambia
A once-thriving lead industry has resulted in lead levels in Kabwe's children of 5–10 times the safe limit.

Acid mine drainage: Johannesburg, South Africa
Acidified water flows from old mines into rivers. It contaminates water supplies and crops and harms wildlife.

Carbon dioxide

The map shows how much CO_2 each country produces per person. Wealthy nations tend to produce the most.

Tonnes of CO_2 per person
- 0–5
- 5–10
- 10–15
- 15–20
- More than 20
- No data

Fukushima, Japan
11 March 2011
An tsunami hit this coastal power plant, triggering explosions. Over 100,000 people had to be evacuated from their homes.

Three Mile Island, USA
28 March 1979
A reactor was damaged when it overheated. The cost of decontaminating the site after the event was US$1 billion.

Idaho Falls, USA
3 January 1961
An explosion at the SL-1 prototype reactor killed three workers – the first in the world to die in a reactor accident.

Lucens reactor, Switzerland
21 January 1969
Built in a cavern, this reactor leaked radiation. None of the workers was contaminated, but the cavern was sealed to contain the radiation.

Pollution hotspots

Puente Hills – Los Angeles, USA
Approximately 10,000 tonnes per day.

Apex – Las Vegas, USA
Approximately 9,500 tonnes per day.

Western Pacific Garbage Patch
A lot of discarded litter ends up in rivers, which take it to the sea, where circular currents called gyres collect it into vast patches in the ocean surface waters. This patch is the largest of these oceanic rubbish dumps.

North Atlantic Garbage Patch
The North Atlantic Garbage Patch measures hundreds of kilometres across. It shifts by as much as 1,600 km (990 miles) north and south with the seasons.

Lagos, Nigeria
Approximately 9,000 tonnes per day.

Gabon
Less wealthy countries, such as Gabon, produce less rubbish because people buy less overall, they buy proportionally more local produce without plastic packaging, and do more recycling.

Rubbish and waste

As living standards improve worldwide and cities grow, so does the amount of rubbish that people produce. Most waste goes to rubbish dumps, which are expensive, use up a lot of land, and are harmful to the environment. Recycling is one way of helping to stop the global rubbish heap growing any bigger.

South Pacific Garbage Patch
So far, the South Pacific Gyre appears to contain less plastic waste than other ocean garbage patches.

South Atlantic Garbage Patch
The first evidence of a South Atlantic Garbage Patch was discovered in 2011. Most plastic particles in ocean garbage patches are too small to be seen with the naked eye.

Top of the recycling table
Switzerland is currently the only country that recycles more than half of its waste. Swiss people are committed recycling but they also have a financial motive – they pay fee for each bag of rubbish that they send to the dump.

RECYCLING ONE ALUMINIUM CAN SAVES ENOUGH ENERGY TO BURN A

KEY
Everyday items discarded by the public per day in each country, shown in kg (lb) per person.

0–0.75 (0–1.65)	**0.75–1.5** (1.65–3.3)	**1.5–2.0** (3.3–4.4)
2.0–2.5 (4.4–5.5)	**Above 2.5** (above 5.5)	**No data**

Sudokwon – Incheon, South Korea
Approximately 16,500–18,000 tonnes per day.

Laogang – Shanghai, China
Approximately 8,000 tonnes per day.

Solomon Islands
Small island nations import a lot of food, so must dispose of a lot of boxes and cartons.

Eastern Pacific Garbage Patch
Together with the Western Garbage Patch, this makes up the Great Pacific Garbage Patch. Scientists estimate that the eastern area contains about 3 million tonnes of plastic litter.

Kuwait
Wealthy countries, such as Kuwait, tend to produce a lot of rubbish per person, since on average, each person buys a lot of packaged products.

Indian Ocean Garbage Patch

RUBBISH RECYCLED

100
90
80
70
60
50
40
30
20
10
0

Switzerland Austria Germany Netherlands Norway Sweden United States

A **plastic** bottle in **landfill** can take **450 years** to **biodegrade**, or rot

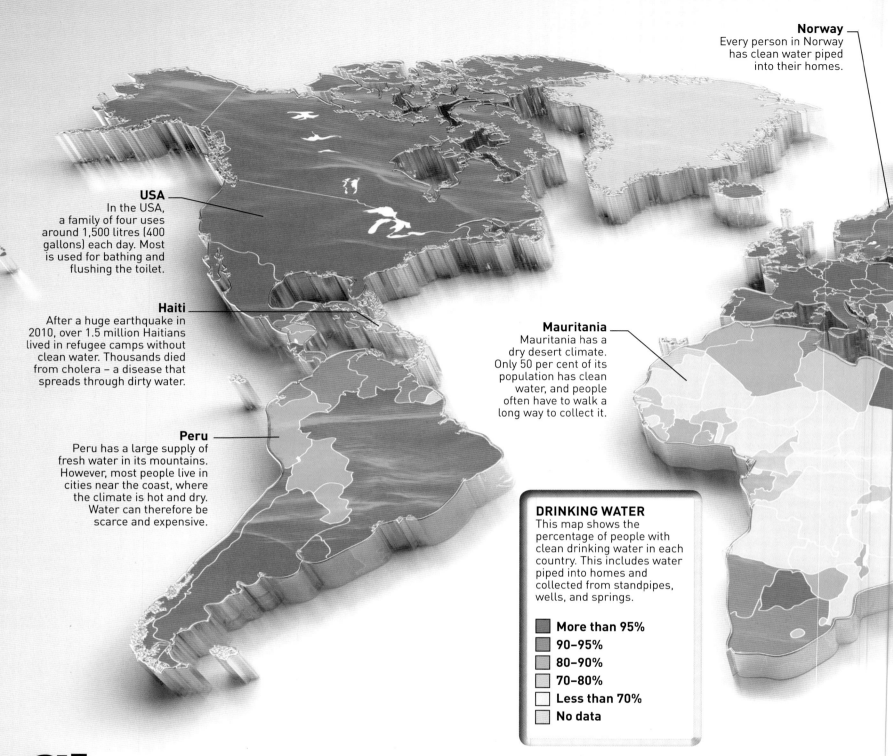

Norway
Every person in Norway has clean water piped into their homes.

USA
In the USA, a family of four uses around 1,500 litres (400 gallons) each day. Most is used for bathing and flushing the toilet.

Haiti
After a huge earthquake in 2010, over 1.5 million Haitians lived in refugee camps without clean water. Thousands died from cholera – a disease that spreads through dirty water.

Mauritania
Mauritania has a dry desert climate. Only 50 per cent of its population has clean water, and people often have to walk a long way to collect it.

Peru
Peru has a large supply of fresh water in its mountains. However, most people live in cities near the coast, where the climate is hot and dry. Water can therefore be scarce and expensive.

DRINKING WATER
This map shows the percentage of people with clean drinking water in each country. This includes water piped into homes and collected from standpipes, wells, and springs.

- More than 95%
- 90–95%
- 80–90%
- 70–80%
- Less than 70%
- No data

Clean water

The tap in your home may give you an instant supply of clean drinking water. However, 90 per cent of the world's population must fetch their water from a standpipe or a well. For 783 million people, their sources of water are contaminated and unsafe to drink.

Thirsty crops

Growing crops in dry climates is by far the thirstiest human activity. It uses much more water than is used in people's homes and dominates water use in many countries. That's why parts of central Asia, where farmers water fields of cotton, top this list of overall water consumers.

IN DEVELOPING COUNTRIES, 70 PERCENT OF INDUSTRIAL WASTE IS

Russia
Russia's rivers and lakes provide plentiful water, but the quality of water supplies is not reliable and most people must buy bottled water to drink.

Water use in the home
These glasses show how many of litres (gallons) of water each person uses a day for such things as drinking, washing, cooking, and cleaning. In Cambodia, each person manages on just 19 litres (5 gallons) of water a day. In the USA, people use 30 times more.

| Cambodia 19.6 (5.2) | Kenya 34.4 (9.1) | Brazil 234 (61.9) | Kuwait 501 (133) | USA 593 (157) |

India
Seventy-two per cent of people live in rural areas without a supply of clean water. Around 1,000 children here under five die every day from diarrhoea.

Indonesia
Many water supplies are polluted by waste from factories and by sewage. Around 70 per cent of people lack clean water.

The **UN** says each person should have **50 litres (13 gallons)** of **clean water** every day

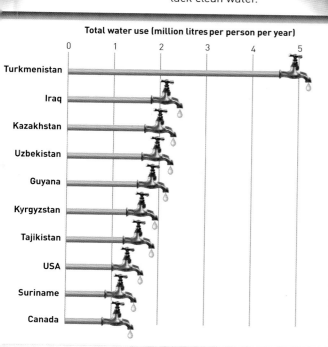

Total water use (million litres per person per year)

Turkmenistan, Iraq, Kazakhstan, Uzbekistan, Guyana, Kyrgyzstan, Tajikistan, USA, Suriname, Canada

Australia
Recent terrible droughts in this dry country have made Australia rethink its water use. Authorities have begun recycling sewage and encouraging grey water recycling (waste water from baths and washing machines) to "drought-proof" the nation.

DUMPED UNTREATED INTO RIVERS, WHERE IT POLLUTES USABLE WATER.

Athabasca oil sands, Canada
The enormous Athabasca oil reserves are in the form of oil shale on the land's surface. To get the oil out of oil shale needs huge amounts of water and energy and causes far more environmental destruction per barrel of oil than normal drilling.

North Sea
Contains western Europe's largest oil and natural gas reserves.

France
France has only small oil reserves and prefers to focus on nuclear power production.

How long left?
Fossil fuels are used up faster all the time, and one day the world's fuel reserves – the fuels remaining in the ground – will run out. Estimates of the size of the fuel reserves go up as well as down, as old reserves are used up and new ones are discovered. Below are the latest estimates of how long they will last.

Coal: 112 years
Natural gas: 64 years
Oil: 54 years

2012 supply estimates

USA
Americans consume one-fifth of the world's fossil fuel energy.

Trinidad and Tobago
Natural gas consumption per person is the highest in the world, and gas reserves are declining fast.

Texas gas fields
The USA is the second-largest producer of gas behind Russia. Texas provides one-quarter of the USA's gas from both onshore and offshore fields.

Venezuela
Has possibly the greatest amount of oil of any single country. Nearly 20 per cent of global reserves are found here.

Nigeria
The largest producer of oil in Africa, but conflict and a lack of resources limit production.

Fossil fuels

Most **fossil fuels** were formed **300–360 million years** ago

Over four-fifths of the world's energy comes from fossil fuels: oil, natural gas, and coal. These are the remains of plants and other life-forms, buried for millions of years. When burned, they release energy, but also waste gases, which pollute the atmosphere.

Falkland Islands
Surveys show that around the British-controlled Falkland Islands there may be double the amount of oil as in the North Sea. Argentina, claims a right to the islands and to the oil.

FROM THE LATE 2ND CENTURY CE, THE ROMANS IN BRITAIN MINED

Russia
Has the world's largest natural gas reserves and second-largest coal reserves. Twice as much gas is consumed in Russia as coal.

FUEL RESERVES
Fossil fuels form in intense underground conditions as remains of dead organisms are compressed over millions of years. Oil and natural gas are found trapped in underground spaces and are extracted by drilling. Coal can be mined at the surface or deep underground. The map shows areas where there are significant oil, gas, and coal fields.

- ■ Oil field
- ■ Gas field
- ■ Coal field

China
Largest producer of coal in the world, though it has the third largest coal reserves.

The Middle East
Richest oil region on Earth – contains almost half the world's oil reserves.

Ghawar oil field, Saudi Arabia
Produces more oil than any other single oil field, providing 60 per cent of Saudi Arabia's vast oil production.

Australia
One of the world's top exporters of coal. Coal consumption per person is the highest in the world.

Top fuel consumers

In 2007, China overtook the USA as the largest burner of fossil fuels, mostly coal. However, because there are fewer people in the USA, the average American burns more than four times as much fuel as the average Chinese citizen.

Top gas consumer
United States

Top coal consumer
China

Top oil consumer
United States

Oil refinery, New Orleans, USA

Alternative energy

There are several types of alternative energy, some of which are also renewable (see opposite page).

Wind
Mounted on tall masts, huge rotating blades called wind turbines harness the wind's energy and use it to drive electricity generators.

Solar
The Sun's energy can be used to heat water in homes or to produce high temperatures for electricity generation. Photovoltaic panels convert sunlight directly into electricity.

Nuclear
The nuclei (cores) of atoms are split apart in nuclear power plants, releasing vast amounts of energy. However, the process also creates dangerous nuclear waste.

Geothermal
A geothermal power plant taps underground steam or hot water, which it uses to generate electricity or to heat buildings directly.

Hydroelectric
A hydroelectric power plant is a dam with generators built into it. Water builds up behind the dam. When gates in the dam are opened, the force of the falling water drives the generators.

Biofuel, biogas, and biomass
Liquid fuel made from plants, rather than oil, is called biofuel. When farm waste, sewage, and rubbish rot, they release biogas, which can be burned as fuel. Biomass is any plant-based material burned for warmth or to generate electricity.

Alternative energy

The world's reserves of fossil fuels – coal, oil, and gas – will not last for ever. To meet the energy shortfall, people are developing alternative energy sources.

Canada
Second-largest producer of hydroelectricity; seventh for nuclear and biofuel; ninth for wind

USA
World's top producer of geothermal, biofuel, and nuclear energy; in second place for wind, fourth for hydroelectricity, and fifth for solar

Mexico
Fourth for geothermal

El Salvador
Ninth for geothermal

Venezuela
Ninth for hydroelectricity

Brazil
Ranked second for biofuel production and third for hydroelectricity

Argentina
Sixth-largest producer of biofuel

Iceland
Seventh on the "top 10" list of geothermal producers

Norway
Number six for hydroelectricity

Germany
First in the world for solar, third for wind and biofuel, and eighth for nuclear

France
Ranked second for nuclear, fourth for biofuel, sixth for wind, and seventh for solar

Spain
Number four for wind and solar, and eight for biofuel

Italy
Ranked second for solar, fifth for geothermal, seventh for wind, and tenth for biofuel

Democratic Republic of Congo
Like many African countries, much of its energy comes from wood burned in people's homes. Biomass and biogas account for over 90 per cent of energy production.

Hydroelectric power plants supply **98 per cent** of **Norway's** energy

KEY
Top 10 alternative-energy producing countries in each field

🗼 **Wind energy**

🏭 **Geothermal energy**

🔲 **Solar energy**

〰️ **Hydroelectric energy**

☢ **Nuclear energy**

🌱 **Biofuel energy**

Sweden
Number ten for hydroelectricity

Russia
World's fourth-largest nuclear producer and the fifth-largest hydroelectricity nation

Ukraine
Number six for nuclear

World's energy sources
Fossil fuels supply more than 80 per cent of the world's energy. Most of the alternative energy we use comes from bio-sources. Nobody knows for sure how much oil, coal, and gas is left in the ground, so many countries are investing heavily in renewable energy.

Alternative energy 19.4%

PERCENTAGE OF WORLD'S TOTAL ENERGY PRODUCTION

Biofuel, biogas, and biomass 12.39%
Hydroelectricity 3.34%
Nuclear 2.70%
Wind 0.51%
Solar 0.23%
Geothermal 0.19%

Fossil fuels 80.6%

China
First in the world for both wind and hydroelectricity, sixth for solar, fifth for biofuel, and ninth for nuclear

South Korea
World's fifth-largest producer of nuclear energy

Japan
A significant producer of solar (third in world), nuclear (third), geothermal (eighth), and hydroelectric (ninth) energy

India
Fourth in the world for wind, seventh for hydroelectricity

Philippines
Second-largest geothermal nation

Kenya
Tenth in the world for geothermal; more than 15 per cent of Kenya's energy comes from this source

Thailand
Ranked ninth in the world for biofuel

Indonesia
Third in the "top 10" of geothermal countries

Australia
Tenth-largest producer of solar energy

New Zealand
Number six in the world for geothermal

Renewable energy
Once fossil fuels have been burned, they cannot be replaced. Energy from natural sources that are always replenished – such as wind, sunlight, water, geothermal, and biomass – is known as renewable energy. However, not all forms of renewable enery are reliable: the Sun does not shine every day, and the wind does not always blow.

TOP RENEWABLE ENERGY SUPPLIERS

China	USA	Brazil	Canada	Russia	India	Germany	Norway	Japan	Spain
764.5	436.4	429.6	360.2	167.4	132.3	121.9	117.7	102.8	90.42

Total energy from renewable sources (terrawatt-hours per year)

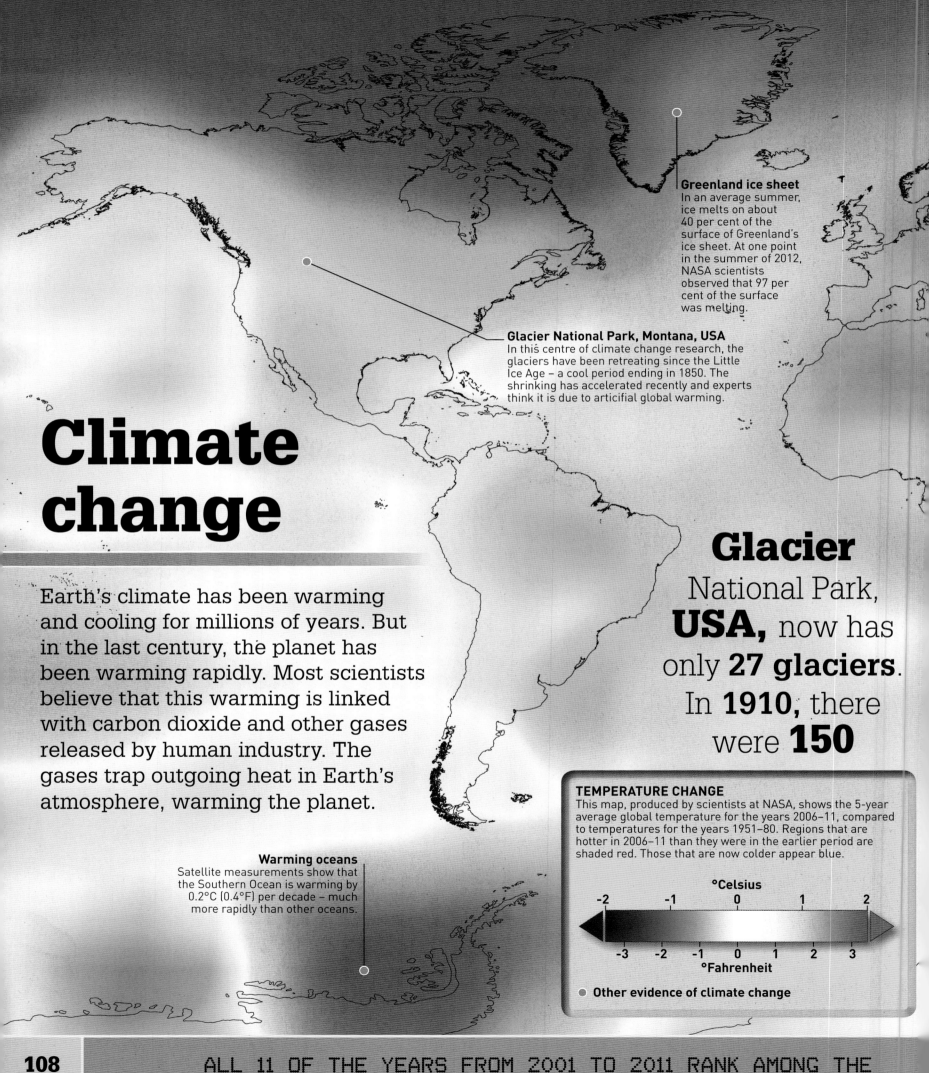

Climate change

Earth's climate has been warming and cooling for millions of years. But in the last century, the planet has been warming rapidly. Most scientists believe that this warming is linked with carbon dioxide and other gases released by human industry. The gases trap outgoing heat in Earth's atmosphere, warming the planet.

Greenland ice sheet
In an average summer, ice melts on about 40 per cent of the surface of Greenland's ice sheet. At one point in the summer of 2012, NASA scientists observed that 97 per cent of the surface was melting.

Glacier National Park, Montana, USA
In this centre of climate change research, the glaciers have been retreating since the Little Ice Age – a cool period ending in 1850. The shrinking has accelerated recently and experts think it is due to artificial global warming.

Glacier National Park, **USA,** now has only **27 glaciers**. In **1910**, there were **150**

Warming oceans
Satellite measurements show that the Southern Ocean is warming by 0.2°C (0.4°F) per decade – much more rapidly than other oceans.

TEMPERATURE CHANGE
This map, produced by scientists at NASA, shows the 5-year average global temperature for the years 2006–11, compared to temperatures for the years 1951–80. Regions that are hotter in 2006–11 than they were in the earlier period are shaded red. Those that are now colder appear blue.

°Celsius
-2   -1   0   1   2

-3   -2   -1   0   1   2   3
°Fahrenheit

○ Other evidence of climate change

Arctic sea ice
The whole Arctic region has warmed more than any other part of the world, and the most obvious effect is on the sea ice. Sea ice is a layer of frozen sea water, 2–3 m (6–9 ft) thick, which forms on the surface of the polar oceans. In 2012, Arctic sea ice fell to its lowest extent since satellites starting monitoring it in 1979.

Rising sea level
Global sea levels are rising, but satellite data tells us that they are rising more in some places than others, because local heating makes the water expand. From 1992–2011, sea levels around the Philippines rose by 5.8 mm (0.2 in) per year, putting the low-lying country third in the UN's list of countries most vulnerable to climate change.

Lake shrinkage
Since 1960, Lake Chad has shrunk by 95 per cent because the pattern of monsoon rainfall has shifted, giving it less rain. With less rain for their crops, people have also taken much more of the lake's water, shrinking it further. Scientists think the rainfall shift could have been triggered by warming of the surface of the oceans.

Retreating Himalayan glaciers
The shrinking of glaciers in the Himalayas north of India has been blamed on the Asian Brown Cloud – a haze of sooty particles released by south Asian cities. Even though the cloud blocks some sunlight reaching Earth, cooling the land below, it has a warming effect overall, because it absorbs and traps heat energy like carbon dioxide does.

Melting glacier
Muir Glacier in Alaska, USA, has been shrinking for over 50 years. It has retreated by more than 12 km (7 miles) and is 800 m (2,860 ft) thinner. In 1941, the glacier was surrounded by bare rock, but it is now covered with trees and shrubs.

13 August, 1941   31 August, 2004

Global sea level
Since 1993, the global sea level has steadily increased by around 3 mm (0.1 in) per year, as measured by satellite. During the 100-year period before 1993, sea levels rose by an average of only 1.7 mm (0.07 in) every year.

Sea level rise since 1993 – 60-day average

Change in sea level (mm): -20, -10, 0, 10, 20, 30, 40, 50

Change in sea level (in): -0.5, 0, 0.5, 1, 1.5, 2

Year: 1994, 1996, 1998, 2000, 2002, 2004, 2006, 2008, 2010

Kluane/Wrangell-St Elias/ Glacier Bay/Tatshenshini-Alsek, Alaska and British Columbia.
Home to some of the world's most spectacualr glaciers.

Maud Gulf Migratory Bird Sanctuary, Arctic Canada

Alert, Canada

Northeast Greenland National Park
World's largest protected area, mostly made up of the Greenland Ice Sheet.

Charlie-Gibbs South Marine Protected Area, Atlantic Ocean

Yellowstone National Park, Wyoming, USA
The first national park in the world, founded in 1872. The large alpine meadows and grass prairies provide ideal habitat for the large herds of bison living in the park.

Northern Canada
Permafrost (permanently frozen soil) makes this vast region inaccessible to people, preserving the Arctic tundra plains for the wolves and caribou.

Sahara desert
World's largest hot desert. Supports little human life other than in scattered oases.

WILDERNESS AREAS

The map shows the level of human influence across the world. The colours are based on the "wilderness value", which measures how far any one place is from permanent human settlements, roads, and manmade structures. This measure of remoteness from human development shows how much wilderness is left.

Key

High wilderness   Low wilderness

Protected areas of the world
The blue areas on the map show some of the world's protected areas of wilderness. Damaging activities, such as hunting and mining, are usually banned. The areas include wildlife reserves, national parks, marine parks, and more.

Galápagos Islands

Aïr and Ténéré Natural Reserves, Niger

Amazon rainforest
The north and west of this great forest have few or no roads and are far from human impact. Some areas are flooded to great depth every year. Some parts have never been logged and are "pristine".

Jaú National Park, Amazonas, Brazil
One of the largest protected rainforest areas in the world and the largest in the Amazon basin. The park includes the entire Jaú River, where the water is black from minerals in dissolved organic matter.

Largest protected areas

While legally protected areas cover 12 per cent of the world's land, global ocean protection covers just 1.6 per cent of the oceans. The world's largest protected area, in Greenland, is three times the size of Italy.

1. **Northeast Greenland National Park**
   Greenland, 927,000 sq km (357,916 sq mi).

2. **Ar-Rub'al-Khali (Empty Quarter)**
   Saudi Arabia, 650,000 sq km (250,966 sq mi).

3. **Chagos Marine Protected Area**
   Indian Ocean, 545,000 sq km (210,426 sq mi).

4. **Phoenix Islands**
   Central Pacific Ocean, 408,250 sq km (157,626 sq mi).

5. **Three Rivers Nature Reserve**
   Qinghai province, China. 363,000 sq km (140,155 sq mi).

About **95 per cent** of the world's **people** live on **10 per cent** of the **land**

Pelagos Sanctuary for Mediterranean Marine Mammals

Yugyd Va National Park, Russia
Largest national park in Europe, made up of forests in the Northern Ural Mountains.

Siberia
The northeastern parts of Russia are cold, remote, and largely untouched forests, mountains, and tundra.

Great Siberian Polynia, Russia

Lake Baikal World Heritage Site, Russia

Qiangtang Nature Reserve, China
The Tibetan Plateau is remote and empty of people. From the most remote point, it is a three-week trip to the nearest cities of Lhasa or Korla – one day by car and the remaining 20 on foot.

Selous Game Reserve Tanzania

Kavango-Zambezi Transfrontier Conservation Area
Includes 17 national parks. Victoria Falls, between Zambia and Zimbabwe, lies at the centre.

Chagos Marine Protected Area, Indian Ocean
A British-controlled cluster of 55 tiny islands. Largest marine reserve in the world.

Outback, Australia
"Outback" describes the hot, dry parts of Australia where very few people live, many of whom are Aboriginals. Several highways pass through even the most remote areas.

Wilderness

Wildernesses are the last places that have been largely unchanged by humans. Indigenous peoples sometimes live in these undeveloped areas, where their lifestyles sometimes impact little on the landscape and wildlife.

Great Barrier Reef Marine Park, Australia
World's largest coral reef system.

Reaching for the sky.
The Burj Khalifa, the world's
tallest building, can be seen
in the distance in this view of
fog-bound Dubai, largest city
in the United Arab Emirates.

Introduction

Engineering and technology enable humans to achieve amazing feats. We build skyscrapers that reach towards the clouds, bridges that span great canyons, and tunnels that pierce mountains and travel under the sea. Our computer networks and transport systems keep people and places connected. We can even explore other planets.

World in motion

Transport has shrunk our world. Thanks to jet airliners, motorways, and high-speed rail routes, we can go on long-distance journeys that would have been unthinkable just a few decades ago. This transport revolution began with the invention of the railway about 200 years ago, and it has continued at speed ever since.

Train collects electricity from power cables suspended above the track.

High-speed electric locomotive
Launched in 1999, the Velaro is now in service in Germany, Spain, China, and Russia. It can reach speeds of more than 400 kph (250 mph). The Velaro is powered by electricity and can pull trains with more than 900 passengers aboard.

Shrinking technology

Few, if any, areas of technology have advanced faster than computing. ENIAC, developed by the US Army in 1946, was the first general-purpose programmable electronic computer. ENIAC contained over 100,000 components. Since then, electronic components have become smaller and smaller. A modern laptop computer is controlled by a tiny microchip that may be etched with more than a billion components.

Modern marvel
This tiny computer, just 1 mm (0.04 in) square, is implanted into the eye to help people with the disease glaucoma.

Enormous ancestor
ENIAC weighed 30 tonnes and occupied an entire room. Operators programmed ENIAC by plugging and unplugging cables and adjusting switches.

Early steam engine
Puffing Billy is the world's oldest surviving steam locomotive. Built in 1813 to haul coal in northern England, it had a top speed of about 10 kph (6 mph).

Coal carried in the tender was burned to heat water in the boiler and produce steam to drive the wheels.

Bullet-shaped nose enables locomotive to cut through the air more easily, increasing speed.

Construction

A steel-and-concrete building revolution began in the late 19th century. Frames made of steel girders allowed taller structures to be built, and the invention of reinforced concrete – concrete with steel rods set into it – introduced an amazingly strong, durable new material. Together, steel and reinforced concrete gave birth to the modern skyscraper, changing the face of the world's cities.

● **Ancient concrete**
The Romans were experts in building with concrete. It was used in the construction of the Colosseum and the Pantheon in Rome.

● **World's oldest skyscraper city?**
Shibam, in Yemen, has about 500 high-rise apartment buildings made of mud brick, most dating from the 16th century.

● **First steel-framed skyscraper**
Completed in 1885, the innovative 10-storey Home Insurance Building in Chicago, USA, used a steel frame to support the walls.

● **Reinforced first**
The first skyscraper built with reinforced concrete was the 15-storey Ingalls Building, in Cincinnati, USA, erected in 1903.

Manhattan, then and now
The Brooklyn Bridge span's New York's East River. The view across to Manhattan Island has changed dramatically since the bridge opened in 1883, and it now bristles with skyscrapers.

Infrastructure

The built and engineered systems that we rely on every day – from sewers and telecommunication networks to power lines, railways, and roads – are collectively known as infrastructure. Without such systems, our modern way of life would be impossible.

● **First telephone exchange**
The first exchange to connect callers was built in New Haven, Connecticut, USA, in 1878.

● **Intercity railway**
Opened in 1830, the Manchester to Liverpool route in England was the first intercity railway.

Ulm–Stuttgart autobahn, 1950
Germany was a pioneer of the freeway, or autobahn, in the 1930s. Cars did not clog the roads until much later!

In **2011**, Hartsfield-Jackson, Atlanta, averaged **184 flights** per hour

Top 10 busiest passenger airports 2011

Around 3.2 billion air passengers passed through the world's top 100 airports in 2011 – around 998 million in Europe and another 989 million in North America. The world's busiest airport, Hartsfield-Jackson International in Atlanta, Georgia, USA, averaged 252,000 passengers per day in 2011, and handled 923,991 flights during the year.

RANK	AIRPORT	PASSENGERS PER YEAR
1	Hartsfield–Jackson Atlanta International, USA	92,365,860
2	Beijing Capital International, China	77,403,668
3	London Heathrow, United Kingdom	69,433,565
4	O'Hare International, Chicago, USA	66,561,023
5	Tokyo International, Japan	62,263,025
6	Los Angeles International, USA	61,848,449
7	Paris Charles de Gaulle, France	60,970,551
8	Dallas Fort Worth International, USA	57,806,152
9	Frankfurt, Germany	56,436,255
10	Hong Kong International, China	53,314,213

Air traffic

Air-traffic controllers have a tough job, ensuring safe routes, takeoffs, and landings for the thousands of planes that crisscross our skies each day. This map shows nearly 6,000 routes carrying scheduled commercial traffic.

WORLDWIDE, THERE WERE 24.79 MILLION PASSENGER AND CARGO FLIGHTS

PASSENGERS PER YEAR

Jeju	9.9 million	Seoul
Rio de Janeiro	7.6 million	São Paulo
Osaka	7.5 million	Tokyo
Sapporo	7.5 million	Tokyo
Melbourne	7.0 million	Sydney
Fukuoka	6.6 million	Tokyo
Beijing	6.6 million	Shanghai
Hong Kong	6.2 million	Taipei
Cape Town	4.5 million	Johannesburg
Mumbai	4.3 million	Delhi

Important airline routes

The map of the world's air traffic resembles a vast spider web, with routes connecting the main financial, commercial, and industrial centres and the most populated regions. The chart shows the most popular routes, by passenger numbers, in 2011.

Los Angeles

Long Beach

New York/
New Jersey

Panama Canal
The canal, built in 1914, connects the Pacific and Atlantic oceans. It is the world's busiest route, with about 14,000 ships passing through it each year.

Shipping

Most countries need to sell the goods they produce and buy in the things they need. Shipping plays an essential role in world trade, carrying food, fuel, chemicals, and manufactured goods between markets.

More than
90 per cent of **global** trade is **carried** by **sea**

Europe's hub

In this expanded view, we can see in greater detail the dense network of shipping lanes serving the major hubs of Europe. Routes criss-cross the North and Baltic seas and the English Channel.

North Sea

Baltic Sea

Hamburg

Rotterdam

Antwerp

English Channel

Tianjin

Qingdao

Busan

Shanghai

Ningbo

Xiamen

Kaohsiung

Shenzhen

Guangzhou

Hong Kong

Suez Canal
The canal links the Mediterranean and the Red Sea. Ships use it to travel between Europe and Asia without the having to sail round the whole of Africa.

Dubai ports

Singapore

Tanjung

Port Klang

World's 20 busiest ports

The ports marked on the map handle more cargo than others worldwide. Cargo is measured in TEUs (twenty-foot container equivalent units). A TEU is one standard container full of cargo. The busiest port in the world is Shanghai in China, which handled more than 30 million TEUs in 2011.

◯ Up to 10 million TEUs per year

⬤ 10–19 million TEUs per year

◯ 20 million or over TEUs per year

Railways

In the early 19th century, railways began to change the world radically by opening up new opportunities for travel and trade. Today, with roads gridlocked by traffic, modern railways are making a comeback.

EN453 (France to Russia)
A trans-European train connecting Paris and Moscow over 3,315 km (2,060 miles).

The Canadian (Canada)
Spectacular 4,466-km (2,775-mile) route between Vancouver and Toronto, travelling through mountains, prairies, and lakeland.

California Zephyr (USA)
Follows the route of the first US transcontinental railway (completed in 1869) from San Francisco to Chicago.

Salta to Antofagasta (Chile to Argentina)
At 941 km (585 miles), this is the longest main line in South America.

Highest railway bridges

Completed in 2001, the Beipanjiang River Railway Bridge will lose its title of "world's highest railway bridge" when India's 359-m- (1,178-ft-) high Chenab River Bridge opens in 2017.

1. Beipanjiang River Railway Bridge, Fa'er Bouyei, Guizhou, China: 275 m (902 ft)
2. Mala Rijeka Viaduct, Podgorica, Montenegro: 198 m (650 ft)
3. Qingshuihe River Railway Bridge, Qingshuihezhen, Guizhou, China: 183 m (600 ft)
4. Pit River Bridge, Shasta Lake, California, USA: 152 m (500 ft)
5. Caijiagou Railway viaduct, Liduzhen, Chongqing, China: 151 m (495 ft)

World's fastest trains

Shanghai's Maglev has no wheels but hovers over the track and is propelled by magnets. It runs for just 30 km (19 miles). The other high-speed contenders listed here travel on long-distance routes.

5. TGV POS, France — 320 kph (199 mph)
4. ICE 3, Germany, Netherlands — 320 kph (199 mph)
3. AVE Class 102, Spain — 330 kph (205 mph)
2. AVE Class 103, Spain — 350 kph (217 mph)
1. Shanghai Maglev, China — 431 kph (268 mph)

SPEED OF TRAIN

Trans-Siberian Railway (Russia)
The world's longest rail journey passes through seven time zones as it runs 9,288 km (5,771 miles) from Moscow in the west to Vladivostock by the Sea of Japan.

The world has **1 million km** (620,000 miles) of **railtrack**

Guangzhou to Lhasa (China)
The Tanggula Pass section is the world's highest track, at 5,072 m (16,640 ft).

Alexandria to Aswan (Egypt)
Travelling via Cairo and Luxor, this line follows the Nile Valley, with its ancient pyramids and temples.

Dibrugarh to Kanyakumari (India)
Longest route in India, at 4,286 km (2,657 miles).

Five longest railway tunnels

In 2016, the Seikan Tunnel will be surpassed by the Gotthard Base Tunnel, a new, 57-km- (35-mile-) long railway tunnel in progress beneath the Swiss Alps.

5 Taihang Tunnel, Taihang Mountains, China: 27.85 km (17.3 miles)

2 Channel Tunnel, English Channel: 50.4 km (31.5 miles)

4 Lotschberg Base Tunnel, Bernese Alps, Switzerland: 34.6 km (21.5 miles)

3 Hakkoda Tunnel, Hakkoda mountains, Japan: 26.4 km (16.4 miles)

1 Seikan Tunnel, Tsugaru Strait, Japan: 53.8 km (33.5 miles)

Blue Train, South Africa
A luxurious train that runs from Cape Town to Pretoria through vineyards, mountains, and the arid landscape of the Karoo.

Indian Pacific (Australia)
This 4,352-km (2,704-mile) route, links Sydney on the east coast with Perth in the west.

Dempster Highway Extension
An ice road built on the frozen Mackenzie River and Arctic Ocean, it provides a winter route to the isolated community of Tuktoyaktuk.

Mountain roads and passes

① Trollstigen, Norway
This dramatic road's name means "Trolls' ladder". It has 11 hairpin bends, which wind up the steep mountainside.

② Stelvio Pass, Italy
One of the highest roads in the Alps, its 60 hairpin bends provide a challenge for both motorists and cyclists.

③ Khardung La, India
This famously high mountain pass in the Ladakh part of Kashmir was built in 1976 and opened to motor vehicles in 1988.

④ Semo La, Tibet, China
Possibly the highest vehicle-accessible pass in the world, it was reliably measured in 1999 at 5,565 m (18,258 ft).

⑤ Irohazaka Winding Road
Each of the 48 hairpin turns on this route in Japan is labelled with one of the 48 characters of the Japanese alphabet.

Bonn-Köln Autobahn
Built in 1932, it was the first road designed exclusively for cars, with separate carriageways and no intersections with other roads.

Tibbit to Contwoyto Winter Road
An ice road built over frozen lakes, it is open for about 10 weeks from late January each year.

Cabot Trail
Looping round the northern tip of Cape Breton Island, Nova Scotia and named after 16th-century English explorer, John Cabot.

Route 66
A 3,940-km (2,448-mile) road that follows the historic route taken by migrants to California during the Great Depression.

Pacific Coast Highway
This world-famous route hugs the Californian coast from Orange County in the south to the forests of giant redwood trees in the north.

Natchez Trace Parkway
A route used by Native Americans and their animals for thousands of years before the modern road was built.

Darién Gap, Panama
A stretch of rainforest that breaks the Pan-American Highway's route.

Pan-American Highway
About 48,000 km (29,800 miles) long, it runs through 18 countries, from Alaska to the southern tip of Argentina.

Yungas Road, Bolivia
A single-track mountain road heavily used by lorries but with unprotected sheer drops of 600 m (1,800 ft). Up to 300 travellers are killed on the route every year.

World's busiest roads

① Kings Highway 401, Canada
The busiest highway in North America – more than 440,000 vehicles pass through the Toronto section every day. It is also one of the widest in the world – some sections of the route have 18 lanes.

② Santa Monica Freeway, USA
Runs from the city of Santa Monica to Los Angeles. It was the world's busiest road until 1993, when the Century Freeway was built a few miles to the south. This reduced traffic and congestion on the freeway, although it still carries up to 329,000 vehicles a day.

KINGS HIGHWAY 401, ONTARIO, CANADA

Roads

The planet is now more accessible by road than it has ever been. There are about 193 million km (120 million miles) of roads on Earth, from multi-lane urban freeways to seasonal ice roads made from frozen lakes and seas.

Estonian Islands
Ice roads between islands and the mainland are only opened to traffic when the ice is 22 cm (8.7 in) thick along the whole route.

Siberia
Siberia has few permanent roads, partly because it is so difficult to build stable foundations on the permafrost soil.

Road of Bones
The M56 Kolyma Highway passes through the coldest inhabited places on Earth, with winter temperatures dropping below -50° C (-58° F).

The **George Washington bridge** in New York carries **106 million** vehicles every year

Karakoram Highway
One of the world's highest roads at an altitude of 4,693 m (15,397 ft), it connects China and Pakistan.

Garden Route
Runs along the South African coast from Cape Town to Port Elizabeth.

Milford Road
Meanders in the stunning scenery of New Zealand's Milford Sound.

Great Ocean Road
Following a beautiful seaside route, this road is a memorial to the Australians who died in World War I.

Record road bridges

△1 Millau Viaduct
This French bridge is the tallest in the world. One mast is 343 m (1,125 ft) tall – taller than the Eiffel Tower.

△2 Sidu River Bridge
With the road 496 m (1,627 ft) above the floor of the Sidu River gorge in China, this is the world's highest bridge.

△3 Bang Na Expressway
This 55-km- (34-mile-) long six-lane elevated highway in Thailand is the world's longest road bridge.

△4 Jiaozhou Bay Bridge
The world's longest road bridge crossing water, it is supported by 5,238 massive concrete pillars.

△5 Lake Pontchartrain Causeway
Two parallel bridges 38 km (23.8 miles) long, near New Orleans, USA.

△6 Akashi-Kaikyò Bridge
The world's longest suspension bridge, it has 300,000 km (190,000 mi) of steel cables and connects two Japanese islands.

MILLAU VIADUCT, FRANCE

KEY
Roads can be paved (covered stones, brick, concrete, tarmac, or another hard surface), or unpaved. Paving makes a road more durable and weatherproof.

— **Famous roads**
— **Scenic routes**
— **Ice roads**

CN Tower
553 m (1,815 ft)
Toronto, Canada
1976

1 World Trade Centre
541 m (1,775 ft)
New York, USA
2013

Istanbul Diamond
261 m (856 ft)
Istanbul, Turkey
2010

Willis Tower
442 m (1,450 ft)
Chicago, USA
1973

Commerzbank
259 m (850 ft)
Frankfurt, Germany
1997

Transamerica Pyramid
260 m (850 ft)
San Francisco, USA
1972

The Shard
310 m (1,020 ft)
London, UK
2012

Trump International Hotel and Tower
357 m (1,170 ft)
Chicago, USA
2009

Torre Caja Madrid
250 m (820 ft)
Madrid, Spain
2008

Trump Ocean Club
293 m (961 ft)
Panama City, Panama
2011

Empire State Building
381 m (1,250 ft)
New York City, USA,
1931

John Hancock Centre
344 m (1,129 ft)
Chicago, USA
1969

The Eiffel Tower
325 m (1,066 ft)
Paris, France
1889

Gran Torre Santiago
300 m (984 ft)
Santiago, Chile
2012

Great Pyramid of Giza
147 m (481 ft)
El Giza, Egypt
c.2560–2540 BCE

Carlton Centre
223 m (732 ft)
Johannesburg,
South Africa
1973

Makka Royal Clock Tower Hotel
601 m (1,972 ft)
Makkah,
Saudi Arabia
2012

Tallest buildings

From ancient pyramids to today's hi-tech hotels, powerful people have shown off their status through impressive buildings. As technology improves, the towers get taller.

Tallest buildings, 2012

To be called a building, a tower must be inhabitable (offices or homes). Buildings do not include "supported structures" such as guyed (tethered) masts. Buildings may be measured to their architectural top, as they are on these pages, or to the tip of any masts or aerials.

828 m
(2,717 ft)

HEIGHT IN METRES

500
450
400
350
300
250
200
150
100
50
0

HEIGHT IN FEET

1,640
1,476
1,312
1,148
984
820
656
492
328
164
0

Jin Mao Tower — Trump International Hotel and Tower — Willis Tower — Nanjing Greenland Financial Centre — Petronas Towers — International Commerce Centre — Shanghai World Financial Centre — Taipei 101 — Burj Khalifa

The Burj Khalifa has **163** floors linked by **57** double-decker lifts

Ostankino Tower
540 m (1,770 ft)
Moscow, Russia
1967

Mercury City Tower
332 m (1,089 ft)
Moscow, Russia
2012

Oriental Pearl Tower
468 m (1,535 ft)
Shanghai, China
1994

Shanghai World Financial Centre
492 m (1,614 ft)
Shanghai, China
2008

Busan Lotte Tower
510.2 m (1,674 ft)
Busan, South Korea
2015

International Commerce Centre
484 m (1,588 ft)
Hong Kong
2010

Shanghai Tower
632 m (2,073 ft)
Shanghai, China
2014

Milad Tower
435 m (1,427 ft)
Tehran. Iran
2007

Burj Khalifa
828 m (2,717 ft)
Dubai, UAE
2010

Taipei 101
509 m (1,670 ft)
Taipei, Taiwan
2004

Tokyo Sky Tree
634 m (2,080 ft)
Tokyo, Japan
2011

Canton Tower
600 m (1,969 ft)
Guangzhou, China
2010

Petronas Towers
452 m (1,483 ft)
Kuala Lumpur, Malaysia
1998

Q1
323 m (1,060 ft)
Gold Coast, Australia
2005

Unsupported towers

Unlike buildings, these structures don't contain offices, homes, or shops. They are observation and communications towers.

● **Tokyo Sky Tree**
This communications tower overtook the Canton Tower in 2011 to become the world's tallest.

● **Canton Tower**
Canton is the former name of Guangzhou, where this tower was completed in 2010.

● **CN Tower**
More than 2 million people visit this tower's glass-floored observation deck every year.

● **Ostankino Tower**
This broadcasting tower was the world's first free-standing structure over 500 m (1,640 ft) tall.

● **Oriental Pearl Tower**
There are 11 spheres in the design of this TV tower, which has 15 observation levels.

Record-breaking buildings

The record for the tallest building (a structure that must be inhabitable) is a fiercely contested prize. These five have all won it.

● **Burj Khalifa, 2010–present**
This building has broken all records, including the tallest building and tallest unsupported structure.

● **Taipei 101, 2004–10**
The world's tallest building until the Burj Khalifa was built, Taipei 101 has 101 floors above ground.

● **Petronas Towers, 1998–2004**
These office blocks were the tallest buildings until 2004. They are still the tallest twin towers.

● **Willis Tower, 1973–98**
Formerly known as the Sears Tower, this 108-storey skyscraper is the USA's tallest.

● **Empire State Building, 1931–72**
This was the first building in the world to have more than 100 storeys – it has 102. It was the tallest building for 40 years.

Internet connections

The Internet has revolutionized the way we live our lives. At the click of a mouse, we can instantly exchange news, ideas, and images with people on the other side of the world, and we can buy or sell goods without having to leave our homes.

The Internet in a minute

Today, there are as many computers, phones, and other devices connected to the Internet as there are people in the world. As a result, an incredible amount of Internet activity can occur in just one minute.

61,141 hours of music

2 million Google searches

6 million Facebook views

20 million photos viewed

6 new Wikipedia articles

US$83,000 in online sales

BY 2015, THE NUMBER OF INTERNET-CONNECTED DEVICES IN THE

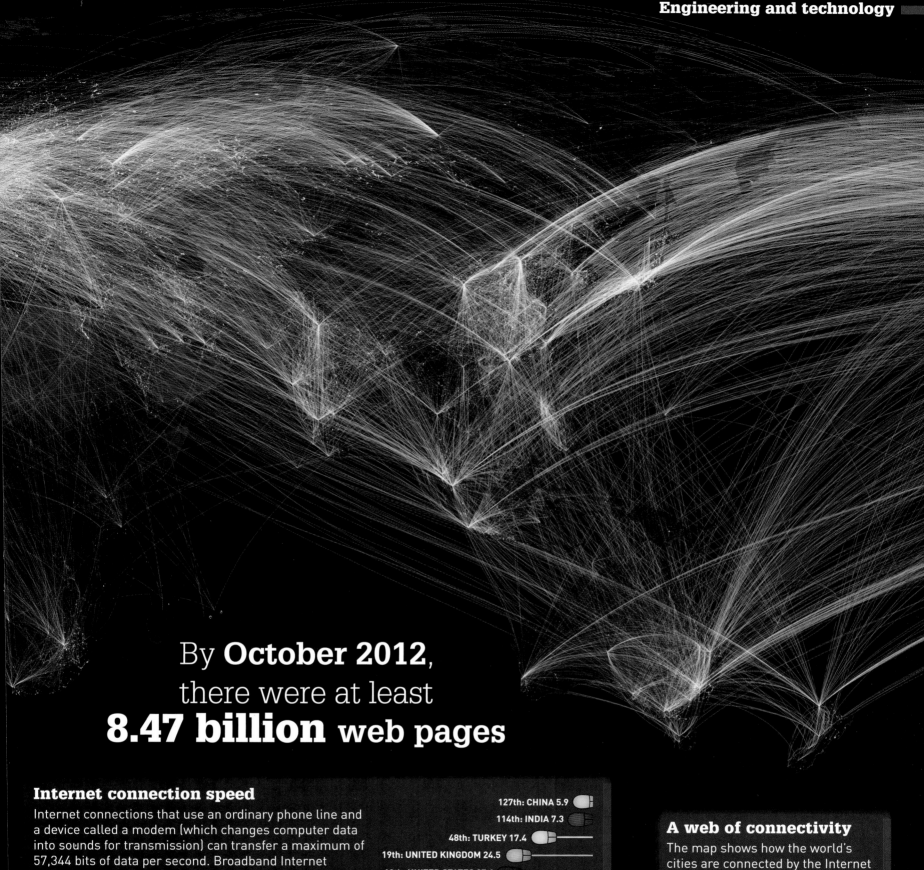

By **October 2012**,
there were at least
8.47 billion web pages

Internet connection speed

Internet connections that use an ordinary phone line and a device called a modem (which changes computer data into sounds for transmission) can transfer a maximum of 57,344 bits of data per second. Broadband Internet connections provided by digital phone lines, satellites, or fibre-optic cables are much faster. Here is a selection of the broadband speeds in different countries in October 2012. Internet users in Hong Kong had the world's fastest broadband, with a peak average download speed of over 49 million bits per second.

127th: CHINA 5.9
114th: INDIA 7.3
48th: TURKEY 17.4
19th: UNITED KINGDOM 24.5
13th: UNITED STATES 27.1
5th: LATVIA 33.5
4th: ROMANIA 38.6
3rd: JAPAN 40.5
2nd: SOUTH KOREA 46.9
1st: HONG KONG 49.2

PEAK CONNECTION SPEED (MILLION BITS PER SECOND) AND WORLD RANKING

A web of connectivity

The map shows how the world's cities are connected by the Internet – the brighter the area, the more connections there are. Connections are not the same as users. Many people, for example, use a single connection in an Internet café.

—— Lines represent Internet connections between cities

Satellites and space junk

The first satellite, *Sputnik 1*, was launched by the Soviet Union in 1957. Since then, thousands of satellites and millions of other objects have accumulated around Earth, creating a serious hazard for space travel.

Geosynchronous ring
This ring-shaped concentration of satellites appears more than 35,000 km (22,200 miles) above Earth's equator. It exists because it is extremely useful for a satellite to "hover" above a point on Earth's turning surface.

High-speed danger

The pattern of spots shows the strikes collected during the entire NASA Space Shuttle program, from 1983–2002. The vast majority of space debris is less than 1 cm (0.5 in) across and includes specks of solid rocket fuel and flakes of paint. But even dust acts like tiny bullets at speeds of up to 42,000 kph (26,000 mph).

Pale spots show damage less than 25 mm (1 in) across

Dark spots show damage more than 25 mm (1 in) across

At least **10 million** pieces of artificial debris are now in **Earth orbit**

KEY
The image shows 12,000 objects monitored by the ESA Space Debris team by radar and telescopes.

Satellites – mostly dead. Around 950 operational

Spent rockets

Mission waste (nuts, gloves, lost items)

Debris from explosions and collisions

Low Earth Orbit
This region is full of orbiting spacecraft, but also full of waste material ejected from spacecraft during missions and countless pieces of debris from collisions.

GPS (Global Positioning System) satellite
One of 31 forming a network, the GPS satellites orbit in one of six orbits. Each orbit is at a different angle to ensure they cover the entire surface of Earth. Someone on the ground is in contact with at least six of them at any one time.

How high are satellites?

Most objects launched into space are in Low Earth Orbit (LEO). At the lowest LEOs (160 km / 99 miles) objects circle Earth in 90 minutes at 28,800 kph (17,900 mph). Certain orbits are particularly useful. Image-taking satellites use polar Sun-synchronous orbits, which pass the equator at the same local time on every pass, so the shadows are the same.

Geosynchronous orbit
35,786 km (22,236 miles)
Satellites at this height orbit at the same speed as Earth turns, so they stay in the same spot over Earth's surface.

Hubble Space Telescope
595 km (370 miles)

Polar Sun-synchronous satellites
600–800 km (373–497 miles)

2,000 km (1,244 miles)

HIGH EARTH ORBIT ZONE

MEDIUM EARTH ORBIT ZONE

LOW EARTH ORBIT ZONE

GPS satellites
23,550 km (14,633 miles)
Objects orbit once every 12 hours, or twice a day.

International Space Station
340 km (210 miles)

A few **countries**, such as Liechtenstein and **Costa Rica**, have **no military forces**

UK
In 2010, the UK spent $59.6 billio on its armed forces, making it the world's fifth-biggest military spender.

France
France holds the world's fourth-largest nuclear arsenal, with 280 active warheads.

USA
The USA spends almost $700 billion per year on its armed forces – more than the next nine-biggest spending countries added together.

Israel
All Israeli men and women must serve for 2 to 3 years in their armed forces. Israel is the only country to make service for women compulsory.

KEY
The total amount of military expenditure by all the countries of the world in 2010 was $1.63 trillion, which is a 50 per cent increase since 2001, and is equivalent to $236 for every person on the planet. The map shows the total number of military vehicles, hardware, and weapons held by selected major countries.

- Up to 10 large warships (including aircraft carriers, cruisers, destroyers, frigates, and corvettes)
- Up to 10 submarines
- Up to 500 combat-capable aircraft
- Up to 1,000 main battle tanks
- Up to 500 nuclear warheads

Egypt
All Egyptian men between 18 and 30 must serve in the army for 1 to 3 years.

Brazil
Brazil's armed forces are the largest in South America. The army takes an active role in education, health care, and the construction of roads and railways.

Armed forces

Almost all countries have a military – an organized force of soldiers and weapons that defends the country against threats from outside or within. Many countries believe that a large, well-equipped military will discourage others from attacking.

Future warfare
Armed forces are increasingly using unmanned drones for surveillance or to launch missiles. Drones are controlled remotely from the ground, so air crew is not risked during missions.

Iran
Iran spends $102 for each member of population on its military budget.

Russia
Russia now holds about 2,700 nuclear warheads, compared to the 45,000 it had stockpiled in 1986. This was at the height of the Cold War, when it was joined to the other republics of the Soviet Union.

North Korea
Has one of the world's largest armies, with an estimated 1.2 million military personnel, compared to 655,000 in South Korea.

South Korea
South Korea keeps a 3-million strong reserve military, in case hostilities break out with North Korea.

China
China spends $106.4 billion on military weapons and personnel – only the USA spends more.

Pakistan
Pakistan's armed forces are one of the largest contributors to United Nations peacekeeping efforts, deploying about 10,000 troops to the UN.

India
India and Pakistan have fought three wars since 1947. Continued tension between them has led India to spend 2.5 per cent of its GDP on defence.

Saudi Arabia
Saudi Arabia's high-technology arsenal of weapons is supplied mainly by the USA, France, and Britain. It is the world's seventh-biggest spender, spending 10 per cent of its income, or GDP, on defence – that's among the world's highest.

Military personnel

China commands the world's largest military force of more than 2 million – but this is only just over three in every thousand people. In North Korea, a massive one-fifth of males aged 17–54 are in the regular armed forces.

TOTAL ARMED FORCES PERSONNEL

2,200,000	
2,000,000	
1,800,000	
1,600,000	
1,400,000	
1,200,000	
1,000,000	
800,000	
600,000	
400,000	
200,000	
0	

USA	UK	France	Russia	China	N Korea	S Korea	Egypt	Israel	Iran	Pakistan	India
1,316,342	178,470	223,622	704,000	2,185,000	1,190,000	655,000	388,500	176,500	398,000	617,000	1,315,550

History

Easter Island statues
The giant statues, or *moai*, on this small Pacific island stand up to 10 m (33 ft) tall. They were carved with stone tools, mainly between 1250 and 1500, by the Polynesian people who settled the island.

Introduction

Human history is crammed full of incident, from civilizations rising and falling, as wars are fought and lost, to revolutions sweeping away the past to begin again. There has also been great architecture and many important innovations, from the first stone tools that enabled people to hunt animals to radio telescopes that can "see" into deep space.

The Great Sphinx
This statue at Giza, in Egypt, has a human head on a lion's body. It is thought to have been made around 4,500 years ago.

c.200,000 years ago
Modern humans
The *Homo sapiens* species (modern humans) evolves in east Africa.

c.2.4 million years ago
Earliest tools
The first stone tools are made by *Homo habilis*, an early human species.

c.100,000 years ago
Jewellery
Early people wear jewellery made from shell beads.

1227
Genghis Khan
At the death of its Mongol leader Genghis Khan, the Mongol Empire stretches across northern Asia.

1095–1272
The Crusades
Christian and Muslim armies fight nine wars to control Jerusalem.

1200
Holy Roman Empire
This "superpower" of the Middle Ages, covers much of central Europe.

900
Khmer dominance, Asia
With their capital at Angkor, the Khmers rule over a large part of Southeast Asia.

1235
Battle of Kirina, Africa
Mandinka forces defeat the Sosso, leading to the birth of the Mali Empire.

1325
Templo Mayor, Mexico
Human sacrifices are mad at this temple in the Aztec capital city of Tenochtitlan

1300
Kanem Empire, Africa
Located north of Lake Chad, Kanem grow powerful and wealthy through its control of trade.

1350
Kingdom of Zimbabwe
The capital of this southern African kingdom is Great Zimbabwe, a stone-walled city.

1949
Chinese Revolution
Led by Mao Zedong, Chinese Communists take power after a long civil war.

1947
Indian independence
After a largely non-violent rebellion, India wins its independence from Britai

1945–54
First Indochina War
Indochina (Vietnam, Cambodia, and Laos) wins independence from France.

1939–45
World War II
Allied forces (Britain, France, USA, USSR, and others) at war with Germany, Japan, and Italy.

1950–53
Korean War
Civil war: China and the USSR help North Korea, the United Nations helps South Korea.

1965
Indo-Pakistani War
Conflict between India and Pakistan over the disputed region of Kashmir.

1955–75
Vietnam War
Communist North Vietnam triumphs over South Vietnam, which is aided by US forces.

1969
Concorde
The world's first supersonic airliner, Concorde, flies for the first time.

2011
World's longest bridge, Chin
Completion of the 164.8-km- (102.4-mile-) long Danyang-Kunshan Grand Bridge.

2011
"Arab Spring"
Revolution and protest sweep through Egypt, Libya, and other Arab countries.

2008
Large Hadron Collider
This huge scientific instrument is designed to detect subatomic particles.

ON 1 JULY 1916, THE FIRST DAY OF THE BATTLE OF THE SOMME

c.90,000 years ago
Burial rites
People begin burying their dead along with meaningful objects such as beads.

c.3200 BCE
Pirámide Mayor, Peru
Built by the Norte Chico civilization at Caral, the most ancient city in the Americas.

1450 BCE
New Kingdom of Egypt
Egypt's empire stretches north to Syria and south to Nubia (modern Sudan).

490 BCE
First Persian Empire
Persia rules territory from the edge of India to Egypt and Greece, linking East with West.

265 BCE
Mauryan Empire, Asia
Under Ashoka, the Mauryan Empire extends over almost all of the Indian subcontinent.

c.40,000 years ago
First music and art
Music is played on simple flutes, and figurines are carved from stone.

c.2589–2500 BCE
Pyramids of Giza, Egypt
Vast tombs are built for the Egyptian pharaohs Khufu, Khafre, and Menkaure.

c.700 BCE
Olmec civilization
Mexico's Olmec culture reaches its peak. It will influence the later Mayan and Aztec cultures.

323 BCE
Macedonian Empire
King Alexander the Great of Macedonia rules lands from Greece to the edge of India.

264–146 BCE
Punic Wars
Three wars erupt between Rome and Carthage, North Africa. Rome emerges victorious.

750
Umayyad Caliphate
The second of four great Islamic dynasties, with its capital in Damascus (Syria).

650
Huari Empire, Peru
The highly organized Huari, in Peru, conquer and control much of the Andean region.

c.300 CE
Mayan culture, Central America
Established by 1000 BCE, Mayan civilization is now at its height. It will last until 1697 CE.

100 CE
Pyramid of the Sun, Mexico
One of two huge stepped pyramids is built in the city of Teotihuacán.

87 BCE
Han Dynasty, China
A time of prosperity in China and an expansion of territories ruled by China.

700
Tihuanaco, Peru/Bolivia
This strong state is centred on a bustling city beside Lake Titicaca in the Andes.

555
Byzantine power
Byzantine rule extends over North Africa and the eastern part of the old Roman Empire.

117 CE
Roman supremacy
Rome now controls much of Europe, north Africa, and the Middle East.

80 CE
Colosseum, Rome
Opening of the stadium in Rome where gladiators fought to the death.

214 BCE
Great Wall of China
Construction begins of this vast defensive wall along China's northern border.

Colosseum, Rome

1453
Fall of Constantinople
The capital of the Byzantine Empire falls to invading Muslim Ottoman forces.

1500
Songhai power, Africa
The Songhai control the Niger Valley, west to Senegal and east to Agades (modern Niger).

1532
Battle of Cajamarca, Peru
Spanish invaders defeat the Inca forces of Atahualpa, leading to 300 years of Spanish rule.

1683
Battle of Vienna
Ottoman expansion finally halts with a defeat by the Holy Roman Empire.

1450
Machu Picchu, Peru
A secret hilltop city of the Incas, who will dominate northern South America.

1500
Ming Dynasty, China
After throwing out the Mongols, China restores its culture and expands its borders.

1519
Aztec rule, Mexico
The Aztecs now rule over 25 million people. In 1521, they are conquered by the Spanish.

1642–51
English Civil War
Parliamentarians defeat Royalists, leading to the execution of King Charles I.

1690
Mughal Empire, India
Under Aurangzeb, the Islamic Mughal Empire of India is at its most powerful.

1922
Height of British Empire
Britain's empire now covers more than 20 per cent of the world's land area.

1914–18
World War I
Britain, France, the USA, and other allies battle Germany, Austria-Hungary, and Turkey.

1880–1902
Boer Wars, Africa
Two wars are fought between Dutch Boer settlers in South Africa and Britain.

1819–30
South American independence
Independence from Spain for Colombia, Peru, Bolivia, Ecuador, and Venezuela.

1789–99
French Revolution
Overthrow of the French monarchy in a bloody revolution. France becomes a republic.

1917
Russian Revolution
Revolt against rule by Tsar Nicholas II; Russia becomes Communist.

1912
Sinking of the *Titanic*
Over 1,500 people die when this luxury liner hits an iceberg and sinks.

1861–65
American Civil War
War between the southern Confederate states and the Union states of the north.

1799–1815
Napoleonic era
France, led by Napoleon Bonaparte, is the dominant military power in Europe.

1775–83
American Revolutionary War
With the help of France and other countries, the USA wins independence from Britain.

1980
Very Large Array
In New Mexico, USA, this giant radio astronomy observatory is completed.

1994
End of Apartheid
South Africa's official segregation policy, Apartheid, ends and equality is reached for black South Africans.

1989–1991
End of Communist bloc
Communist regimes in many countries of eastern Europe are overthrown.

Sydney Opera House
Opened in 1973, this arts venue in Sydney, Australia, was designed by Danish architect Jørn Utzon.

IN WORLD WAR I, THE BRITISH ARMY LOST OVER 57,000 TROOPS.

Australopithecus

Australopithecus hominins evolved about 4.2 million years ago in east Africa. Six species are known. One species, called *A. afarensis*, may be the ancestor of humans. Fossils show that it was up to 1.5 m (5 ft) tall and had a relatively small brain. Crucially, it could walk upright.

Paranthropus

The three *Paranthropus* species had a bony crest on top of the skull to anchor strong chewing muscles. *P. boisei* is nicknamed "nutcracker man" because of its massive jaws and cheek teeth.

Fossil humans

Fossil discoveries have helped scientists to piece together the story of human evolution. Modern humans – *Homo sapiens* – and their ancestors are called hominins. *Sahelanthropus tchadensis*, the first hominin, was an apelike animal that appeared in Africa about 7 million years ago. Later hominin species left Africa and spread out around the world.

Neander Valley, Germany
A partial skeleton of *H. neanderthalensis* found in a cave here in 1856 was the first fossil to be identified as human remains.

Laetoli, Tanzania
Footprints of at least two *Australopithecus afarensis* individuals were discovered here preserved in volcanic ash.

Olduvai Gorge, Tanzania
Stone tools and fossils of *P. boisei* and *H. habilis* were found here.

South Africa
Finds include *Australopithecus*, *Paranthropus*, *H. habilis*, and *H. sapiens* fossils.

Ape-like
Australopithecus –

six species

4 million years ago

Homo – meet the family

We and our extinct relatives belong to the *Homo* genus. A second Latin word, such as *sapiens*, completes each species' name.

Homo habilis
(2.4–1.6 million years ago)
H. habilis ("Handy man") is thought to have been the first hominin species to make stone tools.

Homo georgicus
(1.8 million years ago)
Known only from a single fossil site in Georgia, this may have been the first hominin to leave Africa.

Homo ergaster
(1.9–1.5 million years ago)
As tall as modern humans and with a similar build, it looked very different to its apelike ancestors.

Homo erectus
(1.8 million–30,000 years ago)
Along with *H. ergaster*, *H. erectus* ("Upright man") is known to have used stone handaxes.

Homo antecessor
(1.2 million–500,000 years ago)
Around 780,000 years ago, *H. antecessor* became the first hominin to reach western Europe.

Homo heidelbergensis
(600,000–200,000 years ago)
With a big brain and a muscular body, this species could hunt large animals and make complex tools.

Homo floresiensis
(95,000–17,000 years ago)
Nicknamed "Hobbit", *H. floresiensis* was tiny – just over 1 m (3 ft 3 in) tall. It lived until very recently.

Homo neanderthalensis, or Neanderthals
(350,000–28,000 years ago)
This successful species was skilled at hunting, buried its dead, and knew how to use pigments.

Zhoukoudian Caves, China
Some of the most important fossils of *H. erectus* were found in these limestone caves 50 km (30 miles) from Beijing.

Flores, Indonesia
H. floresiensis remains are known from just one cave on this island.

Java, Indonesia
The earliest known human fossils in East Asia – of *Homo erectus* – come from this island.

Family tree

This chart shows the "family tree" of hominins from *Australopithecus* onwards. Scientists are still working to understand the relationships between different hominin species.

elike *Paranthropus* – three species

Homo (humans) – nine species

Homo habilis ("Handy man") Homo floresiensis

Homo ergaster Homo antecessor

Homo erectus

Homo georgicus Homo heidelbergensis

Neanderthals

Modern people

2   1   0

Prehistoric culture

Earliest music

Music, like art, is far older than writing, since bone flutes and other musical instruments have been made and played for more than 40,000 years.

◇ Early instrument site

Antler flute, Hohle Fels, Germany, 43,000 years ago

First jewellery

People wore jewellery more than 100,000 years ago in sites as distant as Israel and South Africa.

◇ Early jewellery site

Shell beads, Balzi Rossi, Italy

Music, art, religion, and technology all began so long ago, we can't be certain of exactly when. There are clues to early culture, however, such as ritual burial sites, which archaeologists can date.

East Wenatchee, Washington, USA

Horseshoe Canyon paintings, Utah, USA

Clovis, New Mexico, USA

Salado, Texas, USA

Walker, Minnesota, USA

Cactus Hill, Virginia, USA

Wicklow Pipes, Ireland

Shell bead necklace, Cro-Magnon, France

Lascaux Caves, France

Altamira and El Castillo caves, Spain. El Castillo features the oldest known paintings, made 40,000 years ago, possibly by Neanderthals

Lady of Brassempouy carving, France

Ivory horse figurine, Lourdes, France

Shell beads, Grotte des Pidgeons, Morocco

Algerian Sahara

Serra de Capivara paintings, Brazil

Changes in stone tools

2.4 million years ago
The earliest tools, called the Oldowan toolkit, were made by an early human species called "Handy Man", or *Homo habilis*. in Africa. Olduwan-style tools in Europe and Asia are much younger, made by later types of humans, including Neanderthals.

◯ Oldowan site

1.8 million years ago
The Acheulean toolkit of our later ancestors, such as *Homo erectus*, included a new invention – the hand axe, with a finely chiselled edge.

◯ Acheulian site

300,000 years ago
Mousterian tools spanned the Middle Stone Age (ended around 30,000 BCE) and included lots of specialized shapes for different jobs.

◯ Mousterian site

12,000 years ago
The earliest stone tools discovered in America are from the 12,000-year-old "Clovis" people.

◯ Clovis site

Cueva de las Manos paintings, Argentina

Cueva del Milodon, Chile

THE FIRST KNOWN SEWING NEEDLE DATES BACK ABOUT 25,000 YEARS.

Flutes, Hohle Fels Cave,
and Geissenklösterle,
Germany

Bisovava, Russia

"Lion Man" bone
carving, Germany

Sungir Graves, Russia

Carved ivory running lion,
Czech Republic

Tata Plaque (mysterious object
made by a Neanderthal
100,000 years ago), Hungary

Krapina,
Croatia

Balzi Rossi
caves, Italy

Tbilisi, Georgia

Pechka rock shelter, Armenia

Majuangou,
China

Carved
bone disc,
Xiaogushan,
China

Shanidar
Cave, Iraq

Kashafrud,
Iran

Riwat,
Pakistan

Qafzeh,
Israel

Shell beads,
Skhūl, Israel

Bone flutes,
Jiahu, China

Chauvet Cave,
France

Bhimbetka
paintings,
India

Gebelein,
Egypt

Bose, China

Isampur,
India

Gona, Ethiopia
(world's oldest tools)

Island of Socotra,
Yemen

Konso-Gardula,
Ethiopia

Omo,
Ethiopia

Turkana, Kenya

Lokalalei, Kenya

Olduvai Gorge,
Tanzania

Twin Rivers,
Zambia

Inanke Cave,
Zimbabwe

Sterkfontein,
South Africa

"Apollo 11" rock
shelter, Namibia

Swartkrans,
South Africa

Shell beads,
Blombos Cave,
South Africa

Kakadu
National
Park,
Australia

The **oldest known clay pots** were made in **China** about **20,000** years ago

Earliest burials

Our ancestors began burying their dead with meaningful objects, such as beads or other decorations, at least 90,000 ago.

◆ Early burial site

Skull with shells,
25,000 years ago,
Balzi Rossi, Italy

Earliest paintings

Humans have painted and carved rock surfaces since at least 40,000 years ago. Some paintings show people dancing and singing.

◆ Early painting site

Inanke Cave, Zimbabwe,
5,000–10,000 years ago

The first sculpture

The earliest known sculpture consists of figurines carved from stone and bone to look like humans and animals. Some date back up to 40,000 years.

◇ Site of artwork

"Lion Man",
Germany, 32,000
years ago

Ancient empires

In the ancient world, as civilizations grew, some had ambitions to become richer and more powerful by conquering or controlling their neighbours. The most successful conquerors created huge empires.

New Kingdom of Egypt
1550–1069 BCE
The Egyptian New Kingdom grew under Thutmose III, one of the first great generals in history. At its peak, Egypt ruled the southeast Mediterranean.

Stone head of Queen Meritaten of the 18th Dynasty of Egypt

Rise and fall
This map shows the territories of each ancient empire at its peak. Some empires fell as dramatically as they rose, whereas others, such as the Roman Empire, declined gradually over centuries.

BRITAIN
GERMANY
Roman Empire in 117 CE
GAUL
Rome
IBERIA
GREECE
ASIA MINOR
MAURETANIA
MESOPOTAMIA
PERSIA
Babylon
First Persian Empire in 490 BCE
Pasargadae
EGYPT
Thebes

Empires in retreat
The larger an empire grows, the more complex and expensive it becomes to rule. Roman Emperor Trajan seized Mesopotamia in 117 CE, but his successor Hadrian gave it up almost immediately, believing it not worth the expense.

New Kingdom of Egypt in 1450 BCE

Olmec civilization
c.700 BCE

Mayan civilization
c.300 CE

Area of main map

Civilizations of the Americas
The Olmec and Maya cultures, like the empires of Eurasia and Africa, spread, as their communities merged and grew. Trade and cultural exchange, rather than violent conquest, was probably the main way their cultures expanded.

AT ITS HEIGHT, THE HAN EMPIRE OF CHINA RULED OVER 60 MILLION

Olmec civilization
1500–400 BCE
The first major culture in Central America, the Olmecs lived in what is now Mexico. They were expert farmers and traded all over the region. They developed one of the first writing systems in the Americas.

Olmec stone mask

First Persian Empire
550–336 BCE
Cyrus the Great and his army conquered huge swathes of central Asia and grabbed enormous wealth from the kingdoms they conquered. Cyrus's successor, Darius I, built cities, roads, and even a canal from the River Nile to the Red Sea.

Ornate Persian silver bowl

Empire of Alexander the Great
330–323 BCE
Alexander was a general from Macedon, a kingdom north of Greece. At its height, his empire covered most of the world known to Greeks. For centuries after his death, the Greek culture that he introduced continued to dominate the eastern Mediterranean and western Asia.

Coin showing Alexander the Great's head

BACTRIA

Empire of Alexander the Great in 323 BCE

The Silk Road
This trading route from China to Rome was vitally important to both empires. Merchants used it to trade Chinese silk for glass, linen, and gold from the West.

Han Chinese Empire in 87 BCE

Chang'an

CHINA

INDIA

Pataliputra

Mauryan Empire in 265 BCE

Alexander the Great **won** every **battle** he fought

Mauryan Empire
321–185 BCE
Chandragupta Maurya was the first leader to conquer the whole Indian subcontinent. His son Ashoka became a Buddhist and ruled the empire peacefully for 42 years.

Mauryan figure

Han Empire
206–220 CE
The four centuries of Han rule are often called the Golden Age of Ancient China. It was an era of peace and prosperity in which China became a major world power.

Han pot

Roman Empire
27–476 CE
One of history's most influential civilizations, Rome controlled much of Europe, western Asia, and north Africa. Many roads, aqueducts, and canals built by the Romans are still in use today.

Head of Emperor Claudius

Mayan civlization
500–900 CE
One of the most advanced cultures of the ancient world, the Maya developed an accurate yearly calendar based on their sophisticated understanding of astronomy.

Mayan statuette

PEOPLE, OVER ONE-QUARTER OF THE WORLD'S POPULATION AT THE TIME.

Ancient wonders

Ancient Greek travellers and authors such as Herodotus, Antipater, and Philo of Byzantium praised the architectural marvels of the age in their writings. The buildings and statues they described became known as the "Seven Wonders of the World". Today, we recognize many other amazing structures that architects, masons, and sculptors of the past built with relatively simple tools.

Stonehenge
c.2500 BCE, Wiltshire, England

Carnac
c.3200 BCE, Brittany, France. Stone Age monument of more than 3,000 standing stones.

Pont-du-Gard
19 BCE, Nîmes, France

Colosseum
80 CE, Rome, Italy

Bamiyan Buddhas
c.700 CE, Bamiyan, Afghanistan

Great Wall of China
214 BCE

Great Stupa of Sanchi
3rd century BCE, Sanchi, India. Oldest stone structure in India, built by Ashoka the Great to house relics of the Buddha.

Terracotta Army
210 BCE, Xi'an, China

Great Pyramid
300 BCE, Cholula, Mexico

Pyramid of the Sun
100 CE, Teotihuacán, Mexico

Pirámide Mayor, Caral
c.3200 BCE, Supe Valley, Peru. Built by the Norte Chico civilization. Possibly the world's oldest pyramid.

Area of enlarged map

Worldwide wonders

Incredible feats of engineering, building, and sculpture occurred across the globe in ancient times.

THE COLOSSEUM IN ROME COULD HOLD AROUND 50,000 SPECTATORS.

Seven Wonders of the World

Only the pyramids at Giza still stand. Earthquakes destroyed the Hanging Gardens, the Colossus, and the Pharos, flooding and fire ruined the Mausoleum and the Statue of Zeus. The Temple of Artemis was wrecked by the Goths.

Pyramids of Giza
Built as tombs for the pharaohs Khufu, Khafre, and Menkaure.

Hanging Gardens of Babylon
Nebuchadnezzar II built these lush, terraced gardens for his wife, Amytis.

Mausoleum at Halicarnassus
Tomb of Persian governor Mausolos, famed for its size and lavish carvings.

Temple of Artemis
Dedicated to the Greek goddess of hunting, chastity, and childbirth.

Colossus of Rhodes
Vast bronze-and-iron statue, 33 m (110 ft) tall, of the Greek Sun-god Helios.

Pharos of Alexandria
A fire at the top of this huge lighthouse was visible from 50 km (30 miles) away.

Statue of Zeus in Olympia
The sculptor Phidias built this 13 m (430 ft) statue of the king of the gods.

Other ancient wonders

These wonders didn't make the Seven Wonders list, mainly because they were unknown to the Greeks. Some of them were built during later periods.

Colosseum
Stadium where gladiators fought to the death.

Hagia Sofia
Enormous, richly decorated church, later a mosque.

Petra
A city hewn out of rock. Capital of the Nabataeans.

Temples of Abu-Simbel
Two temples built to honour the pharaoh Rameses II.

Pont-du-Gard
Roman aqueduct that carried water to Nîmes.

Acropolis
Greek citadel that includes the Parthenon Temple.

Great Pyramid
World's largest pyramid, now with a church on top.

Pyramid of the Sun
Steep steps up the side led to a temple on the top.

Stonehenge
Prehistoric monument with a circle of enormous stones.

Bamiyan Buddhas
Huge statues chiselled into a cliff; destroyed in 2001.

Great Wall of China
Once ran for 6,259 km (3,889 miles) along China's northern border.

Terracotta Army
8,000 life-size warriors entombed with the first emperor of China.

Hagia Sofia
537 CE, Istanbul, Turkey

Acropolis
5th century BCE, Athens, Greece

Temple of Artemis
c.550 BCE, Ephesus, Turkey

Mausoleum at Halicarnassus
351 BCE, Bodrum, Turkey

Statue of Zeus
456 BCE, Olympus, Greece

Colossus of Rhodes
290 BCE, Rhodes, Greece

Pharos of Alexandria
c.280 BCE, Alexandria, Egypt

Pyramids of Giza
c.2589–2500 BCE, Cairo, Egypt

Petra
4th century BCE, Jordan

Hanging Gardens of Babylon
c.600 BCE, Hillah, central Iraq

Temples of Abu-Simbel
c.1257 BCE, Abu-Simbel, Egypt

The **Great Pyramid**
of Giza weighs
6.5 million tonnes

Famous mummies

Ötzi the Iceman
Around 5,300 years ago, a traveller died when caught in a snowstorm in the Alps. His body became buried in the snow and then froze. In 1991, the corpse was discovered on top of a glacier.

Pharaoh Tutankhamun
The mummy of Tutankhamun was found in a tomb in the Valley of the Kings in 1922. It wore a gold mask and lay inside a nest of three gold cases. The tomb, which had been sealed for 3,200 years, contained statues, furniture, and jewellery.

Tollund Man
Denmark, 400 BCE

Bog bodies

Jeremy Bentham
United Kingdom, 1832

Cladh Hallan skeletons
Scotland, 1600–1120 BCE

Bog bodies

Klement Gottwald
Czech Republic, 1953

Basel Franciscan friars
Switzerland, c. 1550

José dos Santos Ferreira Moura
Portugal, 1887

Guanche mummies
Tenerife, c. 1000–1400

Grottarossa mummy
Italy, 160–180

St Domenico Maggiore mummies
Italy, c. 1490–1570

Uan Muhuggiag
Libya, c. 3500 BCE

Vissarion Korkoliacos
Greece, 1991

Canadian Ice Man
British Columbia, Canada; c. 1450–1700

Aleutian Islands mummies
Alaska, USA, up to about 1800

Anasazi mummies
Arizona, New Mexico, Utah and Colorado, USA; c. 100–1200

Spirit Cave mummy
Nevada, USA; c .7400 BCE

Elmer McCurdy
Oklahoma, USA; 1911

Windover Skeletons
Florida, USA 6000–5000 BCE

Pre-Inca desert mummies
Peru, c.1000

Chiribaya mummies
Peru, c. 1100–1300

Tiwanaku mummies
Chile, 800–1200

Eva Perón
Argentina, 1952

Accidental mummies

Sometimes, bodies are turned into mummies accidentally by naturally dry air and soil, the cold of mountains and polar regions, or the acidic waters of bogs.

1 **The Guanajuato mummies, Mexico**
In 1865–1958, people in Guanajuato unable to pay a grave tax had to dig up long-dead relatives. Some had been mummified by the dry climate.

2 **European bog bodies**
Mummies have been found in the peat bogs of northern Europe, with the oldest dating from around 10,000 years ago.

3 **Lindow Man**
In 1984, a man's body was found in a bog at Lindow Moss, Cheshire, England. He was killed between 2 BCE and 119 CE, perhaps as a religious sacrifice.

4 **Franklin's lost expedition**
Sir John Franklin's 1845 expedition to the Arctic went missing. In 1984, three of his crew were found mummified on Beechey Island, Canada.

5 **The Greenland mummies**
Eight mummified Inuit people who died in around 1475 were found on a cliff at Nuuk, Greenland, in 1972. Their bodies had freeze-dried.

Intentional mummies

Many cultures have preserved the bodies of their dead. Usually, they remove the internal organs and drain the body fluids before embalming the body.

1 **Valley of the Kings**
In the 1890s, 56 mummies – including pharaohs – were found in Egypt's Valley of the Kings. Egyptian priests had hidden the mummies from tomb-raiders.

2 **Philippine fire mumm**
Between 1200 and 1500 the Ibaloi people of the Philippines mummified their leaders by drying them over a fire then put them in caves.

WHEN EGYPTIAN EMBALMERS PREPARED A PHARAOH'S BODY FOR

Juanita the Ice Maiden
In 1995, an Inca girl aged 12–14 was found on Mount Ampato, Peru. The discoverers named her Juanita, or the "Ice Maiden". She was sacrificed to the gods about 500 years ago. The cold had preserved her skin, organs, blood, and stomach contents.

MUMMY DISCOVERIES WORLDWIDE
Some mummies are discovered singly, often in remote locations such as in peat bogs or on high mountains. Other finds involve larger numbers of mummies – for example, in communal graves, tombs, caves, or catacombs.

Accidental mummies

Intentional mummies

0–19 20–39 40–59 60–79 80–99 100–119 120–139 140+

Number of mummies

James Hepburn, 4th Earl of Bothwell
Denmark, 1578

Charles Eugène de Croÿ
Estonia, 1702

Vladimir Lenin
Russia, 1921

Georgi Dimitrov
Bulgaria, 1949

öbnitz Girl
...and,
...0 BCE

Valley of the Golden Mummies Egypt, c. 30 CE

Maronite mummies
Lebanon, 1283

Chehrabad Salt Mine mummies Iran, 4th century BCE–4th century CE

Iufaa and family
Egypt, c.500 BCE

Saqqara mummies
Egypt, 640 BCE

Persian Princess
Pakistan, 1996

Nubian mummies
Sudan, 250–1400

Tarim mummies
China, 200–300 BCE

Siberian Ice Maiden
Russia, c. 400 BCE

Pazyryk ice mummies
Mongolia, c. 200–500 BCE

Mao Zedong
China, 1976

Xin Zhui
China, c. 150 BCE

Ho Chi Minh
Vietnam, 1969

Mummy monk "Luang Phor Daeng"
Thailand, c. 1985

Vu Khac Minh and Vu Khac Truong
Vietnam, c. 1600–1700

Chiang Kai-shek and Chiang Ching-kuo
Taiwan, 1975 and 1998

Buddhist self-mummified nun and monks
Taiwan, 1959–2000

Fujiwara clan mummies
Japan, 1128–1189

Kim Il-Sung and Kim Jong-il
North Korea, 1994 and 2011

Korean mummies
South Korea, c. 1350–1500

Lost mummies of New Guinea
Papua New Guinea, up to 1950s

Mummies

Mummies – the preserved bodies of the dead – have been found the world over. Many were made deliberately, while others formed naturally. More recently, some countries have mummified their leaders.

The Palermo **catacombs** contain at least **8,000** mummies

3 Mummies of Palermo
In 1599, Christian monks in Palermo, Sicily, began to mummify their dead and stored them in catacombs. Later, rich people paid the monks to mummify their bodies.

4 Self-mummified monks
From 1680–1830, some Buddhist monks in Japan mummified themselves. They starved, drank special tea to make their body toxic to maggots, and then were sealed alive in a stone tomb.

5 Chinchorro mummies
The Chinchorro, who lived in what is now Chile and Peru, were the first people known to make mummies. Their oldest mummies date from as early as 5000 BCE.

MUMMIFICATION, THEY PULLED THE BRAIN OUT THROUGH THE NOSE.

The Maya and Aztecs built spectacular pyramid-temples. Human sacrifice took place on the Templo Mayor in the Aztec capital Tenochtitlán (now Mexico City).

Templo Mayor, Mexico

Notre Dame de Paris
Paris, France, 1163–1345

Angel Mounds
Evansville, Indiana, USA, 1000 CE

St Paul's Cathedral (first building)
London, England, 604 CE

Parkin Indian Mound
Parkin, Arkansas, USA, 1350

Cahokia Mounds and Monks Mound
Collinsville, Illinois, USA, 600 CE

Cluny Abbey
Burgundy, France, 940 CE

Taos Pueblo
New Mexico, USA, between 1000 and 1450

Kincaid Mounds
Brookport, Illinois, USA, 1050 CE

Great Houses of the Chacoan people,
Chaco Canyon, New Mexico, USA, 900 CE

Moundville settlement
Alabama, USA, 1000 CE

Alhambra
Granada, Spain, 1350s

Templo Mayor
Mexico City, Mexico, first built 1325, rebuilt six times

Ocmulgee Great Temple Mound
Macon, Georgia, USA, 950 CE

Benin Bronzes
Kingdom of Benin (in modern Nigeria), 13th–16th century

Timbuktu
Mali, 12th century

El Castillo
Chichen Itza, Mexico, 9th–12th century

Calixtlahuaca
Toluca, Mexico, 1476

Temple of the Inscriptions
Chiapas, Mexico, 683 CE

Cusco and the Koricancha
Vilcabamba, Cusco, Peru, 1430

Benin Bronzes

Royal Palaces of Abomey
Dahomey (modern Benin), 1695

Medieval wonders

Machu Picchu
Vilcabamba, Cuzco, Peru, 1450

Isla del Sol
Lake Titicaca, Bolivia, 15th century

El Fuerte de Samaipata
Bolivia, 14th century

"Medieval" means the Middle Ages, which lasted from the 5th century to the end of the 15th century. The period ended when the world became connected by explorers such as Columbus, heralding the start of modern times. Medieval times saw amazing architectural feats worldwide.

Moai figures
Easter Island, Chile, 300–1200

Sacsayhuamán
Cuzco, Peru, mid-15th century

Ollantaytambo
Cuzco, Peru, mid-15th century

By the late 1400s, the Incas had a vast empire in western South America. The city of Machu Picchu occupied a remote hilltop at the edge of the empire.

Machu Picchu

Leaning Tower of Pisa
Italy, 1173–1300

St Basil'sCathedral
Moscow, Russia,
1555–61

Moscow Kremlin
Moscow, Russia,1450

**Papal Basilica of
St Peter**
Vatican City, Rome,
Italy, 1506–1626

**The Great
Mosque of
Djenné**
Djenné, Mali,
1200–1330

EUROPE

St Peter's Basilica, built at the start of the Renaissance, is one of the world's largest and most ornate churches. Its enormous dome is 137 m (448 ft) high.

Papal Basilica of St Peter, Italy

KEY
Locations and dates of medieval wonders.

Pictured wonders

● **Other wonders**

Imam Reza Shrine
Mashhad, Iran,
818 CE

**Ani,
Armenian City**
Kars Province,
Turkey, 5th century CE

Taj Mahal
Agra, India,
1642–53

**Great Wall of China
(Ming Dynasty)**
14th century

**Kiyomizu
Temple**
Kyoto, Japan,
798 CE

Grand Canal
China,
5th to 13th
centuries

**Porcelain
Tower of Nanjing**
River Yangtze,
Nanking, China,
early 15th century,
reconstructed 2010

**Prophet's Mosque
(Al-Masjid al-Nabawi)**
Medina, Saudi Arabia, 622 CE

**The Grand Mosque
(Al-Masjid al-Haram)**
Mecca, Saudi Arabia,
7th century CE

**Konark Sun
Temple**
India, 13th century

Angkor Wat
Angkor, Cambodia
1113–50

The Leaning Tower of Pisa tilts by **3.97** degrees

ASIA

The vast Buddhist temple at Borobudur, Java, has six stepped rectangular storeys, three circular terraces and is decorated with 2,672 carved panels and 504 statues.

Borobudur

**Sigiriya
palace**
Sri Lanka,
5th century CE

**Rock hewn churches
at Lalibela**
Ethiopia,
13th century

**City of Great
Zimbabwe**
Near Masvingo,
Zimbabwe,
11th century

Borobudur
Central Java,
Indonesia,
9th century CE

AFRICA

At Lalibela, 11 churches – complete with windows, doors, and roofs – were hewn (cut) into rocky hills. Each is cut from a single block of stone and linked by trenches.

Rock-hewn church at Lalibela

IS BUILT ON A PLAFTORM TO PREVENT DAMAGE FROM RIVER FLOODS.

Medieval empires

Ottoman battle helmet

At times between 500 and 1500 CE, one power or another controlled vast parts of Europe and Asia and spread Islam and Christianity across the world as they knew it. Little known to them, African rulers connected large regions for the first time, while empires in the Americas grew in isolation from the rest of the world.

Holy Roman Empire in 1200 CE

Frankfurt

Byzantine Empire in 555 CE

Ottoman Empire in 1683 CE

Constantinople

Istanbul

Damascus

Umayyad Caliphate in 750 CE

Songhai Empire in 1500 CE

Mali Empire in 1350 CE

Gao

Ka-ba (Kangaba)

Njimi

Asante Empire in 1750 CE

Kanem Empire in 1300 CE

Mali Empire
c. 1230–1600
A west African empire that became wealthy through trading gold and developing agriculture along the banks of the Niger.

Kumasi

Asante Empire
1670–1902
A sophisticated and disciplined society. Clever strategies and adoption of western firearms helped bring about military expansion.

Asante trophy head

São Salvador (M'banza-Kongo)

Kingdom of Kongo in 1625 CE

Kingdom of Kongo
1390–1914
Ruled by a "manikongo" (king) and divided into six regions. The Atlantic slave trade weakened the empire, and eventually the Portuguese took control.

Kingdom of Zimbabwe 1350 CE

Great Zimbabwe

Kingdom of Zimbabwe
1220–1450
Famous for its capital, Great Zimbabwe, where the elite lived in a stone enclosure. The rulers controlled gold mines and ivory and traded with the Middle East and China.

The Americas

Aztec Empire in 1519 CE

Huari Empire in 650 CE

Chimu Empire in 1470 CE

Inca Empire in 1525 CE

Tihuanaco Empire in 700 CE

Eurasia and Africa

THE AZTECS SACRIFICED TENS OF THOUSANDS OF THEIR OWN

At its **peak**, the **Mongol Empire** ruled over **100 million** people

Mongol Empire in 1227 CE

Mongol Empire
1206–1368
Founded by Genghis Khan in 1206. Numerous violent conquests led to the largest continuous land empire in history.

Karakorum

Mongol horde helmet

Ming China in 1500 CE

Beijing

Ming China
1368–1644
Founded by Zhu Yuanzhang, the leader of an uprising that overthrew the Mongols. A socially stable era during which the Grand Canal and the Great Wall were rebuilt.

Mughal Empire in 1690 CE

Shahjahanabad (Old Delhi)

Mughal sword

Angkor

Khmer Empire in 900 CE

□ **Holy Roman Empire**
962–1806
One of the longest-lasting empires in history, this was a Christian state with no capital. In 1356 Frankfurt became the home of imperial elections.

□ **Byzantine Empire**
518–1453
Evolved from the Eastern Roman Empire. A Christian, Greek-speaking empire that preserved both Roman and Greek cultures.

Byzantine necklace pendant

□ **Mughal Empire**
1526–1857
The Mughals brought centralized government, education, and religious tolerance to south Asia.

□ **Khmer Empire**
802–1400s
A Hindu and Buddhist empire influenced by Indian culture. Architecture of the empire reached its height with the construction of the temple at the capital, Angkor.

□ **Aztec Empire**
1430–1521
From their capital built on artificial islands on a lake, the Aztecs, who called themselves Mexica, conquered most of modern-day Mexico.

Statue of Aztec god of death

□ **Inca Empire**
1438–1533
The largest empire of pre-Spanish Americas. Incas worshipped Inti, the Sun-god, and were skilled at building cities high up in the Andes mountains.

□ **Songhai Empire**
1340–1591
Rose up in the wake of the declining Mali Empire. The city of Timbuktu became a centre of Islamic learning.

Songhai coin

□ **Chimu Empire**
c.1200–1470
Skilled in pottery, textiles and metalwork. Territory covered coastal regions by the Andes mountains. Conquered by the rival Inca Empire in 1470.

□ **Umayyad Caliphate**
661–750
The second of four great Muslim dynasties of the Arab caliphate, meaning "kingdom".

□ **Kanem Empire**
700–1387
One of the most powerful African empires. The main religion became Islam during the second dynasty under the rule of the Sayfawa.

□ **Huari Empire**
500–1100
The first of the New World powers to use large cities to run the empire and to live in, rather than just for religious ceremonies.

Huari wooden figure

□ **Tihuanaco Empire**
550–950
Began as a small town on the shores of Lake Titicaca on the border of Peru and Bolivia before rapidly expanding to the surrounding areas.

□ **Ottoman Empire**
1299–1922
Sometimes called the "Turkish Empire", a long-lasting Islamic state with the wealthy city of Constantinople (modern-day Istanbul) as its capital.

PEOPLE AND ENEMY PRISONERS EACH YEAR TO APPEASE THE GODS.

Castles

From castles and forts to walled cities, rulers and nations throughout history have tried to build impregnable structures to keep their enemies at bay and strengthen their grip on power.

KEY
Flags pinpoint some of the world's most impressive fortifications.

Selected castles, forts, citadels, and fortified cities

Fort Columbia, Washington, USA

Fort Union, New Mexico, USA

Castle of Santa Maria da Feira, Portugal

Castle of São Jorge, Portugal

Ribat of Monastir, Tunisia

Loropéni, Burkina Faso

Cape Coast Castle, Ghana

Elmina Castle, Ghana

Castillo San Felipe de Barajas, Colombia

Chan Chan ancient walled citadels, Peru

Fortifications of Valdivia, Chile

European castles

Most were fortified residences of nobles or monarchs; others were purely defensive.

Burghausen, Germany
Europe's longest castle complex, consisting of a main castle and inner courtyard protected by five outer courtyards.

Krak des Chevaliers, Syria This 12th-century crusader castle has an outer wall with 13 towers separated from the inner wall and keep by a moat.

Forts after the age of castles

Forts became vital military centres. Their low, thick, angled walls were able to deflect cannonballs.

THE OTTOMAN TURKS BESIEGED THE FORTIFIED TOWN OF CANDIA,

Asian castles

Castles in Asia reflect local building styles and look different to those in Europe, but they served the same purpose.

Himeji, Japan Originally dating from 1333, Himeji was rebuilt in the 17th century. With a network of 83 buildings protected by 26-m- (85-ft-) high walls and 3 moats, Himeji is Japan's largest castle.

Mehrangarh Fort, India This fort, 122 m (400 ft) above the city of Jodhpur, hides several palaces within its walls. Built by the ruler Rao Jodha in 1459, it is entered through a series of seven gates.

Fortified cities

Cities surrounded by defensive walls, often incorporating a castle or royal residence.

Forbidden City, China The former imperial palace in Beijing has 980 buildings ringed by a wall and a 52-m- (171-ft-) wide moat.

Great Zimbabwe Once the capital of the Kingdom of Zimbabwe, the stone walls of this royal city were built without using mortar.

Moscow Kremlin, Russia

Kirkuk citadel, Iraq

Uqair, Saudi Arabia

Bam citadel, Iran

Rohtas Fort, Pakistan

Gyantse fortress, Tibet, China

Wan Ping fortress

Tuon Cheng fortress, China

Fort Glanville

Fort Queenscliff

Fort Denison

Windsor Castle,
England, has been a royal residence for **900** years

Fort Independence, USA This star-shaped fort, completed in 1851, defended the harbour of Boston. Guns were mounted on its five pointed bastions.

Castle of Good Hope, South Africa A star fort built by the Dutch East India Company in 1666–79 to protect Dutch settlers on the Cape of Good Hope.

PERIOD OF BATTLE

WWI and beyond
1914–

Modern revolutionary
1780–1914

Early modern
1500–1780

Medieval
500–1500

Ancient
Before 500 CE

Yorktown, 1781
French–American victory over the British led to independence for the USA.

Waterloo, 1815
Napoleon defeated by a coalition of European nations, marking an end to his domination of Europe.

Vienna, 1683
Holy Roman Empire's defeat of the Ottoman Empire halted the spread of Islam in Europe.

Antietam, 1862
Bloodiest single-day battle in American history, with 23,000 casualties.

Spanish Armada, 1588
English defeat of a vast Spanish fleet, causing the loss of 63 ships.

The Little Bighorn, 1876
Victory for the Lakota, Northern Cheyenne, and Arapaho peoples over the US Army led by General Custer.

Battle of France, 1940
German invasion and occupation of France during World War II.

Algiers, 1957
Campaign of guerrilla warfare against French–Algerian authorities.

The Alamo, 1836
Texan revolutionaries inflicted heavy losses on Mexican forces storming the Alamo Fort. Mexico won, but Texas gained independence the next year.

Alcazar Quivir, 1578
Morocco and Ottoman Empire defeated the Portuguese Empire. Almost all Portuguese killed or imprisoned.

Gettysburg, 1863
Turning point of the US Civil War. Paved the way for a Union victory over the Confederate states.

Military milestones

Changes in weapon technology have affected how battles are fought. As weapons get deadlier, the two sides in a battle grow farther and farther apart, until today, they sometimes don't meet or glimpse each other at all.

Bay of Pigs, 1961
CIA-trained force of Cuban exiles tried to invade Cuba and overthrow Communist leader Fidel Castro.

Carabobo, 1821
Victory for Simón Bolívar's Patriots over the Royalists, who supported Spanish rule. Led to Venezuela's independence.

Kirina, 1235
Mandinka forces beat the Sosso king and created the Mali Empire over west Africa.

1. **Battle of Crécy, 1346**
A key battle in the Hundred Years' War between England and France. New long-range bows made close hand-to-hand combat, and the chivalry that went with it, a thing of the past.

Cajamarca, 1532
Defeat of the Inca Empire by Spanish conquistadors led to Spanish rule for the next three centuries.

2. **The Somme, 1916**
The British and French attacked the German Army during World War I in what was the world's first major tank battle. It was also one of the bloodiest military operations ever.

Riachuelo, Paraguay River, 1865
A naval battle far upriver. Defeat for Paraguay by Brazil (allied with Argentina and Uruguay) during the ruinous Paraguayan War (1864–70).

3. **Battle of Britain, 1940**
Between Britain and Germany during World War II, this was the first major campaign fought entirely in the air.

4. **Battle of the Coral Sea, 1942**
For the first time, ships in this sea battle never once sighted or directly fired on one another.

The **Ottoman Turks** took Constantinople in 1453 using **cannon** for the **first time** in a major battle

AFTER THE BLOODY BATTLE OF KALINGA, INDIAN EMPEROR ASHOKA

Sieges

Not strictly a battle, a siege is a military blockade of a city or fortress. The aim is to conquer the city by waiting for those inside to surrender. Sometimes, the side laying siege attacks to speed things up.

① Siege of Carthage 149–146 BCE
One of the longest sieges in history. The Romans surrounded Carthage (in modern Tunisia) and waited 3 years for its surrender, then enslaved the Carthaginian population.

② Capture of Jerusalem, 1099
During the Crusader wars between Christians and Muslims, the Muslim defenders of Jerusalem lost control when the Christians built two enormous siege engines (towers on wheels) and scaled the walls.

Austerlitz, 1805
With smaller forces, the French Empire crushed Russia and Austria. One of Napoleon's greatest victories.

Actium, 31 BCE
Rome declared war on Antony and Cleopatra of Egypt. The Roman victory led to the beginning of the Roman Empire.

Thermopylae, 480 BCE
Vastly outnumbered Greek forces held the Persian Emperor Xerxes at bay for a vital 3 days.

Badger Mouth, 1211
Mongol ruler Genghis Khan's victory over the Jin Dynasty of China. One of history's bloodiest battles.

Huai-Hai, 1948
Final major fight in Chinese Civil War that led to the Communist takeover of China

Stalingrad, 1942–43
Long siege of this Soviet city caused immense suffering on both sides and led eventually to crippling defeat for Nazi Germany.

Fall of Constantinople, 1453
After a 4-month siege, Byzantine Empire fell to the invading Ottoman Empire.

Battle of Phillora, 1965
One of the largest tank battles of the Indo-Pakistani War. Decisive victory for Indian Army.

Battle of Inchon, 1950
A clear victory for the United Nations against North Korean forces in the Korean War.

Iwo Jima, 1945
The USA captured this island as a way of possibly invading Japan. Over 21,000 Japanese died.

Wuhan, 1938
Soviet and revolutionary Chinese forces totalling 1,100,000 troops and 200 aircraft failed to stop Japan capturing the city.

Omdurman, 1898
Small British and Egyptian forces massacred a huge, but ill-equipped, Sudanese Army.

El Alamein, 1942
Major tank battle of World War II. British-led victory over Axis Powers (Italy and Germany).

Dien Bien Phu, 1954
Viet Minh communist revolutionaries besieged and defeated the French to end the First Indochina War. The next year began another 20 years of fighting in Vietnam.

Kalinga, 262–261 BCE
The Mauryan Empire under Ashoka the Great fought the republic of Kalinga. At least 100,000 Kalingans were killed.

Isandlwana, 1879
Crushing victory for the Zulu nation over the British, despite relying mainly on spears and cowhide shields.

Surabaya, 1945
Heaviest battle of the Indonesian Revolution against the British and Dutch. Celebrated as Heroes' Day in Indonesia.

Coral Sea, 1942
World War II naval battle between Japan and the USA and Australia. The battle was the first time aircraft carriers engaged each other.

Battlegrounds

At one time, armies met in formation on a single field of battle and fought for one to several days. By the 20th century, long-range weapons had changed warfare. Battlefields in places became theatres of war the size of countries.

IS SAID TO HAVE REJECTED WARFARE AND TURNED TO BUDDHISM.

The last empires

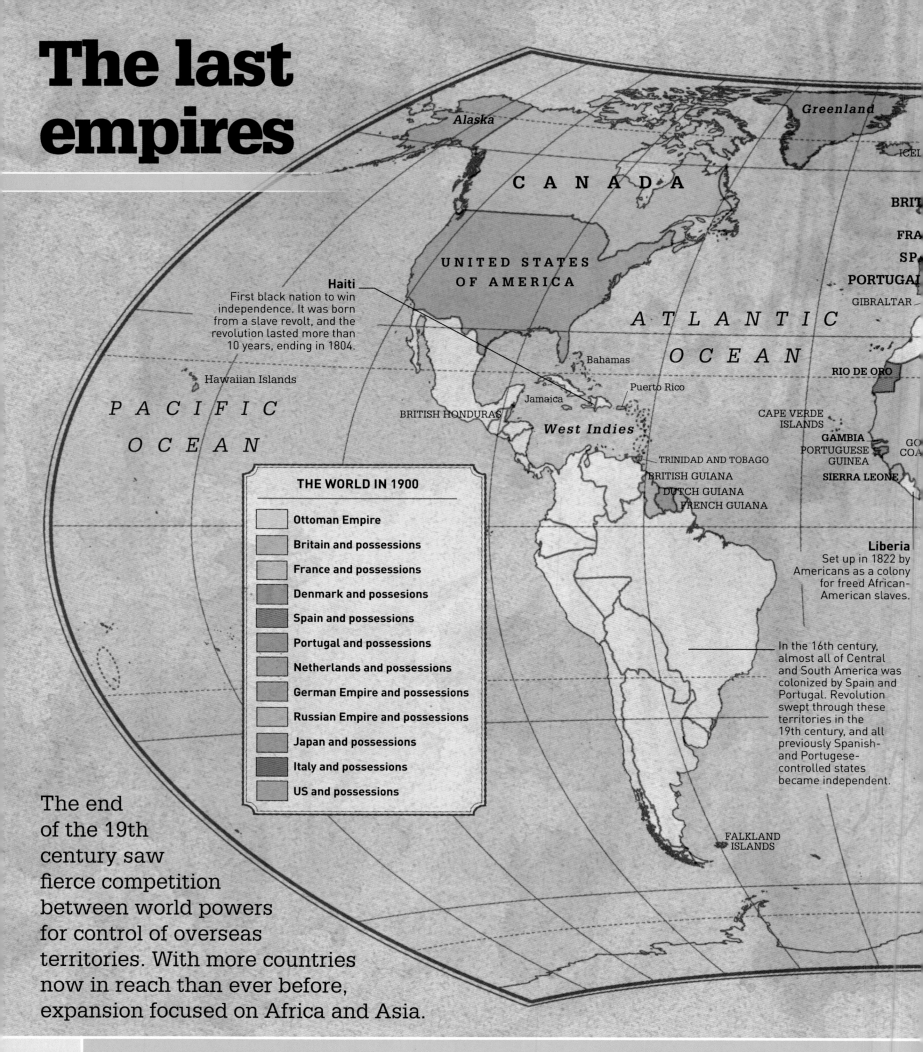

THE WORLD IN 1900

- Ottoman Empire
- Britain and possessions
- France and possessions
- Denmark and possesions
- Spain and possessions
- Portugal and possessions
- Netherlands and possessions
- German Empire and possessions
- Russian Empire and possessions
- Japan and possessions
- Italy and possessions
- US and possessions

Greenland

ICEL

CANADA

BRIT

FRA

SP

PORTUGAL

GIBRALTAR

UNITED STATES
OF AMERICA

Alaska

Haiti
First black nation to win
independence. It was born
from a slave revolt, and the
revolution lasted more than
10 years, ending in 1804.

ATLANTIC

OCEAN

RIO DE ORO

Hawaiian Islands

Bahamas

Puerto Rico

Jamaica

BRITISH HONDURAS

CAPE VERDE
ISLANDS

GAMBIA

PORTUGUESE
GUINEA

GO
COA

PACIFIC

OCEAN

West Indies

TRINIDAD AND TOBAGO

BRITISH GUIANA

DUTCH GUIANA

FRENCH GUIANA

SIERRA LEONE

Liberia
Set up in 1822 by
Americans as a colony
for freed African-
American slaves.

In the 16th century,
almost all of Central
and South America was
colonized by Spain and
Portugal. Revolution
swept through these
territories in the
19th century, and all
previously Spanish-
and Portugese-
controlled states
became independent.

FALKLAND
ISLANDS

The end
of the 19th
century saw
fierce competition
between world powers
for control of overseas
territories. With more countries
now in reach than ever before,
expansion focused on Africa and Asia.

In 1900, Europeans controlled 90 per cent of Africa

RUSSIAN EMPIRE

DENMARK

NETH.

GERMAN EMPIRE

BELGIUM

AUSTRO-HUNGARIAN EMPIRE

ITALY

TUNIS

ALGERIA

OTTOMAN EMPIRE

CYPRUS

EGYPT

AFGHANISTAN

PERSIA

KUWAIT

BAHRAIN

TRUCIAL OMAN

OMAN

QING EMPIRE

JAPAN

INDIA

FRENCH WEST AFRICA

NIGERIA

TOGO

KAMERUN

RIO MUNI

FRENCH CONGO

CONGO FREE STATE

ANGOLA

NORTHEASTERN RHODESIA

BAROTSELAND-NORTHWESTERN RHODESIA

GERMAN SOUTHWEST AFRICA

BECHUANA-LAND

ANGLO-EGYPTIAN SUDAN

ERITREA

FRENCH SOMALILAND

BRITISH SOMALILAND

ITALIAN SOMALILAND

BRITISH EAST AFRICA

GERMAN EAST AFRICA

BRITISH CENTRAL AFRICA

SOUTHERN RHODESIA

MADAGASCAR

PORTUGUESE EAST AFRICA

Ethiopia
The only African nation never to have been colonized.

CEYLON

FRENCH INDOCHINA

PHILIPPINE ISLANDS

MALAYA

BRITISH NORTH BORNEO

BRUNEI

SARAWAK

DUTCH EAST INDIES

PORTUGUESE TIMOR

KAISER WILHELM'S LAND

BISMARCK ARCHIPELAGO

PAPUA

PACIFIC OCEAN

INDIAN OCEAN

AUSTRALIAN COLONIES

CAPE COLONY

NEW ZEALAND

Scramble for Africa

The Atlantic slave trade, in which Africans were forcibly sold to people in the Americas, ended in the 1800s. European powers went into Africa to wipe out the trade, but at the same time, took control. Europeans raced each other to claim territory.

- **1871:** Germany and Italy are both unified. No more territory available for expansion of empires in Europe.
- **1884–85:** Berlin Conference, where European powers decide rules on carving up Africa.
- **1900:** Only Liberia and Ethiopia remain non-European. Britain rules 30 percent of Africa's population.

The Great Game

In the 1830s, Britain feared Russia was planning on invading British-ruled India through controlling India's neighbour, Afghanistan. The "Great Game" was the rivalry for power in Asia between the British and Russian empires.

- **1839–42:** First Anglo-Afghan War. Terrible defeat at Kabul for the British.
- **1878–80:** Second Anglo-Afghan War. Russia is defeated and Britain withdraws but takes control of Afghanistan's foreign affairs.
- **1907:** Russia and Britain sign a peace treaty in the face of the German threat of expansion in the Middle East.

At least **1 million** people died in the **1910 Mexican Revolution**

Norway
1905 (from Sweden)

Iceland
1944 (from Denmark)

England
1642–51

Ireland
1922 (from Britain)

Belgium
1830–31
(from Netherlands)

France
1789–99

Spain
1936–39

Portugal
1974

Tunisia
2011

Algeria
1954–62
(from France)

Thirteen colonies of North America
1776 (from Britain)

Cuba
1953–59

Mexico
1910–20

Haiti
1791–1804 (from France)

Nicaragua
1979–90

Venezuela
1823 (from Spain)
1830 (from Gran Colombia)

Panama
1903 (from Colombia)

Colombia
1819 (from Spain)

Equador
1822 (from Spain) and
1830 (from Gran Colombia)

Peru
1824 (from Spain)

Bolivia
1825 (from Spain)

Ghana
1957 (from Britain)

Angola
1961–75
(from Portugal)

Namibia
1968–88
(from South Africa)

Famous revolutionaries

Revolutionary leaders are driven by passionate ideals. They inspire people to rise up against governments. Such people are key in organizing effective group action against the authorities.

1. **Che Guevara, 1928–67**
   Argentinian-born idealist – helped Fidel Castro overthrow Cuban dictator Fulgencio Batista. Now a global symbol of rebellion.

2. **Kwame Nkrumah, 1909–72**
   Oversaw Ghana's independence from Britain. Ghana was the first in a wave of sub-Saharan African nations to break free of colonial rule.

3. **Simón Bolivar, 1783–1830**
   Venezuelan politician and general who led Venezuela, Colombia, Ecuador, Peru, and Bolivia to independence. One of South America's most influential leaders.

4. **Vladimir Lenin, 1870–1924**
   After being exiled to Siberia, Lenin returned to Russia to support and then lead the 1917 revolution.

5. **Mao Zedong, 1893–1976**
   Founder of the People's Republic of China. Ruthless in bringing about modernization with the "Great Leap Forward" and enforced Communism with the "Cultural Revolution".

6. **Mahatma Gandhi, 1869–1948**
   Devoted his life to bringing peace to India. Has inspired nonviolence and civil rights movements worldwide.

Revolutions and uprisings

Powerful nations that overpower other countries are often met with resistance from the people they conquer. In some cases, this can lead to revolutions. Sometimes a country's own government becomes so unpopular that a revolution occurs.

Internal uprising
Countries that have had internal revolutions

Uprising against an outside power
Countries achieving independence from a foreign ruling power through revolution

Countries not involved in revolutions on these pages

THE AMERICAN REVOLUTION OF 1776 GAVE HOPE TO POVERTY-

Revolutions

People all over the world have risen up against oppressive rulers. Revolutions can be sudden or lengthy, bloody or peaceful, but have one thing in common: they are all an attempt to change the way a country is ruled.

Lithuania
1989 (from USSR)

Finland
1917 (from Russia)

Estonia
1989 (from USSR)

Latvia
1989 (from USSR)

Belarus
1989 (from USSR)

Ukraine
1989 (from USSR)

Moldova
1989 (from USSR)

Turkmenistan
1989 (from USSR)

Uzbekistan
1989 (from USSR)

Russia
1917
4

Georgia
1989 (from USSR)

Kazakhstan
1989 (from USSR)

Armenia
1989 (from USSR)

Kyrgyzstan
1989 (from USSR)

Korea
1945
(from Japan)

Greece
1821–32
(from Ottoman Empire)

Iran
1979

Tajikistan
1989 (from USSR)

5

China
1949

Vietnam
1975 (Socialist Republic of Vietnam created after war between North and South Vietnam)

Libya
2011

Egypt
2011

Azerbaijan
1989 (from USSR)

Burma
1962

Philippines
1896–98 (from Spain)

Eritrea
1961–91
(from Ethiopia)

Yemen
2011

India
1947 (from Britain)
6

Laos
1975
(from USSR)

Cambodia
1979 (Khmer Rouge)

Somalia
1986–92

Singapore
1965 (from Malaysia)

Papua New Guinea
1975 (from Australia)

Kenya (Mau Mau)
1952–60 (from Britain)

Rwanda
1961
(from Belgium)

Indonesia
1945–49
(from the Netherlands)

East Timor
1975 (from Portugal) and 2002 (from Indonesia)

Madagascar
1960 (from France)

South Africa
1994

Collapse of Communism

The USSR was a Communist state that incorporated Russia and 14 other Soviet republics (shown in red on the map). The USSR also had great influence over several other European states that collectively were known as the "Communist bloc" (in yellow on the map). In 1989, revolution spread through all these states, and in 1991 the USSR was dissolved.

▼ **Fall of communism**
Indicates countries in which Communism collapsed in 1989–91

Arab Spring

The "Arab Spring" revolutions and protests swept through the Arab world in 2011. As the map shows, in some countries rulers were forced out, while in others there were failed uprisings. In many cases, the demonstrations and protests were violent. The Arab Spring was the first uprising where protestors used social media – online applications such as Facebook and Twitter – to coordinate their actions.

〰 **Arab Spring**
Indicates countries involved in the Arab Spring

STRICKEN EUROPE AND INSPIRED THE 1789-99 FRENCH REVOLUTION.

KEY

Major shipwrecks with known coordinates

Scapa Flow (1919)
After World War I, the German navy sank 52 of its own ships here, rather than surrender them to Britain.

SS *Islander* (1901)
Its cargo of gold, which some estimate is worth up to £500 million today, has never been found.

SS *Sultana* (1865)
This river steamer exploded in the Mississippi River with the loss of around 1,700 lives.

Medusa (1816)
When the *Medus...* sank, 147 crewm... built a life raft, b... only 15 survived... be rescued.

HMS *Agamemnon* (1809)
A former command of Admiral Nelson, she struck an uncharted group of rocks in a bay off Uruguay.

Shipwrecks

The beds and shores of the world's seas, lakes, and rivers are littered with shipwrecks. Some are famous either for the huge loss of life they caused or the enormous value of their cargo.

Natural shipwrecks

Sailors battle constantly against the phenomenal forces of nature, and one of the most common causes of shipwrecks is bad weather. Storms and hurricanes batter ships and blow them off course, and fog, rain, or snow reduce visibility. Ice is another big risk. An iceberg can inflict fatal damage to a ship if it collides with one; also ice that builds up on the body of a ship can cause it to become unstable Fnd capsize.

ONE OF THE WORLD'S LARGEST WRECKS IS THE AMOCO CADIZ, WHICH

Notorious wrecks

1 RMS _Titanic_
On 14 April, 1912, this ship struck an iceberg and sank two hours and forty minutes later.
Death toll: 1,517

2 USS _Arizona_
Sunk in the opening minutes of the Japanese attack on the US Navy at Pearl Harbor in 1942.
Death toll: 1,177

3 RMS _Lusitania_
British liner sunk by a World War I German submarine in 1915.
Death toll: 1,200

4 _Bismarck_
German battleship, lost after a hard battle with HMS _Hood_ in May 1941.
Death toll: 2,085

5 _Nuestra Señora de Atocha_
Spanish galleon, laden with treasure, caught in a hurricane in 1622.
Death toll: 260

6 _Wilhelm Gustloff_
German passenger ship torpedoed by a Russian submarine in 1945.
Death toll: approx. 9,100

7 HMS _Sussex_
Royal Navy ship lost in a storm off Gibraltar in 1694, carrying over 10 tonnes of gold coins.
Death toll: 500

8 MV _Doña Paz_
Passenger ferry that collided with an oil tanker off the Philippines in 1987.
Death toll: 4,375

9 HMS _Birkenhead_
British ship that sank after striking rocks at Danger Point in 1852.
Death toll: 460

10 _Batavia_
Dutch ship that sank off Australia in 1629, on its maiden voyage.
Death toll: wreck 40; later mutiny 233

Battle of Midway (1942)
US ships _Yorktown_ and _Hammann_ were lost here, along with four Japanese aircraft carriers and a cruiser, in one of World War II's fiercest naval battles.

Eduard Bohlen (1909)
Ran aground in fog and now lies 400 m (1,300 ft) inland, half-buried in huge sand dunes.

HMS _Pandora_ (1791)
Sank while on a mission to find the HMS _Bounty_ and her mutinous crew.

Artificial shipwrecks

Humans can be responsible for shipwrecks in many different ways. War is one of the main causes – missiles, mines, air attacks, and sabotage have all been used to destroy ships. Other factors can be bad design, shoddy construction, or poor maintenance and repairs; navigation errors that cause a ship to run aground or hit other traffic; and overloading cargo so that the vessel tips over.

SANK IN 1978, SPILLING OVER 200,000 TONNES OF CRUDE OIL.

Industrial wonders

Golden Gate Bridge
San Francisco, California, USA, 1937. World–famous steel bridge and longest suspension bridge in the world when built.

Boeing Everett Factory
Everett, Washington, USA, 1968. Aircraft assembly building and the largest building in the world.

Great Belt Bridge
Denmark, 1998. Connects islands of Zealand and Funen. World's longest suspension bridge carrying both rail and road traffic.

Bell Rock Lighthouse
Inchcape, Scotland, 1810. Oldest surviving lighthouse.

The Langeled Pipeline
2006. Undersea pipeline pumping Norwegian natural gas to Britain.

Hibbing Taconite Company Mine
Hibbing, Minnesota, USA, 1895. World's largest open pit mine.

Lockheed SR-71 Blackbird
Beale, California, USA, 1964. Fastest manned jet aircraft.

London Sewage System
Late 19th century. Declared an engineering triumph for successfully diverting raw sewage away from the Thames.

Channel Tunnel
Folkestone, UK – Calais, France, 1994. International undersea rail tunnel.

Hoover Dam
Nevada/Arizona, USA, 1936. Largest concrete structure ever built at the time of construction.

Guggenheim Museum
New York, USA, 1959. Architectural and design feat.

Graf Zeppelin

Guggenheim Museum
Bilbao, Spain, 1997. Important work of modern architecture.

WM Keck Observatory
Mauna Kea, Hawaii, USA, 1993 and 1996. Second-largest optical telescopes on Earth.

Very Large Array
Socorro, New Mexico, USA, 1973–80. Astronomical observatory made up of 27 radio antennas arranged in a Y-shape.

Concorde

Sagrada Familia
Barcelona, Spain, 1882–current. Huge church designed by Antoni Gaudí, considered a masterpiece, and still under construction.

Large Hadron Collider
Geneva, Switzerland, 1998–2008. Giant scientific instrument for testing particles.

Panama Canal
1914. 77 km (48 miles) long. Among the most difficult engineering projects in history.

Itaipu Dam
Brazil/Paraguay, 1984. Largest hydroelectric producer of energy in the world.

San Alfonso del Mar swimming pool
Algarrobo, Chile, 2006. 1 km (0.6 mile) long and 35 m (115 ft) deep. Largest swimming pool in the world.

The Industrial Revolution of the 18th and 19th centuries saw remarkable advances in technology and materials. This led to extraordinary design and engineering feats, the likes of which had never been seen before.

Industrial pioneers

First transatlantic cable, Canada – Ireland, 1858
Cable that transported messages from one end to the other. The first of its kind to be laid across the Atlantic, meaning messages could be received in a matter of minutes.

Transcontinental Railroad, California – Nebraska, USA, 1869
Connected the east coast railways of the USA with the Pacific coast for the first time. Considered to be one of the greatest technological feats of the 19th century.

Home Insurance Building, Chicago, Illinois, USA, 1885
First ever steel-framed building, and first tall building to be supported by a fireproof metal frame. Although not very tall, the technology used make it the first "skyscraper".

FRENCH ENGINEER ALBERT MATHIEU PUT FORWARD A PROPOSAL

Over **16,000** people **built** the **Hoover Dam**

Soviet Submarine K-222
Severodvinsk, Russia, 1968. The world's fastest submarine. Record of 82.8 kph (51.4 mph).

Shanghai Underground Bunker
Shanghai, China, 2006. The *Shanghai Morning Post* reported the existence of an underground bunker capable of sheltering over 200,000 people.

Jiaozhou Bay Bridge
Jiaozhou, China, 2007. Longest bridge over water, at 42.5 km (26.4 miles) long.

Neuschwanstein Castle
Schwangau, Germany, 1892. Iconic "fairy tale" palace of King Ludwig II of Bavaria.

The Bailong Elevator
Zhangjiajie, China, 2002. World's highest and heaviest outdoor lift, built on the side of a cliff.

Three Gorges Dam
Yangzte, China, 2008. Most powerful hydroelectric power station in the world, but water shortages in the dry months mean the Itaipu Dam in South America produces more energy.

Seawise Giant
Yokosuka, Japan, 1979. Longest ship ever built, at 458 m (1,503 ft).

Danyang–Kunshan Grand Bridge
Jiangsu, China, 2011. Carries the Beijing – Shanghai high-speed railway for 164.8 km (102.4 miles), making it the world's longest bridge.

Great Manmade River
Libya, 1991. Network of pipelines that transport water from ancient underground reservoirs in the Sahara to coastal Libyan cities.

Terminal 3 at Dubai International Airport
Dubai, United Arab Emirates, 2008. World's largest airport terminal.

Istana Nurul Iman
Bandar Seri Begawar, Brunei, 1984. Palace of the Sultan of Brunei and the largest palace ever built.

TauTona Mine
Carletonville, South Africa, 1962. At 3.9 km (2.4 miles) deep, the deepest gold mine in the world. Can take one hour to get to the rock face from the surface.

Bahá'í House of Worship
New Delhi, India, 1986. World famous temple with a lotus flower design.

Sydney Opera House
Sydney, Australia, 1973. Great 20th-century architectural work.

Graf Zeppelin airship, Friedrichshafen, Germany, 1928
Made the first non-stop transatlantic passenger flight and flew regular commercial flights from 1932–37 from Germany to Brazil. The first aircraft in history to fly over 1.6 million km (1 million miles), and no passengers or crew were ever injured.

Concorde, Toulouse, France, 1969
The first commercial passenger aircraft to fly faster than sound. Its average speed was 2,140 kph (1,334 mph), more than twice that of conventional aircraft. Only 20 were ever built and the last Concorde flight was in 2003.

● Other industrial wonders

FOR THE CHANNEL TUNNEL IN 1802, 192 YEARS BEFORE IT OPENED.

Culture

Holi Festival, Jodhpur, India
During the Hindu spring festival of Holi – known as the Festival of Colours – people throw pigments and coloured water over each other.

Introduction

The word "culture" is a broad idea, and includes the values, beliefs, and behaviour of a society, or group of people. Culture includes many things, including customs, language, religion, music, art, food, and clothing. Some points of culture are traditional, having survived virtually unchanged for centuries. Others are short-lived, such as fashion styles and trends in pop music.

Headdress, called a *kiritam*, varies in size and design, according to the character being portrayed.

Hand gestures (known as *mudra*) are the dancer's main way of telling the story.

Noble-hearted characters always have green faces; dark red signifies a treacherous nature.

Kathakali dancer Indian kathakali dancers enact stories from two epic poems, the *Ramayana* and the *Mahabarata*. Dealing with the constant struggle between good and evil, dances end with the destruction of a demon.

Heroes always wear red jackets

Dancer's skirt is made up of many layers of white cotton.

Modern culture

Today's culture is fast moving and ever-changing, thanks in part to the instant communication offered by the Internet. But long before the Internet, the migration of people around the world began introducing people to cultures different from their own. Global broadcasting then accelerated this effect in the 20th century. The cultural contact often creates a fusion (uniting) of different cultural styles, especially in the fields of music, fashion, and cooking.

Live performances Huge crowds watch singers, such as Eva Simons (right), perform live, just as they have always done. But today the "live" audience can number many millions, with most watching remotely via radio, TV, and the Internet.

Stadium spectators For many sports fans, being part of a passionate, noisy, banner-waving stadium crowd makes them feel an important part of the event.

SAID TO HAVE BEEN WRITTEN BY THE HINDU WISE MAN VALMIKI,

Traditional culture

Older people can pass culture on to the next generation, enabling a society's traditions to be preserved for many years. The *Ramayana*, a Hindu poem written in the 5th or 4th century BCE, tells the story of Rama and Sita, and their battle against the demon-king Ravana. Over many generations, the *Ramayana* and its values have been kept alive in India and southern Asia through writing, story telling, painting, sculpture, festivals, music, and dance.

Literature

The *Ramayana* was originally written in Sanskrit, the language of Hinduism and ancient Indian literary texts.

Sculpture

The great warrior Rama, holding his bow, stands next to his wife Sita. Both hold up their right hands in blessing.

Festival

At the Hindu festival of Diwali, people light lamps to commemorate Rama's return from exile and his victory over Ravana.

Painting

In this scene from the *Ramakie*n, a Thai version of the *Ramayana*, the monkey god Hanuman uses his body as a bridge for Rama to cross.

Music

Musicians in Bali, Indonesia, provide accompaniment to kecak dancers, who perform parts of the *Ramayana*.

California, USA
Two hundred years ago, up to 90 languages were spoken in California by Native Americans. Today, only around 50 survive, and all of them are endangered.

Yuchi, USA
This Native American tongue is called a "language isolate". This means that experts can't find any connection between this and any other living language.

Spanish, USA
Spanish is the main language of 12 per cent of Americans, making the USA the world's fifth-largest Spanish-speaking nation.

Chamicuro, Peru
Typical of endangered languages, this aboriginal language is now spoken by only two members of the Chamicuro people.

Dutch, Suriname
Suriname's official language is Dutch, but 40 per cent of the people speak a local language, Sranan Tongo.

Guarani, Paraguay
Spanish dominates in most South American countries, but in Paraguay, it is rivalled by Guarani, a Native American language.

Cameroon
More than 280 different languages are spoken in Cameroon. Sixteen are critically endangered.

SPREADING LANGUAGES

These languages have not only taken hold as the main language of one country – they have spread to become the main language of other countries as well. In each of these countries, there may also be important second and third languages, and sometimes many more.

LANGUAGE WITH THE GREATEST NUMBER OF SPEAKERS IN EACH COUNTRY

- English
- Spanish
- Chinese
- Arabic
- Russian
- French
- Portuguese
- German
- Dutch
- Korean
- Malay
- Kiswahili
- Italian
- Persian

Countries with a unique main language
Each of these countries has a main language that is not the main language of any other country.

Continent by continent

Some parts of the world have been more affected than others by the shift towards more popular languages. Europe's population of about 740 million has only 234 living languages, whereas more than 1 billion people of Africa still speak over 2,000.

- 284 **Europe**
- **Americas** 1,060
- **Number of languages spoken worldwide** 7,105
- 2,304 **Asia**
- **Africa** 2,146
- 1,311 **Pacific**

Ter Saami, Russia
This is one of the languages spoken by the Sami, the indigenous people of the Arctic. Research in 2010 found that there are only two speakers left.

Russia
Apart from the main language, Russian, there are five languages in Russia each with 1 million or more speakers: Tatar, Ukrainian, Bashkir, Chechen, and Chuvash. At least 10 of Russia's minority languages are nearly extinct.

On average, **two languages** die out **every month**

Chinese
Around 1 billion people speak Mandarin Chinese. It has more native speakers than any other language.

Papua New Guinea
Several hundred languages are spoken here, making it the most varied place on Earth for languages.

India's languages
There are 22 official languages in India, although the national government uses only Hindi and English.

ENDANGERED LANGUAGES
A language disappears when its speakers no longer exist. Factors such as war and urban growth can cause old languages to die out. Languages are quickly going extinct – over 200 languages are spoken by fewer than 10 people each.

● **Languages with ten or fewer native speakers**

Vanuatu
A total of 18 languages in Vanuatu now have fewer than 10 fluent speakers.

Languages

Languages were developed by humans so that they could communicate with each other within their groups. As communities began to interact more, some languages spread and became more widely spoken, whereas others were used less or even died out.

Australia's languages
Almost 400 languages were spoken by Aboriginal people before European settlers arrived. Only about 15 are now spoken by all age groups. Only older people speak the remaining 72, meaning these will quickly die out without help.

MAJORITY RELIGIONS

Each country is coloured according to the religion that is most popular there. In many countries, however, millions of people follow religions that are not the majority religion, and many more are not religious at all.

- ■ **Judaism**
- ■ **Orthodox Christianity**
- ■ **Catholic Christianity**
- ■ **Protestant Christianity**
- ■ **Sunni Islam**
- ■ **Shi'a Islam**
- ■ **Hinduism**
- ■ **Chinese traditional religion**
- ■ **Christianity and native religions**
- ■ **Buddhism**
- ■ **Shinto**

Holy places

A place that religious followers think of as "holy" may be the spiritual centre of the religion. It could be the place where it all began, a site of pilgrimage, or the religion's official headquarters.

JERUSALEM

Contains sites holy to three major world religions.

✡ **Western Wall (Judaism)**
(1) Remains of the Temple in Jerusalem, and sacred site of prayer for Jews.

♇ **Church of the Holy Sepulchre**
(1) Said by Christians to contain the burial site of Jesus Christ.

☪ **Dome of the Rock (Islam)**
(1) Shrine built where the Prophet Muhammad rose to heaven.

NEW FAITHS

New religions have emerged in the last 200 years.

✿ **BAHA'I, 1866**
(30) **Shrine of the Bab, Haifa**
Resting place of the Bab, revered by the Baha'i faith as a Messenger.

🦁 **RASTAFARI, 1930**
(31) **Jamaica**
Home of Rastafari, whose followers worship Haile Selassie I of Ethiopia as God in human form.

🪷 **ISKCON, 1966**
(32) **New York City**
The International Society for Krishna Consciousness, known as Hare Krishna, began here.

Religious followers

Most of the world's people identify with a religion, whether or not they take part in religious services. Their beliefs, customs, or ancestors link them to their religious community.

Judaism
14 million

Sikhism
23 million

Buddhism
376 million

Hinduism
900 million

Islam
1.5 billion

Christianity
2.1 billion

♇ CHRISTIANITY

Followers worship Jesus Christ as the son of God. Christianity is split into these major branches: Orthodox, Catholic, and Protestant.

(2) **St Mary of Zion Church**
Heart of the Ethiopian Orthodox Church and said to hold God's 10 Commandments in the Ark of the Covenant.

(3) **Saint Sava, Belgrade**
The world's largest Eastern Orthodox church, built in 1989 in Serbia.

(4) **Vatican City**
Headquarters of the Roman Catholic Church.

(5) **Our Lady of Guadelupe**
Mexico City's famous image of the Virgin Mary and site of a Roman Catholic pilgrimage.

INDIAN RELIGIONS
Many world religions began in India, or, like Zoroastrianism, have taken up home there.

ॐ HINDUISM

18 Varanasi
Holiest Hindu city. Steps lead bathers down to the sacred River Ganges.

19 Dwarka
Pilgrimage site, holy city, and one of the Char Dam ("four seats") of Hinduism.

20 Ujjain
One of seven places (also including Dwarka and Varanasi) of "sacred ground".

☸ BUDDHISM

21 Bodh Gaya
Place where the Buddha, the founder of Buddhism, found enlightenment.

22 Jokhang, Lhasa, Tibet
The most important and sacred temple in Tibetan Buddhism.

23 Shwedagon Pagoda
In Yangon, Myanmar, this huge gold-plated building houses relics of the Buddha.

☬ SIKHISM

24 Harmandir Sahib
Known in English as the Golden Temple of Amritsar and sacred to Sikhs.

✋ JAINISM

25 Pawapuri
Sacred to the Jain faith, the site where a key teacher achieved enlightenment.

⚱ ZOROASTRIANISM

26 Iranshah Atash Behram, Udvada, India
An important fire temple of the Zoroastrian faith, which began in Persia (Iran).

FAR EASTERN RELIGIONS
Many beliefs coexist in China and Japan. These are the most common.

木 CONFUCIANISM

27 Dacheng Hall, Qufu
The largest and oldest temple of the teacher, Confucius.

☯ TAOISM

28 White Cloud Temple
Headquarters of the Chinese Taoists, Beijing.

⛩ SHINTO

29 Izumo Taisha, Japan
The Japanese emperor's family shrine.

---

6 Our Lady of Aparecida, São Paulo, Brazil
Eight million Catholic pilgrims a year visit this celebrated statue of the Virgin Mary.

7 San Agustin Church, Manila
The Philippines' oldest church has survived bombs and earthquakes since 1607.

8 All Saint's Church, Germany
In Wittenberg, Martin Luther began Protestantism by nailing his ideas on the church door.

9 Canterbury Cathedral
Place of pilgrimage and world centre of the Anglican Protestant Church.

10 St Peter's Church
The oldest Anglican church outside Britain, in Bermuda.

11 Salt Lake Temple
Largest centre of worship of the Church of Jesus Christ of Latter-day Saints, known as the Mormon Church.

☪ ISLAM

Muslims, followers of Islam, believe in one god and that Muhammad (570–632 CE) is His prophet. This religion split into Sunni and Shi'a faiths early on.

12 Makkah
Sacred to all Muslims as Muhammad's birthplace.

13 Medinah
The burial site of Islam's prophet, Muhammad.

14 Kairouan, Tunisia
Fourth city of Sunni Islam, and seat of Islamic learning.

15 Najaf, Iraq
Third city of Shi'a Muslims. Features the tomb of their first imam, Imam Ali.

16 Konya, Turkey
Home of Sufi mystic Rumi, whose followers perform the "Whirling Dervish" dance.

17 Demak Great Mosque
One of Indonesia's oldest mosques, built in the 15th century.

Raft the Salmon River, Idaho, USA
Ride the rapids as you travel through spectacular canyons on the "River of No Return".

Surf at Mavericks, California, USA
Only a select few are prepared to risk the big, wild waves at Mavericks, which can reach 15 m (50 ft).

Gran Cenote, Mexico
Divers can marvel at stalactites and stalagmites in this huge undersea cave formation.

Kauna'oa Bay, Hawaii
As well as swimming and sunbathing, you can snorkel to investigate local marine life. At night, you can even watch manta rays feeding in the bay.

Bora Bora, French Polynesia
Just 29 km (18 miles) long, this little island – the remnant of an extinct volcano – has beautiful white sandy beaches in a turquoise lagoon fringed by palm trees.

Galápagos Islands, Ecuador
These isolated islands boast many unique species, including giant tortoises, marine iguanas, and many different types of finch.

Hike the Inca Trail, Peru
Hike through mountains and jungles to the wonderfully preserved remains of the Inca city of Machu Picchu. Lost for hundreds of years, this 15th-century settlement was rediscovered in 1911.

Palm Beach, Florida, USA
Loved by millionaires, Palm Beach offers warm water, a fine climate, and bright city lights close to hand.

London Eye, UK
At its highest point, 135 m (443 ft) above the ground, the London Eye offers a panoramic view that stretches 40 km (25 miles) to the horizon.

Wiener Riesenrad, Vienna, Austria
Built in 1897, this 65-m- (213-ft-) tall structure was one of he first Ferris wheels ever made.

Bonaire, Caribbean
There are over 80 superb dive sites around this small island, which is home to three species of sea turtle.

Pantanal, Brazil/Bolivia/Paraguay, South America
The world's greatest concentration of jaguars – and much more besides. Over 1,000 bird species, including storks and macaws, and 300 types of mammal such as tapirs and anteaters.

Skydivers
in freefall reach
200 kph
(124 mph)

KEY

Adventure destinations
If you like your holidays thrill-packed, try these extreme activities, from white-water rafting and skydiving to surfing and trekking in remote regions.

World's top big wheels
Why not take a city break and ride one of the world's amazing observation wheels? Watch the world turn and take in the incredible views from the top.

Best diving and snorkelling sites
Take the plunge and immerse yourself in the magical worlds of coral reefs and undersea caverns. Swim with the fish ... but watch out for the venomous ones!

Top 5 Beaches
Relax, stretch out, and catch some rays on a sandy shore somewhere. Can't decide where to go? No worries – we've done the hard work for you and picked the best of the bunch.

Top 5 Safari sites
Get right up close to nature on a safari. See wild animals in their natural habitats, experience incredible animal migrations, and marvel at unique species.

Trek Annapurna, Nepal
Enjoy stunning scenery as you trek through the Himalaya mountains in the shadow of the mighty peaks of Annapurna.

Tempozan Ferris Wheel, Osaka, Japan
Opened in 1997, this 112.5-m- (369-ft)-tall wheel has coloured lights that provide a weather forecast for the next day: orange signifies sunshine, green means cloudy, and blue equals rain.

Aqaba, Jordan
See stunning corals and a rich array of colourful fish in water just 1.5 m (5 ft) deep.

Bwindi Park, Uganda
Half of the world's mountain gorillas live here. Also good for giraffes and lions.

Star of Nanchang, China
A trip round this 160-m- (525-ft)- high wheel in an eight-person gondola takes 30 minutes.

Maldives
Find reefs, caves, and abundant marine life.

Sipadan Island, Malaysia
Nutrient-rich waters make this one of the best sites in the world to see marine animals, including sea turtles; hammerhead, reef, and leopard sharks; barracudas; and parrotfish.

Seychelles
Northeast of Madagascar, this beautiful archipelago is made up 155 islands.

Masai Mara, Kenya
See lions, leopards, and cheetahs, and the spectacular mass migration of zebras, gazelles, and wildebeest.

Singapore Flyer
The world's tallest observation wheel, at 165 m (541 ft), gives views of 45 km (28 miles).

Okavango Delta, Botswana
Watch large roaming herds of buffaloes and elephants, and endangered animals such as African wild dogs.

Tourism

Fraser Island, Australia
This World Heritage Site has 1,660 sq km (640 sq miles) of unspoiled natural beauty.

Today, many people travel the globe in search of holidays that provide adventure, fun, and an unforgettable glimpse of the world's natural wonders. Here is a selection of the best tourist destinations the world has to offer.

Skydive in Queenstown, New Zealand
Step out of a plane 4,500 m (15,000 ft) above Queenstown and freefall for 60 seconds, until a pull on the ripcord opens your parachute and you float gently to the ground.

MARA, ALONG WITH 500,000 ZEBRA, GAZELLE, AND ELAND.

Edward Hopper
1882–1967; USA.
Hopper painted in the Realist style – a style that tries to show things as they are in real life. Hopper used simple colours and often painted solitary, lonely-looking people.

Andy Warhol
1928–1987, USA.
Warhol pioneered Pop Art – the "pop" refers to popular culture. His art used familiar images of famous people and everyday items such as soup cans. Warhol took his inspiration from advertising, TV, and comic strips.

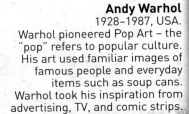

Edvard Munch
1863–1944; Norway.
Munch was an Expressionist artist. Expressionists tried to express feelings in their work, rather than portray people and objects accurately. Munch's most famous painting is *The Scream* (1893), which shows a person with an agonized expression.

Thomas Gainsborough
1727–88; England.
Founder of the 18th-century British Landscape school, Gainsborough made portraits as well as scenes. *Mr and Mrs Andrews* (1750; right) is an early masterpiece.

Claude Monet
1840–1926; France.
Impressionists such as Monet painted their view of brief moments in time. They often used small, thin, visible brushstrokes.

Frida Kahlo
1907–1954; Mexico.
Frida Kahlo began painting after she was badly injured in an accident. She is best known for her self-portraits. Her work used bold, bright colours and was influenced by Mexican folk art.

Pablo Picasso
1881–1973; Spain.
Among many other things, this famous artist was one of the founders of Cubism – a style of art that used geometric shapes to depict people and objects, often showing them from multiple viewpoints at the same time.

Victor Meirelles
1832–1903; Brazil.
Meirelles' religious and military paintings and depictions of episodes from Brazilian history won him fame and praise in the 19th century. His painting *The First Mass in Brazil* (1861; right) still appears in primary-school history books in Brazil.

Eugène Delacroix
1798–1863; France.
Delacroix was one of the Romantics, who stressed imagination and emotion. *Liberty Leading the People* (1830; above) marks the overthrow of Charles X of France in 1830.

Art

People the world over value art because it allows them to express their emotions and their culture, record history and everyday life, and explore what it means to be human. The works of the world's great artists often sell for huge sums of money.

Sculpture
15th century–present; Nigeria.
The people of the Kingdom of Benin, in what is now Nigeria, sculptured bronze heads and figures. They also made masks out of wood, bronze, and ivory. The tradition continues: on the right is a wooden mask of the late 20th century.

Marc Chagall
1904–89; Russia.
Chagall produced Expressionist and Cubist paintings, and also stained-glass windows. He is known for his paintings of village scenes and of lovers floating in the air.

Yue Minjun
Born 1962; China.
Based in Beijing, Yue Minjun is best known for his oil paintings, which show him frozen with laughter in various poses and in different settings. He has also represented himself in sculptures, watercolour paintings, and prints. He first exhibited his work in 1987; by 2007, he had sold 13 paintings for over US$1 million each.

Tamara de Lempicka
1898–1980; Poland.
In the 1920s and 1930s, de Lempicka was the most famous painter in the Art Deco style, which featured geometric shapes and intense, bright colours. She lived a flamboyant life and associated with the rich and famous.

Caravaggio
1570–1610; Italy.
Caravaggio was one of the Baroque artists, who revolutionized art by painting realistic rather than idealized people and scenes. He is one of the most influential painters in art history.

Katsushika Hokusai
1760–1849; Japan.
Hokusai is perhaps the most famous Japanese printmaker. His wood-block prints included landscapes, such as *The Great Wave of Kanagawa* (1831; above), and scenes from everyday life.

Basawan
c.1580–1600; India.
A painter of miniature scenes, Basawan illustrated the *Akbarnama* (right) – the official chronicle of Akbar, the third Mughal Emperor.

Willie Bester
Born 1956; South Africa.
Bester's collages and sculptures use recycled material and objects found in scrap yards and flea markets. His 1992 *Tribute to Biko* (above) commemorates Stephen Biko, who campaigned for racial equality in South Africa.

Yannima Tommy Watson
Born c.1935; Australia.
Despite starting painting only in 2001, when he was in his mid-60s, Tommy Watson rapidly became one of Australia's foremost Aboriginal artists. His paintings relate to the stories of the Dreamtime – the creation period in Aboriginal mythology.

It is estimated that **Picasso** produced about **148,000 works of art** during his **lifetime**

US$120 MILLION, MAKING IT THE WORLD'S MOST EXPENSIVE PAINTING.

173

Christt the King
36 m (120 ft)
Swiebodzin, Poland
2012

4. Statue of Liberty
Liberty was a gift
from the people
of France to
the USA.

Angel of the North
20 m (66 ft) high,
54 m (175 ft) wingspan
Gateshead, UK
1998

Great Sphinx
20 m (66 ft)
Giza, Egypt
2500 BCE

KEY
Heights exclude the plinths
on which the statues stand.

- Above 40m (131 ft)
- 30–40m (98–131 ft)
- 20–30m (66–98 ft)
- 16–20m (52–66 ft)
- 5–16m (16–52 ft)

Moai (statues)
Up to 10 m (33 ft)
Easter Island
c.1500

Christ the Redeemer
30 m (98 ft)
Rio de Janeiro, Brazil
1931

Political statues
Some statues are built to remind people
of their freedoms, promote a sense of
unity, or reinforce political ideas.

1. The Motherland Calls
85 m (279 ft); Volgograd, Russia; 1967
Marks the Soviet Union's victory over German
forces in the Battle of Stalingrad (1942).

2. Mother of the Fatherland
62 m (203 ft); Kiev, Ukraine; 1981
The female statue represents the strength and
victory of the Soviet Union in World War II.

3. African Renaissance Monument
49 m (161 ft); Dakar, Senegal; 2010
Africa's tallest statue shows a man gazing out
to sea as he holds a woman and child.

4. Statue of Liberty
46 m (151 ft); New York, USA; 1886
"Lady Liberty" stands with a torch in one hand
and a stone tablet in the other.

5. Juche Tower statues
30 m (98 ft); Pyongyang, North Korea; 1982
Three figures represent a peasant, an
industrial worker, and an intellectual.

African Renaissance Monument

Statues

Since ancient times, humans have built
grand statues of great rulers, heroic
figures, and gods and goddesses. We
are still doing it, and statues today are
getting bigger and bigger.

The **Angel of the North** has a bigger wingspan than a **Boeing 767** jet

1. The Motherland Calls
The statue beckons fighters to come to the defence of their nation.

Spring Temple Buddha
128 m (420 ft); Lushan, China; 2002
The world's tallest statue. Named after the nearby Tianrui hot spring.

Religious statues

Many religious movements use statues to inspire belief and to aid worship.

Guanyin, Hainan, China

11. Buddha
116 m (381 ft); Monywa, Myanmar; 2008
Depicts the Buddha standing. World's second-tallest statue.

12. Guanyin
108 m (354 ft); Sanya, Hainan, China; 2005
Represents the goddess Guanyin blessing the world.

13. Virgin of Peace
47 m (154 ft) Trujillo, Venezuela; 1983
The Virgin Mary, mother of Jesus, is shown holding a dove of peace in her hand.

14. Shiva
44 m (143 ft); Chitapol, Kathmandu, Nepal; 2012
Hindu god Shiva stands with a trident in his left hand. His right hand offers a blessing.

15. Murugan
43 m (141 ft); Batu Caves, Gombak, Malaysia; 2006
Statue stands by a cave shrine to the Hindu god Murugan.

Historical statues

Nations often use statues to celebrate the most famous people – both real and legendary – from their past.

6. Yan Di and Huang Di
106 m (348 ft); Zhengzhou, China; 2007
Shows the heads of two legendary kings regarded as the early founders of the Chinese nation.

7. Peter the Great
96 m (315 ft); Moscow, Russia; 1997
Erected to celebrate 300 years of the Russian Navy, which was founded by Tsar Peter I.

8. Guan Yu
61 m (200 ft); Yucheng, Shanxi, China; 2010
Statue of the general Guan Yu (160–219), later deified as Chinese god of war, at his birthplace.

9. José Maria Morelos
40 m (131 ft); Janitzio, Michoacán, Mexico; 1934
Mexico's rebel leader in the War of Independence (1810–21) is shown with a raised, clenched fist.

10. Genghis Khan
40 m (131 ft) Tsonjin Boldog, Mongolia; 2007
This statue depicts the famous Mongol leader (r.1206–1227) mounted on a horse.

Peter the Great

Tulip Time Festival
Michigan, USA
This festival is held in cities that were founded by the Dutch or had large numbers of Dutch settlers. Tulips line the streets and special tulip gardens are created for the event.

Vancouver, Canada

Thanksgiving
USA and Canada
This harvest celebration in November (October in Canada) usually involves a turkey dinner. It was first held to give thanks for the harvest of 1621.

Toronto, Canada

San Francisco, USA

New York, USA

Mardi Gras, New Orleans USA

Noche de Rábanos
Oaxaca, Mexico
When radishes first were brought to the Americas in the 16th century, market traders made radish sculptures to advertise the new vegetables. The "Night of the Radishes" has celebrated that custom since 1897.

Cuba

Haiti

Jamaica

Barranquilla, Colombia

Mazatenango, Guatemala

Trinidad

Panama

French Guiana

Tapati Festival
Easter Island
Tapati includes dancing, ritual chants, art exhibits, carving competitions, horse and boat races, body-painting, a string figure (*kai-kai*) contest, the selection of a queen, a parade, and *haka pei* – sliding down a steep hillside on banana-tree trunks at high speed.

Ambato, Ecuador

Cajamarca, Peru

Inti Raymi Day
Cuzco, Peru
The Festival of the Sun dates back to the Incas. People celebrate the winter solstice and the start of the new year.

Oruro, Bolivia

Coastal cities, Brazil

Cologne, Germany

Binche, Belgium

Notting Hill London, UK

Cheese Rolling Festival
Gloucestershire, UK
Contestants chase a roll of cheese down a steep, muddy hill.

Venice, Italy

Tomatina
Buñol, Valencia
Since 1944, tomato fights have been held on the last Wednesday of August. Over 100 tonnes of tomatoes are hurled each year!

Ovar, Portugal

Malta

Festival of the Sahara
Tunisia
A festival celebrating nomadic life and traditions. Events include camel marathons and performances of Bedouin song, dance, and poetry.

Madeira

Santa Cruz, Tenerife

Cape Verde Islands

Festival-au-Desert
Mali
Three days of traditional Tuareg art, music, and dance. Everyone camps in the desert, with their camels close by.

Montevideo, Uruguay

Festivals

Festivals give people a chance to celebrate their religious and cultural traditions. Above all, they are a great opportunity to throw a party!

Carnival
Carnival is marked by parades, such as in Rio de Janeiro, Brazil (left). It comes just before Lent – a time of fasting and avoiding rich foods that leads up to the Christian festival of Easter.

Major Carnival locations

MORE THAN 45 MILLION TURKEYS ARE EATEN ON THANKSGIVING DAY

Wife-Carrying World Championships
Sonkajärvi, Finland
Male entrants carry their wives over an obstacle course. The winner receives his wife's weight in beer.

Baltai
Tatarstan, Russia
Baltai means "feast of honey". The festival marks the start of the mowing season and is celebrated by decorating a bear with birch leaves.

Chinese New Year

Called the Spring Festival in China, since it marks the end of winter, this festival typically involves street processions with lanterns and Chinese dragons. Families clean their houses to sweep away bad fortune and welcome in the New Year. The festival is celebrated in all countries with significant populations of Chinese people.

 Locations with important Chinese New Year celebrations

Rijeka, Croatia

Patras, Greece

Limassol, Cyprus

Beijing

Ghost Festival, *China*
Part of "Ghost Month", when the ghosts and spirits of dead ancestors are said to emerge from the underworld.

Boryeong Mud Festival
Boryeong, South Korea
At this mucky festival, which dates from 1998, people cover each other in mud. The mud is said to contain minerals that are good for the skin.

Asakusa district, Tokyo

Awa Odori
Tokushima, Japan
Awa Odori began in 1586, when Tokushima's residents decided to celebrate their town's new castle. Today, more than 1 million tourists visit to watch performers in traditional dress dance in the streets.

Kolkata, India

Goa, India

Janmashtami
Mumbai, India
Marks the birthday of the Hindu god Krishna. Boys and men clamber to the top of a pole, trying to smash a clay pot full of curd and spill its contents. Krishna is said to have stolen curd from pots as a boy.

Philippines

Singapore

Indonesia

Bendigo Easter Festival
Bendigo, Australia
Dating from 1871, this is Australia's longest continuously running festival. During the festival's Easter procession, the *Sun Loong*, the longest imperial dragon in the world, dances through the streets of Bendigo.

Esala Maha Perahera
Kandy, Sri Lanka
The 10-day "Festival of the Tooth" celebrates the Tooth Relic of the Lord Buddha. Dancers, acrobats, and fire performers gather in Kandy. On the last night, an elegantly dressed elephant carries the tooth.

Mauritius

Incwala
Swaziland
At the "Festival of the first fruits", the king eats pumpkins and other fruits. People dance and sing in his honour and to bring blessings on the harvest.

World parties

Some festivals draw people from far and wide. They may be messy, such as Tomatina (left), or involve unusual competitions, such as wife-carrying.

 Key world party sites

Sydney, Australia

Prickly Pear Festival
Mandela Bay, South Africa
This is a day for celebrating (and eating!) traditional foods such as ginger beer, pancakes, potjiekos, bunnychow, and fish braai.

Te Matatini
New Zealand
A Māori dance festival in which performers come together from all over New Zealand to compete in the national finals. *Te Matatini* means "many faces".

Television

Televisions provide us with entertainment and news 24 hours a day. People also watch TV programmes on mobile devices such as laptops, smartphones, and tablets.

United Kingdom
In a 65-year lifetime, a person in the UK may spend up to 9 years watching television.

United States
Ninety-nine per cent of US homes have at least one TV, and 66 per cent have three or more TV sets.

French Guiana
There are around 30,000 TV sets serving a population of 173,000.

Ghana
Around 2 million Ghanaian households have a television.

Argentina
Ninety-seven per cent of Argentinian homes possess a television.

Falkland Islands
TV ownership is relatively high among the tiny population of about 2,500 islanders.

Broadcast channels chart

TOTAL NUMBER OF BROADCAST CHANNELS

- China 3,240
- USA 2,218
- Ukraine 647
- Turkey 635
- Romania 623
- France 584
- India 562
- South Africa 556
- Mongolia 456
- Germany 373

Broadcast channels

The number of broadcast TV channels varies greatly around the world. China has over 3,000 – the most of any country. Deciding what to watch must be a real headache!

COLOUR TELEVISIONS PER 10 PEOPLE

There are more than 1.5 billion TVs around the world, but they are not distributed equally among the nations.

- Less than 1
- 1–2
- 2–3
- 3–4
- 4–5
- 5–6
- 6–7
- 7 or more
- Data not available

Hours per week

Experts say that watching over 2 hours of TV per day (14 hours per week) can be bad for your health, yet in the UK and USA, people watch twice that.

United Kingdom	United States	Italy	France	Germany	Ireland	Australia	Denmark	Netherlands	Belgium	Finland	Norway	Sweden
28	28	27	23	23	23	22	20	20	19	18	18	18

HOURS PER PERSON PER WEEK

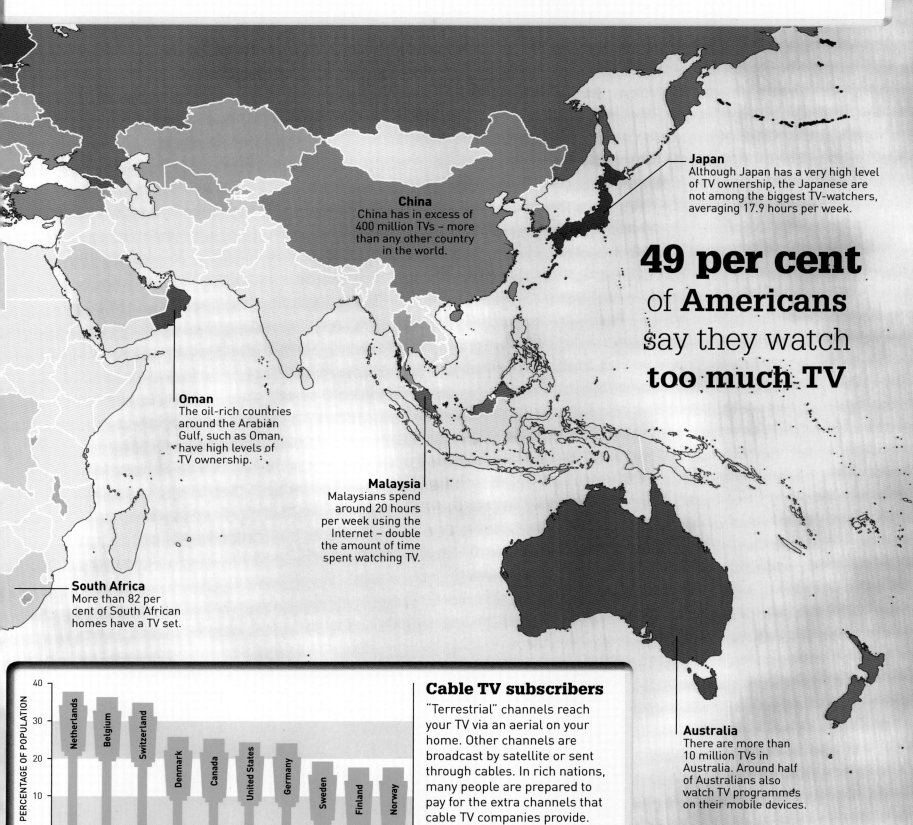

Japan
Although Japan has a very high level of TV ownership, the Japanese are not among the biggest TV-watchers, averaging 17.9 hours per week.

China
China has in excess of 400 million TVs – more than any other country in the world.

49 per cent
of **Americans**
say they watch
too much TV

Oman
The oil-rich countries around the Arabian Gulf, such as Oman, have high levels of TV ownership.

Malaysia
Malaysians spend around 20 hours per week using the Internet – double the amount of time spent watching TV.

South Africa
More than 82 per cent of South African homes have a TV set.

Australia
There are more than 10 million TVs in Australia. Around half of Australians also watch TV programmes on their mobile devices.

Cable TV subscribers

"Terrestrial" channels reach your TV via an aerial on your home. Other channels are broadcast by satellite or sent through cables. In rich nations, many people are prepared to pay for the extra channels that cable TV companies provide.

PERCENTAGE OF POPULATION

(Bar chart categories: Netherlands, Belgium, Switzerland, Denmark, Canada, United States, Germany, Sweden, Finland, Norway)

REGULARLY WATCH TELEVISION WHILE EATING DINNER.

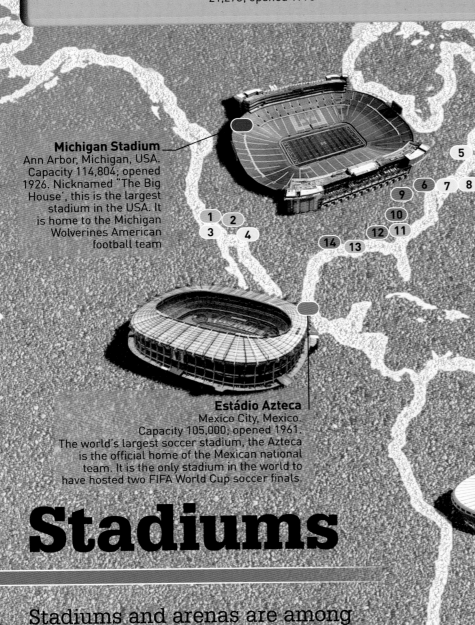

Americas

1 Los Angeles Memorial Coliseum
California, USA. Capacity 93,607; opened 1921

2 Rose Bowl
Pasadena, California, USA. Capacity 92,542; opened 1922

3 Dodgers Stadium
California, USA. Capacity 56,000; opened 1962

4 University of Phoenix Stadium
Arizona, USA. Capacity 63,400; opened 2006

5 Bell Centre
Quebec, Canada. Capacity 21,273; opened 1996

6 Beaver Stadium
Pennsylvania, USA. Capacity 106,572; opened 1960

7 Madison Square Garden New York, USA. Capacity 22,292; opened 1968

8 Arthur Ashe Stadium
New York, USA. Capacity 23,200; opened 1997

9 Ohio Stadium
Ohio, USA. Capacity 102,329; opened 1922

10 Neyland Stadium
Tennessee, USA. Capacity 102,455; opened 1921

11 Sanford Stadium
Georgia, USA. Capacity 92,746; opened 1929

12 Bryant–Denny Stadium
Alabama, USA. Capacity 101,821; opened 1929

13 Tiger Stadium
Louisiana, USA. Capacity 92,542; opened 1924

14 Darrell K. Royal – Texas Memorial Stadium Texas, USA. Capacity 100,119; opened 1924

Michigan Stadium
Ann Arbor, Michigan, USA. Capacity 114,804; opened 1926. Nicknamed "The Big House", this is the largest stadium in the USA. It is home to the Michigan Wolverines American football team

KEY
The colours show capacity (numbers of spectators).

- 110,000 and above
- 100,000–109,999
- 90,000–99,999
- 80,000–89,999
- Fewer than 80,000

Camp Nou
Barcelona, Spain. Capacity 99,354; opened 1957. The biggest stadium in Europe and the world's 11th largest.

Estádio Azteca
Mexico City, Mexico. Capacity 105,000; opened 1961. The world's largest soccer stadium, the Azteca is the official home of the Mexican national team. It is the only stadium in the world to have hosted two FIFA World Cup soccer finals.

Estádio do Maracanã
Rio de Janeiro, Brazil. Capacity 82,238; opened 1950. Built for the 1950 football FIFA World Cup, the Maracanã was the world's biggest stadium at the time, with room for nearly 200,000 people. Capacity was greatly reduced in the 1990s after part of the stadium collapsed. It is now being renovated in time for the 2014 FIFA World Cup.

Stadiums

Stadiums and arenas are among the largest and most impressive buildings on the planet. They not only enable us to experience the thrills and drama of competition between the best sports players, teams, and athletes, but also host pop concerts and other shows.

Europe

15 Millennium Stadium
Cardiff, UK. Capacity 74,500; opened 1999

16 Wembley Stadium
London, UK. Capacity 90,000; opened 2007

17 Allianz Arena
Munich, Germany. Capacity 69,901; opened 2005

18 Estádio Santiago Bernabéu
Madrid, Spain. Capacity 85,454; opened 1947

THE LARGEST EVER "MEXICAN WAVE" INVOLVED 157,574 PEOPLE AT

The record for the loudest crowd roar of **131.76 decibels** was set at the **Türk Telekom Arena**, Istanbul, Turkey, during a Galatasaray–Fenerbahce football match in 2011

Rungrado May Day Stadium
Pyongyang, North Korea.
Capacity 150,000; built 1989.
Said to look like a magnolia
blossom, the stadium is used
for sport and military parades.

22
23

Record crowd sizes
Crowds were even larger before
the modern safety-conscious era,
and standing and overcrowding
were common. The largest-ever
crowds at sports events are below.

Football: 135,000. Estádio da Luz, Portugal. Benfica vs Porto, January 1987.

Football: 149,415 (plus 20,000 without tickets). Hampden Park, Scotland. Scotland vs England, 1937.

Wrestling: 190,000. May Day Stadium, North Korea. Pro-Wrestling event, April 1995.

Football: 199,854. Maracanã Stadium, Brazil. Brazil vs Uruguay, World Cup Final, July 1950.

19

20

21

FNB Stadium (Soccer City)
Johannesburg, South Africa.
Capacity 94,736; opened 1989.
Nicknamed "The Calabash" because it looks like
the African pot of the same name, the FNB is
the largest stadium in Africa. It was extensively
renovated for football's 2010 FIFA World Cup.

Melbourne Cricket Ground
Victoria, Australia.
Capacity 100,018; opened 1854.
This stadium holds the record
for the highest floodlight towers
of any sporting venue. It is
known to locals as "The G".

Asia
19 Azadi Stadium
Tehran, Iran. Capacity
100,000; opened 1971

20 Salt Lake Stadium
Kolkata, India. Capacity
120,000; built 1984

21 Lumpinee Boxing Stadium
Bangkok, Thailand. Capacity
9,500; opened 1956

22 Beijing National Stadium ("Bird's Nest")
China. Capacity: 80,000;
opened 2008

23 Gwangmyeong Velodrome
South Korea.
Capacity 30,000;
opened 2006

Michigan International Speedway
Brooklyn, Michigan, USA

Chicagoland Speedway
Joliet, Illinois, USA

Indianapolis Motor Speedway
Speedway, Indiana, USA

Iowa Speedway
Newton, Iowa, USA

Bristol Motor Speedway
Bristol, Tennessee, USA

Kansas Speedway
Kansas City, Kansas, USA

Las Vegas Speedway
Las Vegas, Nevada, USA

Auto Club Speedway
Fontana, California, USA

Kentucky Speedway
Sparta, Kentucky, USA

Darlington Raceway
Darlington, South
Carolina, USA

Circuit of the Americas
Austin, Texas, USA

Homestead–Miami Speedway
Homestead, Florida, USA

Circuit Gilles Villeneuve Québec,
Montreal, Canada

Dover International Speedway
Dover, Delaware, USA

Charlotte Motor Speedway Concord,
North Carolina

Atlanta Motor Speedway
Hampton, Georgia, USA

Daytona International Speedway
Daytona Beach, Florida, USA

Hockenheimring
Hockenheim, Germany

Nürburgring
Nürburg,
Germany

Circuit de Spa-Francorchamps
Spa, Belgium

Silverstone Circuit
Silverstone, UK

Autodromo Nazionale Monza Monza, Italy

Circuit de la Sarthe
Le Mans, France

Circuit de Catulunya
Montmeló, Spain

Valencia Street Circuit
Valencia, Spain

Circuit de Monaco
Monte Carlo, Monaco

Autódromo José Carlos Pace
São Paolo, Brazil

Great champions

F1 is the pinnacle of "open-wheel" racing and the winner each season is called the world champion. NASCAR remains the top stock-car competition.

Dale Earnhardt Snr.
Nationality: US
Killed while racing at Daytona in 2001, Earnhardt had already won seven NASCAR titles.

Motor racing

With engines roaring, race cars provide a thrilling spectator sport as they hurtle down the track, weave through chicanes, and hug hairpin bends. The highly tuned Formula 1 cars draw big crowds in many countries. In the United States, stock-car racing is more popular.

NASCAR Sprint Cup

The Sprint Cup Series is the world's premiere stock-car racing competition. It involves 36 races over 10 months. As in F1, points awarded throughout the series decide the winner.

Michael Schumacher
Nationality: German
Record seven-time F1 World Champion. Schumacher has won over 90 F1 Grand Prix races – more than any other driver in history.

Ayrton Senna
Nationality: Brazilian
Three-time F1 World Champion. Third-most-successful driver of all time in terms of F1 race wins (41). Died in an accident at the 1994 San Marino Grand Prix.

Fernando Alonso
Nationality: Spanish
Became the youngest driver to win back-to-back F1 World Championships (2005 and 2006). In 2012, he passed 30 Grands Prix wins.

A Formula 1
steering wheel costs
about **£20,000**

Hungaroring
Budapest, Hungary

Korean International Circuit
Yeongam, South Korea

Buddh International Circuit
Greater Noida, India

Bahrain International Circuit
Sakhir, Bahrain

Yas Marina Circuit
Abu Dhabi, UAE

Shanghai International Circuit
Shanghai, China

Suzuka Circuit
Suzuka City, Japan

Le Mans

The French town of Le Mans hosts the world's toughest endurance race. Teams of three drivers keep their sports cars racing for 24 hours, grabbing what food and rest they can in between two-hour stints behind the wheel.

Sepang International Circuit
Kuala Lumpur, Malaysia

Marina Bay Street Circuit
Marina Bay, Singapore

KEY
Location of major race tracks worldwide

⮎ **Formula 1 sites**

⬭ **NASCAR sites**

⬭ **Le Mans**

Kyalami
Midrand, South Africa

Albert Park
Melbourne, Australia

Formula 1 (F1)

In the annual F1 World Championship, ultra high-performance "open-wheel" race cars compete in a series of Grand Prix races worldwide. Cars finishing in the top-10 positions in each race win points. At the season's end, trophies are awarded for the driver and manufacturer with the most points.

Top Thrill Dragster
Cedar Point, Ohio, USA
193 kph (120 mph); 128 m (420 ft) high
853 m (2,800 ft) long

Intimidator 305
Kings Dominion, Virginia, USA
145 kph (90 mph)
93 m (305 ft) high
1,554 m (5,100ft) long

Leviathan
Canada's Wonderland, Ontario
148 kph (92 mph)
93 m (306 ft) high
1,672 m (5,486 ft) long

Superman: Escape from Krypton
Six Flags Magic Mountain, California, USA
161 kph (100 mph)
126 m (415 ft) high
376 m (1,235 ft) long

Vortex
Carowinds, North Carolina, USA; 80 kph (50 mph)
27m (90 ft) high
622 m (2,040 ft) long

Colossus
Thorpe Park, England
72 kph (45 mph); 30 m (100 ft) high
850m (2,789 ft) long

Alpengeist
Busch Gardens, Florida, USA
107 kph (67 mph)
59 m (195 ft) high
1,148 m (3,828 ft) long

Apocalypse,
Six Flags America, Maryland, USA
89 kph (55 mph)
30 m (100 ft) high
884 m (2,900 ft) long

Ultimate
Lightwater Valley, UK
80 kph (50 mph)
33 m (107 ft) high
2,268 m (7,442 ft) long

Kingda Ka
Six Flags Great Adventure, New Jersey, USA
206 kph (128 mph)
139 m (456 ft) high
950 m (3,118 ft) long

Colossos
Heide-Park Soltau, Germany
102 kph (75 mph)
60 m (197 ft) high
1,344 m (4,409 ft) long

Kingda Ka

This ride goes from 0-206 kph (128 mph) in 3.5 seconds, catapulting riders as high as a 45-storey building.

Montezum
Hopi Hari, Brazil
103 kph (64 mph)
42 m (139 ft) high
1,030 m (3,380 ft) long

Tower of Terror
Gold Reef City, South Africa
95 kph (59 mph)
34 m (112 ft) high
100 m (328 ft) long

TOP 5
Numbers indicate ranking from 1-5.

Fastest   **Highest**   **Longest**

Roller coasters

Breakneck speeds, hair-raising twists and turns, stomach-churning drops – roller coasters can satisfy even hardened thrill-seekers. This map shows some of the world's biggest and best coasters.

Highest steel
Kingda Ka, USA
139 m (456 ft)

2nd highest
Top Thrill Dragster, USA
128m (420ft)

Most inversions: 10
Colossus, UK, and 10 Inversion Roller Coaster, China

Fastest
Formula Rossa, UAE; 241 kph (150 mph)

Flying roller coasters

These coasters –such as Manta at SeaWorld, Florida, USA (right) – make you feel as though you are flying. The cars run on the underside of the track. Riders start in a seated position, but as the ride starts they are rotated to face the ground.

Steel Dragon 2000
Nagashima Spa Land, Japan
153 kph (95 mph)
97 m (318 ft) high
2,437 m (8,133 ft) long

Dinoconda
China Dinosaurs Park, China
128 kph (80 mph)
76 m (249 ft) high
1,058 m (3,471 ft) long

Formula Rossa
Ferrari World, UAE
241 kph (150 mph)
52 m (171 ft) high
2,000 m (6,562 ft) long

Ten Inversion Roller Coaster
Chimelong Paradise, China
72 kph (45 mph); 30 m (100 ft) high
850 m (2,789 ft) long

Fujiyama
Fuji-Q Highland, Japan
130 kph (81 mph)
70 m (260 ft) high
2,045 m (6,709 ft) long

Takabisha
Fuji-Q Highland, Japan
100 kph (62 mph)
43 m (141 ft) high
1,000 m (3,281 ft) long

29 kph
(18 mph): speed of the word's oldest coaster, **Leap the Dips**

4-D roller coasters

Fourth-dimension (4-D) coasters, such as China's Dinoconda, give theme parks an extra level of thrills. The seats on a 4-D coaster can rotate forwards or backwards, so as the riders hurtle along the track they also spin in a full circle. Eejanaika (below) is a 4-D ride at Japan's Fuji-Q Highland theme park.

Tower of Terror II
Dreamworld, Queensland, Australia; 161 kph (100 mph)
114 m (377 ft) long; 376 m (1,235 ft) high

Roller coaster records

Opened in 1902, the world's oldest coaster is the wooden Leap-the-Dips, at Lakemont Park, Pennsylvania, USA. Since then, coasters have become taller, longer, faster – and scarier! Today's coasters are usually made of steel. Wood is less flexible than steel, so wooden coasters tend to be less complex and extreme than steel ones.

● **Steepest drop**
Takabisha, Japan
121 degrees

● **Highest G-force**
Tower of Terror, South Africa
6.3G

National flags

 CANADA

 UNITED STATES OF AMERICA

 MEXICO

 BELIZE

 COSTA RICA

 EL SALVADOR

 GUATEMALA

HONDURAS

SOUTH AMERICA

 GRENADA

 HAITI

 JAMAICA

 ST KITTS & NEVIS

 ST LUCIA

 ST VINCENT & THE GRENADINES

 TRINIDAD & TOBAGO

COLOMBIA

AFRICA

 URUGUAY

 CHILE

 PARAGUAY

 ALGERIA

 EGYPT

 LIBYA

 MOROCCO

TUNISIA

 LIBERIA

 MALI

 MAURITANIA

 NIGER

 NIGERIA

 SENEGAL

 SIERRA LEONE

TOGO

 BURUNDI

 DJIBOUTI

 ERITREA

 ETHIOPIA

 KENYA

 RWANDA

 SOMALIA

 SUDAN

 NAMIBIA

 SOUTH AFRICA

 SWAZILAND

 ZAMBIA

 ZIMBABWE

 COMOROS

MADAGASCAR

MAURITIUS

 LUXEMBOURG

 NETHERLANDS

 GERMANY

 FRANCE

 MONACO

 ANDORRA

 PORTUGAL

 SPAIN

 POLAND

 SLOVAKIA

 ALBANIA

 BOSNIA & HERZEGOVINA

 CROATIA

KOSOVO (disputed)

 MACEDONIA

 MONTENEGRO

ASIA

 LATVIA

LITHUANIA

CYPRUS

MALTA

RUSSIAN FEDERATION

ARMENIA

AZERBAIJAN

GEORGIA

TURKEY

 QATAR

 SAUDI ARABIA

 UNITED ARAB EMIRATES

 YEMEN

IRAN

KAZAKHSTAN

KYRGYZSTAN

TAJIKISTAN

 CHINA

 MONGOLIA

 NORTH KOREA

 SOUTH KOREA

TAIWAN

JAPAN

BURMA (MYANMAR)

CAMBODIA

AUSTRALASIA & OCEANIA

SINGAPORE

MALDIVES

AUSTRALIA

NEW ZEALAND

PAPUA NEW GUINEA

FIJI

 SOLOMON ISLANDS

 VANUATU

A SOVEREIGN STATE IS A COUNTRY INDEPENDENT OF OTHER STATES,

Of all the flags of the world's **196 sovereign states**, only **Nepal's** has more than **four sides**

NICARAGUA PANAMA ANTIGUA & BARBUDA BAHAMAS BARBADOS CUBA DOMINICA DOMINICAN REPUBLIC

GUYANA SURINAME VENEZUELA BOLIVIA ECUADOR PERU BRAZIL ARGENTINA

BENIN BURKINA FASO CAPE VERDE GAMBIA GHANA GUINEA GUINEA-BISSAU IVORY COAST

CAMEROON CENTRAL AFRICAN REPUBLIC CHAD CONGO DEM. REP. CONGO EQUATORIAL GUINEA GABON SÃO TOMÉ & PRÍNCIPE

SOUTH SUDAN TANZANIA UGANDA ANGOLA BOTSWANA LESOTHO MALAWI MOZAMBIQUE

EUROPE

SEYCHELLES DENMARK FINLAND ICELAND NORWAY SWEDEN IRELAND UNITED KINGDOM BELGIUM

ITALY SAN MARINO VATICAN CITY AUSTRIA LIECHTENSTEIN SLOVENIA SWITZERLAND CZECH REPUBLIC HUNGARY

SERBIA BULGARIA GREECE MOLDOVA ROMANIA UKRAINE BELARUS ESTONIA

IRAQ ISRAEL JORDAN LEBANON SYRIA BAHRAIN KUWAIT OMAN

TURKMENISTAN UZBEKISTAN AFGHANISTAN PAKISTAN BANGLADESH BHUTAN INDIA NEPAL SRI LANKA

LAOS PHILIPPINES THAILAND VIETNAM BRUNEI INDONESIA EAST TIMOR MALAYSIA

MARSHALL ISLANDS MICRONESIA NAURU PALAU KIRIBATI TUVALU TONGA SAMOA

Index

Acknowledgements

Dorling Kindersley would like to thank: Caitlin Doyle for proofreading, Helen Peters for indexing, Haisam Hussein, Anders Kjellberg, Peter Minister, Martin Sanders, and Surya Sarangi for illustration, Deeksha Miglani and Surbhi N. Kapoor for research, and David Roberts for cartographic assistance.

The publisher would like to thank the following for their kind permission to reproduce their photographs:

(Key: a-above; b-below/bottom; c-centre; f-far; l-left; r-right; t-top)

2 Andy Biggs: www.andybiggs.com (tc). **Corbis:** Alaska Stock (tr). **3 Corbis:** Floris Leeuwenberg (ftr); SOPA / Pietro Canali (tl). **Getty Images:** Art Wolfe (tr). **Sebastian Opitz:** (tc). **4–5 Andy Biggs:** www.andybiggs.com. **22 Getty Images:** Mark Garlick (br). **23 Corbis:** Charles & Josette Lenars (cr). **24–25 Robert J. Hijmans:** Hijmans, R.J, S.E. Cameron, J.L. Parra, P.G. Jones and A. Jarvis, 2005. *Very high resolution interpolated climate surfaces for global land areas.* International Journal of Climatology 25: 1965–1978 (base-map data). **26–27 Robert J. Hijmans:** Hijmans, R.J, S.E. Cameron, J.L. Parra, P.G. Jones and A. Jarvis, 2005. *Very high resolution interpolated climate surfaces for global land areas.* International Journal of Climatology 25: 1965–1978 (base-map data). **28–29 Adam Sparkes:** Data of the tropical cyclones projected by Adam Sparkes. Base image: NASA Goddard Space Flight Center Image by Reto Stöckli (land surface, shallow water, clouds). Enhancements by Robert Simmon (ocean color, compositing, 3D globes, animation). Data and technical support: MODIS Land Group; MODIS Science Data Support Team; MODIS Atmosphere Group; MODIS Ocean Group Additional data: USGS EROS Data Center (topography); USGS Terrestrial Remote Sensing Flagstaff Field Center (Antarctica); Defense Meteorological Satellite Program (city lights). **29 NOAA:** (tc). **30 Dorling Kindersley:** Rough Guides (tl, tr). **Shutterstock:** Edwin van Wier (crb). **31 Dreamstime.com:** (tc). **PunchStock:** Digital Vision / Peter Adams (tr). **35 NASA:** Goddard Space Flight Center, image courtesy the NASA Scientific Visualization Studio, (bl). **36 Dorling Kindersley:** Rough Guides / Tim Draper (bl). **Dreamstime. com:** Darryn Schneider (tr). **40–41 Corbis:** Alaska Stock. **42 Alamy Images:** Martin Strmiska (bl). Getty Images: Werner Van Steen (c). **43 NHPA / Photoshot:** Ken Griffiths (cr). **45 Corbis:** Science Faction / Louie Psihoyos (tr). Dorling Kindersley:

Christian Williams (tc). **48 Alamy Images:** National Geographic Image Collection (bl). **Dorling Kindersley:** Courtesy of the Weymouth Sea Life Centre (bc). **49 Dreamstime.com:** Francesco Pacienza (tr). **53 Corbis:** Roger Tidman (bc). **55 Corbis:** Paul Souders (ca). **56 Corbis:** Minden Pictures / Mike Parry (cl); National Geographic Society / Ben Horton (tc). **60 Dorling Kindersley:** Courtesy of the Natural History Museum, London (cra, c). **Getty Images:** Visuals Unlimited, Inc. / Alex Wild (cr). **61 Alamy Images:** Premaphotos (tl). **Corbis:** Visuals Unlimited / Robert & Jean Pollock (tr). **Getty Images:** Mint Images / Frans Lanting (tc). Photoshot: Gerald Cubitt (br). **62–63 Dreamstime.com:** Jezper. **62 Alamy Images:** Tim Gainey (bc); John Glover (br). FLPA: Imagebroker / Ulrich Doering (cb). **Getty Images:** Shanna Baker (clb); Alessandra Sarti (bl). **64 Dorling Kindersley:** Courtesy of Oxford University Museum of Natural History (clb). **64–65 Dr. Clinton N. Jenkins:** Data: IUCN Red List of Threatened Species / www.iucnredlist.org / BirdLife International; Processing: Clinton Jenkins / SavingSpecies.org; Design & Render; Félix Pharand–Deschênes / Globaia.org. **66 Dorling Kindersley:** Rough Guides (cl). **67 Corbis:** Ocean (crb). **Dorling Kindersley:** Roger and Liz Charlwood (crb/New Caledonia). **72–73 Corbis:** SOPA / Pietro Canali. **74–75 Getty Images:** Doug Allan. **75 Corbis:** Aurora Photos / Bridget Besaw (tl); Frank Lukasseck (ftl); Minden Pictures / Ch'ien Lee (tc); John Carnemolla (tr). **76–77 Center for International Earth Science Information Network (CIESIN):** Columbia University; International Food Policy Research Institute (IFPRI); The World Bank; and Centro Internacional de Agricultura Tropical (CIAT). **84 Corbis:** Dennis Kunkel Microscopy, Inc. / Visuals Unlimited (tc); Dr. Dennis Kunkel Microscopy / Visuals Unlimited (tr). **85 Getty Images:** Kallista Images (cr). **89 Dreamstime.com:** Cammeraydave (tr). **90 Corbis:** dpa / Horst Ossinger (br); James Leynse (bc). **91 Corbis:** epa / Justin Lane (bl); Kim Kulish (cra); epa / Mario Guzman (br). **Getty Images:** AFP (cr); (bc). **93 Dreamstime.com:** Kheng Guan Toh (br). **101 Corbis:** Peter Adams (bl). **105 Corbis:** Shuli Hallak (bc). **107 Dreamstime.com:** Milosluz (bc). **108–109 NASA:** Goddard Space Flight Center Scientific Visualization Studio. **109 NASA:** 1941 photo taken by Ulysses William O. Field; 2004 photo taken by Bruce F. Molnia. Courtesy of the Glacier Photograph Collection, National Snow and Ice Data Center / World Data Center for

Glaciology. (bl). **110–111 UNEP–WCMC:** Dataset derived using the Digital Chart of the World 1993 version and methods based on the Australian National Wilderness Inventory (Lesslie, R. and Maslen, M. 1995. National Wilderness Inventory Handbook. 2nd edn, Australian Heritage Commission. Australian Government Publishing Service, Canberra) (base-map data). **112–113 Sebastian Opitz. 114–115 Dreamstime. com:** Dmitry Mizintsev (c). **114 Corbis:** (bc); Science Faction / Louie Psihoyos (br). **115 Corbis:** Bettmann (crb); Cameron Davidson (br). **Dorling Kindersley:** Courtesy of The Science Museum, London (tc). **Getty Images:** Three Lions (bc). **116–117 Michael Markieta:** www.spatialanalysis.ca. **118–119 Prof. Dr. Bernd Blasius:** Journal of the Royal Society Interface, *The complex network of global cargo ship movements*, p1094, 2010 (base-map data). **122 Getty Images:** Radius Images (bc). **126–127 Chris Harrison** (base-map). **128–129 ESA. 128 NASA: Columbia Accident Investigation Report, (bc). 129 ESA: (cra). NASA:** Image created by Reto Stockli with the help of Alan Nelson, under the leadership of Fritz Hasle (br). **130 Corbis:** DoD (br). **132–133 Getty Images:** Art Wolfe. **134 Corbis:** Radius Images (bl); Peter Turnley (br). Getty Images: (cr). **135 Corbis:** Sodapix / Bernd Schuler (b). **136–137 Corbis:** W. Cody. **137 Science Photo Library:** MSF / Javier Trueba (crb). **138 akg-images:** Oronoz (clb/Mousterian Tool). **Dorling Kindersley:** The American Museum of Natural History (bl); Natural History Museum, London (cl, clb). **Getty Images:** AFP (tc); De Agostini (tr). **139 akg-images:** Ulmer Museum (bc). **Getty Images:** De Agostini (crb). **141 Dorling Kindersley:** Courtesy of the University Museum of Archaeology and Anthropology, Cambridge (tl); Ancient Art / Judith Miller (bc/Urn); Alan Hills and Barbara Winter / The Trustees of the British Museum (tc); Stephen Dodd / The Trustees of the British Museum (tr). **Getty Images:** De Agostini (bl). **144 Alamy Images:** Ancient Art & Architecture Collection Ltd (tc). **Getty Images:** Copper Age (tl). Rex Features: (tr). **148 Dorling Kindersley:** © The Board of Trustees of the Armouries (tr); The Wallace Collection, London (cb). **149 Dorling Kindersley:** © The Board of Trustees of the Armouries (cla); Lennox Gallery Ltd / Judith Miller (cra); William Jamieson Tribal Art / Judith Miller (bl); Courtesy of the Royal Armories (tc); The Trustees of the British Museum (cb); Peter Wilson / CONACULTA–INAH–MEX. Authorized reproduction by the Instituto Nacional

de Antropología e Historia (clb). **150 Corbis:** Walter Geiersperger (cl); Robert Harding World Imagery / Michael Jenner (clb). **151 Alamy Images:** Peter Titmuss (bc). **Corbis:** Design Pics / Keith Levit (cra). **Dreamstime.com:** (bl). Getty Images: AFP (cr). **156 Corbis:** Bettmann (cb, cra). **Getty Images:** (c). **157 Corbis:** Bryan Denton (bl); Peter Turnley (cr). Getty Images: AFP (ca); (c); (clb). **159 Dreamstime.com:** (bc). **162–163 Corbis:** Floris Leeuwenberg. **164 Dreamstime.com:** Randy Miramontez (c); Constantin Sava (bl). **165 Alamy Images:** Hemis (br). **Corbis:** Godong / Julian Kumar (tr). **Dreamstime.com:** F9photos (cr); Teptong (crb). **Getty Images:** Philippe Lissac (tc). **172 Alamy Images:** GL Archive (tr); The Art Archive (cb). **Corbis:** Bettmann (cl, cr); Oscar White (cla); The Gallery Collection (crb). **Dorling Kindersley:** Philip Keith Private Collection / Judith Miller (br). Getty Images: De Agostini (cra, cra/ Gainsborough); Stringer / Powell (tc). **172–173 123RF.com. 173 Corbis:** (cl, cr, cb); Contemporary African Art Collection Limited (clb). **Getty Images:** AFP (bc); (tl, tr); (cla). **174 Corbis:** In Pictures / Barry Lewis (br). **175 Corbis:** JAI / Michele Falzone (cra). **Dorling Kindersley:** Rough Guides (bc); Surya Sankash Sarangi (c). **176 Dorling Kindersley:** Alex Robinson (br). **177 Corbis:** Jose Fuste Raga (bc). **178–179 Dreamstime.com:** Luminis (background image). **180 Alamy Images:** Aerial Archives (cl). **Getty Images:** (ca). **180–181 Getty Images:** AFP (cb); (ca). **181 Corbis:** Arcaid / John Gollings (br). **Getty Images:** (ca). **182 Corbis:** GT Images / George Tiedemann (tr); Icon SMI / Jeff Vest (br). **182–183 Dreamstime.com:** Eugenesergeev (tyre tracks on the map). **183 Getty Images:** AFP (tr); (tl, tc, cr, bc). **184 Alamy Images:** David Wall (tr). **Dreamstime.com:** Anthony Aneese Totah Jr (c). **Getty Images:** AFP (cl). **185 Alamy Images:** G.P.Bowater (tr); Philip Sayer (tc). Getty Images: AFP (br)

All other images © Dorling Kindersley For further information see: www.dkimages.com

ARCTIC OCEAN

Chukchi Sea

Beaufort Sea

Queen Elizabeth Islands

Ellesmere Island

Greenland

Greenland Sea

Victoria Island

Baffin Bay

Baffin Island

Davis Strait

Denmark Strait

Iceland

Norweg Sea

Brooks Range

Mackenzie

Great Bear Lake

Péninsule d'Ungava

Labrador Sea

Bering Strait

Yukon

△ Mount McKinley (Denali) 6,194 m (20,320 ft)

Great Slave Lake

Hudson Bay

Bering Sea

Rocky Mountains

Canadian Shield

Laurentian Mountains

North Sea

Aleutian Basin

Coast Mountains

Lake Winnipeg

NORTH AMERICA

Grand Banks of Newfoundland

British Isles

Aleutian Islands

Gulf of Alaska

Vancouver Island

Great Plains

Missouri

Great Lakes

Bay of Biscay

Aleutian Trench

Snake

Ohio

Appalachian Mts

North American Basin

Azores

Iberian Peninsula

Medi

Mendocino Fracture Zone

Colorado

Mississippi

Bermuda

Madeira

Atlas Mountains

Sah

Murray Fracture Zone

Lower California

Sierra Madre Occidental

Sierra Madre Oriental

Gulf of Mexico

West Indies

Greater Antilles

Canary Islands

Ahag

Sah

Yucatán Peninsula

Caribbean Sea

Lesser Antilles

Cape Verde Islands

ATLANTIC

PACIFIC

Middle America Trench

Orinoco

Guiana Highlands

Mid-Atlantic Ridge

OCEAN

OCEAN

Galápagos Islands

Caquetá

Río Negro

Amazon

Gulf of Guinea

Niger

Amazon Basin

Ascension Island

SOUTH AMERICA

Height above sea level

8,000 m

25,000 ft

Peru Basin

Andes

Peru-Chile Trench

Planalto de Mato Grosso

Brazilian Highlands

Brazil Basin

Angola Basin

St Helena

7,000 m

20,000 ft

6,000 m

Nazca Ridge

Gran Chaco

Paraná

Río Grande Rise

Ca Bas

5,000 m

15,000 ft

East Pacific Rise

Easter Island

Uruguay

4,000 m

3,000 m

10,000 ft

2,000 m

Aconcagua 6,959 m △ (22,837 ft)

Pampas

Tristan da Cunha

1,000 m

5,000 ft

Juan Fernandez Islands

Andes

Gough Island

Sea level

Sea level

-1,000 m

-5,000 ft

Chile Rise

Mid-Atlantic Ridge

Walvis Ridge

-2,000 m

Patagonia

Argentine Basin

-3,000 m

-10,000 ft

-4,000 m

-15,000 ft

Falkland Islands

-5,000 m

Tierra del Fuego

South Georgia

-6,000 m

-20,000 ft

Mornington Abyssal Plain

Cape Horn

South Sandwich Islands

-7,000 m

Eltanin Fracture Zone

-25,000 ft

-8,000 m

Drake Passage

△ mountain

river

seasonal river

Southeast Pacific Basin

Antarctic Peninsula

Weddell Plain

SOUTH